D0365630

ANGER

HOW TO LIVE WITH AND WITHOUT IT

ANGER

HOW TO LIVE WITH AND WITHOUT IT

Albert Ellis, Ph.D.

BARNES & NOBLE BOOKS
NEW YORK

For Janet L. Wolfe
With love

Fine Communications
322 Eighth Avenue
New York, NY 10001

Anger: How to Live With and Without It
LC Control Number 2004111300
ISBN 1-56731-698-0

This special edition is published by MJF Books in arrangement with Citadel Press Books, an imprint of Kensington Publishing Corp.

Manufactured in the United States of America on acid-free paper ∞

MJF Books is a trademark of Fine Creative Media, Inc.

QM 10 9 8 7 6 5 4 3 2 1

Contents

Preface

Why another book on anger? Although numerous books tell us how to deal with anger, none of them seems to work effectively and efficiently in most situations. These books generally support one of two positions. Some advise you to assume a passive, nonresistant attitude when you think others treat you unfairly. Such an attitude may give people the impression that you very much control yourself and the situation, but it hardly helps you achieve anything else. Many people may assume that your passivity and acceptance of their "unfair" treatment means that you do not object to their treating you shabbily or unfairly. Therefore, they have no reason to stop their mistreatment. Your passivity will give others a green light, so to speak, to deal with you as they please.

On the other hand, a multitude of books advise you to openly and freely give vent to and fully express your feelings of anger and rage. They fail to indicate that when you express these feelings it will encourage others to return your resentment.

You can easily see that both of these approaches have many weak points and that neither of them succeeds in presenting an effective solution to the problem of anger.

The solution? Epictetus, a remarkably wise Stoic philosopher, pointed out some two thousand years ago that you *choose* to overreact to the obnoxious behavior of others while you could more wisely choose to react differently. Rational Emotive Behavior Therapy (REBT) has found that by following the age-old wisdom of many philosophers and by combining it with the most modern methods of psychotherapy, you can learn to reduce self-defeating, angry reactions and to live successfully with the feelings that you may still experience.

Can you do this by yourself? Yes, you definitely can—as Dr. Robert Harper and I particularly show in a previous book, *A Guide to Rational Living*. Here I will explain exactly how you can create your own *philosophy of anger* by consciously and unconsciously subscribing to absolutistic thinking and how, by changing your thoughts, feelings, and behaviors that underlie and accompany your rage, you can greatly reduce it. Through careful attention to REBT theory and practice, you can learn effectively to deal with your anger in a remarkably short period of time.

The first edition of this book was published in 1977 and was a pioneering self-help book that explained what anger is, what harm it frequently does to people and their relationships, and how to use Rational Emotive Behavior Therapy to significantly reduce it. This edition has sold very well for twenty-five years, has been useful to many of my psychotherapy clients, and has helped to minimize the rage of hundreds of people who have enthusiastically written me about it.

A revised version of this book, *How to Control Your Anger Before It Controls You*, authored by me and Raymond Chip Tafrate, was published in 1997 and has also done very well. To my surprise, however, both the first edition *and* the revised one continue to sell many copies. Readers find the first uniquely persuasive and often use both books to help them overcome their anger. The two books, though containing some of the same material, supplement each other. So the publisher has decided to keep both of them in print and has asked me to bring *Anger: How to Live With and Without It* up to date.

I have been happy to do this, especially since many serious forms of rage have increased considerably in recent years. Thus, we now have more child abuse, wife battering, child and teenage violence (including murder) than ever before. National and international warring has led to the terrorism of September 11, 2001. Unhappily no end is in sight—nor is any easy solution. An immense reeducation of practically all children and adults throughout the world is required to stem this tremendous tide of violence.

The theory and practice of Rational Emotive Behavior Therapy, which is espoused in this book, is no panacea or miracle cure for personal and group violence. But it and several closely related philosophies may importantly contribute to stemming it. Read this book, help yourself by its messages of collaboration and peace, and do what you can to spread them widely to your relatives, friends, and everyone else. What better can you do for yourself and the world?

Albert Ellis, Ph.D.
Albert Ellis Institute
45 East 65th Street
New York, NY 10021
aiellis@aol.com

Acknowledgments

Just about all published books, these days, result from collaboration between the author and several other important contributors. So with this one. First, I want to thank the many clients I have cited, though quite anonymously, in this book for their invaluable contributions. My editors at Citadel Press have been particularly helpful. Although I take full responsibility for all the ideas in the book, these and my clinical associates at the Albert Ellis Institute in New York have contributed mightily to them and to this book.

ANGER

HOW TO LIVE WITH AND WITHOUT IT

"What disturbs people's minds is not events but their judgments on events."

—Epictetus

1

Must You Feel Angry?

You'd better face the hard reality that situations that frustrate or prevent you from attaining your goals and from enjoying what you want really do exist. But have you no choice but to feel angry at these everyday "horrors"?

Most mental health experts agree that you must feel anger. They see the newborn infant as expressing emotions comparable to anger and rage in the first hours of life. And throughout all ages of development humans confront almost daily their own feelings of anger and those of other people whom they encounter. Most authorities say you need your anger to protect yourself from the onslaughts of a hostile and aggressive world. If you do not always remain on your guard, you will stay vulnerable to others who will dominate and exploit you, jeopardize your freedom and property, and take advantage of your passivity by abusing you for their own personal gain with no regard to your welfare.

What, exactly, is anger? It is a special *combination* of your thoughts, feelings, and behaviors, when you are (or think you are) severely frustrated by unfortunate conditions and by people's "unfair" behavior. As Howard Kassinove and his collaborators point out and as Mark Terjesen and Raphael Rose agree, when you feel angry, you have a negative internal feeling state accompanied by thinking and perceptual distortions and deficiencies (especially misappraisals and attributions of other people's injustice). Your angry thoughts and feelings lead you to physiological arousal and tendencies to act against your "aggressors."

Many authorities on anger, including Raymond DiGiuseppe, believe that angry (and depressed) individuals "are unstable in the way they assign blame and have an unstable sense of self." Raymond Chip Tafrate and his research associates found that subjects high on trait anger were more prone to dysfunctional thinking and also experienced a greater number of physical sensations than people who were low on trait anger. Aron Siegman and Selena Snow discovered that the full-blown expression of anger is a form of emotional disturbance while the mere inner experience of anger is not.

At the same time, as I shall show throughout this book, anger is often self-protective, is a very normal human response, and has helped preserve the human race.

Your failing to fight for what you want leaves you the alternative of remaining passive when others take advantage of and prevent you from achieving your goals. Thus, most authorities today generally leave you with one of two alternatives for dealing with anger:

Feel the anger but sit on it, squelch it, deny and repress it.

Feel the anger and freely express it.

Squelching your anger doesn't get you much of anywhere, and unexpressed rage will do you more harm than candidly and freely expressed feelings. Sigmund Freud's *hydraulic theory* states that anger and other emotions have a tendency to increase in intensity—to expand under pressure like steam in a kettle—so that if you squelch your emotions, if you don't give free vent to them, you run the risk of doing some real harm to yourself. Physical harm such as stomach ulcers, high blood pressure, or other sometimes more severe psychosomatic reactions result. In addition, refraining from giving honest expression to your feelings—keeping these feelings pent up inside you—doesn't help you lose your anger. Quite the contrary. You will, in all probability, feel much worse. For your anger hasn't gone away, but stays right there in your "gut." And now you can easily turn overly critical of yourself for not standing up for your rights with those who have caused the injustice.

Conversely, if you let yourself feel authentically angry and let others know about your feelings, you may encounter problems of quite another nature. For people will receive your free expression of anger in most instances as an outwardly aggressive or hostile action, and will probably close themselves off from you and defensively respond to you with *further* hostility.

Some therapists in the field have attempted to solve the problem with still another alternative, what they call *creative aggression* (or *constructive anger*). This differs from the above *free-expression* method in that you express yourself more controllably and hope (often against hope!) that others will willingly listen to your point of view.

In the following example I will attempt to illustrate the dynamics of the other theories and then, using the same example throughout the book, will investigate the alternatives and solutions that Rational Emotive Behavior Therapy offers. I am confident that if you pay close attention to these principles, you will see that you can deal with problems relating to anger and other emotions effectively and efficiently by use of the REBT guidelines.

Let us say that I have promised to share an apartment with you as a roommate and to share the rent, provided you fix up and furnish the place. This seems agreeable to you. You go to a good deal of trouble and personal expense to keep your part of the bargain. At the last minute I inform you that I have made other plans and cannot, will not keep my part of the agreement. You feel extremely angry with me; not only have you gone to considerable expense to keep your agreement, but you are distinctly inconvenienced in that you must at the last minute look for another roommate.

You may at first keep your feelings of anger to yourself. But because you have those feelings, unexpressed, your underlying resentment greatly interferes with our friendship. So you see that nothing gets resolved, that your seething interferes with your other activities as well, and that this solution won't work.

You decide to confront me with your feelings, to *express* them. "Look here," you say, "I won't have you treating me like this! After all, you said you'd share the apartment with me after I had furnished it. I would never have fixed it up had you not agreed to share it with me in the first place. You've clearly done me in, and acted really rottenly. How could you have done a thing like that to a friend? I've never done anything so nasty to you, and I really don't see how you can expect anyone's friendship if you treat people so terribly."

Or instead, given the convenience of my having the capacity and willingness to play it with you, you use *creative aggression*, express your anger controllably, and "prepare" me for what will come. Receiving my permission to open up about your feelings, you go ahead to express your anger.

Although your perception of my unfairness to you may be correct, your presentation of it (either through the free-expression method or through creative aggression) *can* do more harm than good. Both approaches focus on my wrong, even if creative aggression allows for a softening of the blow. Through that focus, you can easily set the stage for additional problems with me.

By openly criticizing me for my "outrageous" behavior, you can push me to *defend* it. Then any steps I might take to treat you more fairly would be halted.

Remember also that I, like most people, may have strong self-downing tendencies. When you point out to me my "error" or my unappealing characteristics, I may carry your implications farther than you even intended. Hence, from your critical remarks, no matter how well, how creatively put, I may feel guilt or self-downing, and will frequently try to make you equally self-blaming. We'd better acknowledge these very real problems as inherent in either of the two approaches that recommend expressing your anger. Nonetheless, acknowledging this still does not solve your problem: What do you *do* with your anger?

So far we have seen holding in your anger brings dubious results. Yet freely expressing it creates many other problems. Creative aggression seems a more workable solution but still shares some of the same difficulties.

Another alternative—that of *Christian forgiveness*—involves the turning of the other cheek. But in this often hostile world in which we live, this is somewhat impractical. People may feel far less intimidated by you and thus all the more tempted to take advantage of your "good nature." You may behave beautifully, but unfortunately, that does not mean that others will respect you and treat you equally well.

After examining the above alternatives in dealing with your anger, you may see that each approach may work in a given situation, but not in *all* situations. Further, each one of these approaches has serious and destructive drawbacks. So let us look for a formula that will allow you to deal with difficult situations and get what you want without damaging your own integrity or inciting anger in others.

The following chapters will introduce methods that are free of the drawbacks of the other approaches already discussed. If you read carefully and give your full attention to the techniques presented in this book, if you take the time and trouble to think seriously about, experiment with, and test out these concepts in your own life, and if you energetically and conscientiously practice them over a period of time, I believe that you, too, will see and enjoy the changes that REBT has helped bring about in the anger problems of my clients and readers.

2

How You Create Your Own Anger: The ABCs of REBT

The ABCs of REBT (Rational Emotive Behavior Therapy) can give you what I call an elegant approach to the problem of dealing with your anger. Not a magical formula—quite the contrary, since REBT concerns itself with seeking solutions and dealing with your problems in a realistic manner. It prefers to stick with hardheaded facts of reality—not with airy theories.

How exactly did the theory of REBT evolve? What does it have that makes it different from and often more effective than other forms of psychotherapy?

The basic principles of REBT have evolved from my own extensive clinical research and experience, further supported by numerous experiments done in this area. During my career as a psychotherapist I have had occasion to use many different techniques in treating my many clients. These years have shown me and my trainees that most of the psychoanalytic approaches are ineffective, inefficient, and fail to meet the problems of most people who seek therapy. I say this from my own personal experience. Although the field of psychotherapy includes many techniques and approaches to helping people, most of its methods are too expensive and time consuming for both clients and therapists. Naturally, emotional problems themselves have enormous costs, and if long drawn-out types of therapy show positive and lasting results, the investment seems well worth it. But alas, such therapies, according to my own observations, do not appear to work out.

I have drawn many of the important principles of REBT from the wisdom of philosophy as well as from the most modern psychological advances. Since my youth I have made the in-depth study of philosophy a hobby; and by incorporating some of its principles into my therapeutic approach, I discovered that my clients could achieve more effective results in far less time than when I used other approaches. I found that by my presenting a philosophical as well as a psychological analysis, the client could enjoy the fruits of two sciences and benefit considerably from our efforts.

Although I'd naturally advise you to consult a competent rational therapist when you have a serious problem, you can use REBT to efficiently "therapize" yourself with little outside help. In this book I will explain how you create your own anger *philosophically*—by consciously or unconsciously subscribing to absolutistic, demand-oriented thinking. If you understand exactly how to control and operate your thinking, you will enable yourself, with the guidance of this book, to undercut and change the counterproductive and destructive aspects of your anger. REBT has designed methods in which you can dissolve your rage no matter what unjust events happen to you.

Perhaps the most distressing fault that I realized while using the usual techniques of psychotherapy was this: Upon termination of many years of therapy, clients still could not confront life's difficult situations on their own without the continued help of their therapist. I felt that after spending all that time and money my clients certainly deserved better results. Rather than continue with these methods, I began to experiment with some ideas of my own. By combining philosophy with various approaches used in therapy, I devised the fundamental principles of REBT. The results were rewarding: Instead of depending on me to give them useless interpretations, my clients now had a realistic perspective with which to think and behave. In a relatively short time they began to show more rapid and lasting progress than from previous methods.

With most of my clients, I use realistic examples to help them work through their problems. Here, for the sake of clarity, I shall mainly stick to one consistent example throughout the book; so we shall continue with the illustration already introduced in chapter 1. I have promised to share an apartment with you if you go ahead and fix it up and furnish it. We have agreed that from then on we will share the expenses. You have so far lived up to your half of the agreement, but at the last minute, without ample notice or explanation, I withdraw from my portion of the agreement. You become enraged with me.

How, by using REBT methods, can you overcome your hostility?

We begin by locating C—the *Emotional* (or *Behavioral*) *Consequence:* your anger.

Next we look for A—your *Adversity* or *Activating Event*. I failed to uphold my portion of an important agreement between us.

As we look at A and C, it may appear that A causes C. REBT theory assumes, however, that although your Adversity or Activating Event directly *contributes* to your Emotional Consequence, it does not really *cause* it. We do not always easily see the dynamics of cause and effect. Yet if we look closely at this relationship between A and C—as we will throughout this book—we will find other factors involved and find that although my withdrawing from our agreement may have inconvenienced and disappointed you greatly, my "unjust" action alone does not necessarily make you feel angry with me.

If we conclude that C directly results from A, then we would have to assume that whenever we encountered any one particular A, we would always expect a particular C. For instance, we know that water boils at one temperature and freezes at another, and we find this true for all situations involving water and temperature. Yet when people and various situations interact together, such laws of causality do not hold true. Most of us know occurrences in which we were surprised by a person's reaction to a given situation. For instance, we have often heard of victims of brutal crimes who, instead of cooperating with the police and courts to bring their assailant to justice, have done just the opposite. They have gone so far as to actually help their assailant avoid prosecution. If we examine one hundred people, all victims of the same crime, we would surely find a large variation of responses among these people. Some would act in the above manner, others would obsess themselves with the arrest and prosecution of the perpetrator, and yet others would respond at various points between these two extremes. An Emotional and Behavioral Consequence, although affected by an Activating Event or Adversity, does not directly and exclusively result from it.

Another important point to keep in mind: We do, in fact, have choices and control over our responses to every situation, and our feelings and responses often remain much more within our control than we realize. The more aware we are of our existing alternatives, the more likely our ability to consider the situation in its proper perspective before we take action. The intermediate thought process that we carry on *between* A and C is an evaluation in which we make a decision that will determine our response. The more aware we make ourselves of this intermediate phase, the better chance we have of making a choice that makes us likely to achieve our goals. Through such choices we minimize the possibility of interfering with our progress by impulsive behavior.

The sciences of linguistics, philosophy, and psychology have each attempted some explanation of the dynamics of thought and cognition as they affect our Emotional Consequences. We rarely give much consideration to cognition, or how we think, and therefore we seldom are aware of the influence it has upon our actions and reactions.

You, like every other person, have developed a *Belief System* that you rely upon to assist you in making judgments and evaluating situations, ideas, people, and events. Although you have your own personal belief or value system, you also have many beliefs consistent with others in your given society or culture. Yet in some important ways the Belief Systems of different cultures significantly differ. We continually discover that customs and behavioral patterns that we judge barbaric and crude exist in civilized cultures. We also know that an individual may hold a number of different Belief Systems at once, that cultural norms change during an individual's lifetime, and that individuals can change, sometimes radically, their feelings and opinions about many things in order to remain happy and productive in an ever-changing world.

As each society establishes sets of beliefs, values, and norms that bind its inhabitants together cooperatively, its religious, political, and parental teachers pass on guidelines that serve as foundations for the development of our own personal Belief Systems. Therefore, our individual Belief Systems include ideas not entirely our own. Much of what we think good or bad, right or wrong, we have imbibed from others.

Even though beliefs are influenced by environment, no universal norm exists. No action or person rates as either good or bad in and of itself, but instead is rated by somewhat arbitrary and changeable standards.

Let us turn our attention to B, your Belief System. Before advancing a detailed explanation of B, let us clarify one main point. Although B exerts an extremely strong influence upon your reactions at C, we'd better not see B as the only factor in determining C but always remember that A *also* influences your reactions. Your behavior at C, then, follows a combination of A and B. As we shall see later, you often cannot influence A although you can determinedly try!

Your conception of reality is not merely your responses to current external stimuli. This conception instead stems from a vast storehouse of your previous experiences and your personal beliefs and associations related to these experiences. Every action you take follows a series of thoughts, no matter how independent these actions appear. You tend to avoid those situations that you consider repulsive, harmful, or distasteful, while you seek those that seem to you desirable.

Actually, the ABCs of your feelings and actions are more complicated than I have just indicated. As I pointed out in 1956 in my first paper on REBT at the American Psychological Association's annual convention, your Consequences (C's) include thoughts, feelings, and behaviors—all of which integrally influence each other. When you think, you *also* feel and behave; when you feel, you *also* think and behave; and when you behave, you *also* think and feel. Activating Events (A's) also include and interact with Beliefs (B's), and with Consequences (C's). We shall discuss this in detail later.

Using the REBT model and once knowing what is happening at B and what are your Consequences at C, I have found it easy to locate quickly and accurately important details about what you are most likely telling yourself at B, your Belief System. Then I can show you (and other people) how to deal with life's difficult situations and teach you to use the REBT model yourself. Of course, literally thousands of Activating Experiences and Emotional Consequences exist. Yet REBT has discovered that in almost any situation you may place B in one of a few categories. Once aware of both A and C, you can find B with little difficulty—as I shall show you farther on in this book.

If your C (Consequence) is anger, REBT shows you that your feelings of anger (or any other self-defeating feeling) largely result from your perceiving a "negative" experience at A. It also shows you that your Belief System has strongly influenced your feelings at C. At this point REBT seeks to help you discover exactly what beliefs contribute to this anger and show you how you can alter them by examining their unreality and irrationality. You then can change your unhealthy and unproductive feelings of rage to healthy and productive feelings of sorrow, disappointment, and frustration.

Who actually originated the ABCs of anger and of other human disturbances? Probably the ancient Asian, Greek, and Roman philosophers, from whom I first derived them. Lao-tzu and Gautama Buddha, both of whom lived in the sixth century B.C., saw that people partly create and can choose to uncreate their angry feelings; and Seneca and Epictetus, in the first century A.D., and following the Greek Stoic philosophers from the fourth century B.C., were quite clear about people's ability to construct and deconstruct their angry feelings and actions. Seneca wrote a book, *On Anger*, in which he gave scores of examples of how we make ourselves feel angry and how we can change our thinking and action to change our feelings.

After I developed Rational Emotive Behavior Therapy (REBT) between 1953 and 1955 and presented my first paper on it in 1956, a good many therapists started working with and researching the cognitive-behavioral approach to anger and produced many studies and case histories supporting it. These included Aaron Beck, Jerry Deffenbacher, Raymond DiGiuseppe, Chris Eckhardt, Howard Kassinove, Raymond Novaco, and Chip Tafrate. As a result of their studies and many others, the ABCs of inducing and reducing rage have been well established in the psychological literature. Ready for you to use!

3

The Insanity of Anger

In this chapter I will attempt to show how your rational and irrational Beliefs fall into only a few major categories, and how you can learn to recognize and amend these beliefs. We have learned that in REBT we start at C. Thus, to give as clear an explanation as possible of your Belief System, let us first consider an important point about C that we have so far neglected.

In REBT we can divide all negative feelings into two major categories. At point C (Consequence), we have what we call:

Healthy negative feelings
and
Unhealthy negative feelings

Although no strict or inflexible definition exists for either category, we can simply say that when any Adversity (A) occurs in your life, healthy negative feeling consists of attitudes or approaches that will help you get what you want and help you deal with what you don't want. They will encourage feelings and behaviors that will help you remain alive and live in a reasonably happy and productive manner. It follows, then, that unhealthy negative feelings tend to sabotage or inhibit you from achieving what you desire.

We can also divide your Belief System into two basic categories:

Rational Beliefs (RBs)
and
Irrational Beliefs (IBs)

Let us begin with your Rational Beliefs (RBs). We may safely assume that all human beings have some rational, self-helping and social-aiding beliefs. Our cooperative interaction with other people strongly testifies to the fact that almost all of us have strong sets of rational beliefs that we use to control and direct our personal and social behavior. If we did not, the human race would have progressed very little during its history. As noted in chapter 2, we often learn our Rational Beliefs from our elders, and they vary greatly in many respects from culture to culture. The major guidelines for civilized norms and Belief Systems have undergone a process of evolution just as our bodies and cultures have changed throughout history. Human development and the development of our Belief Systems constitute processes in which many factors interact.

Almost every time something happens to you at A (Activating Event), you respond in one of two ways: rationally or irrationally. Although your response often includes a combination of both modes, you can sometimes affect your actions more by one mode than the other. For instance, you may ignore your Rational Beliefs and respond to a situation on a largely irrational level. Your Irrational Beliefs about an event may have, thus, had an extremely strong, "winning" influence.

Let us return now to our illustration and see if we can locate your Rational Beliefs. We know that you feel angry with me at C due to your perception of my behavior at A, in that I "unfairly" withdrew from an important agreement with you. Because of this situation, you may say to yourself something like: "What a bad thing he has done to me. How terrible of him to treat me in such a shoddy and inconsiderate manner!" This may seem a rational or reasonable statement. Nonetheless, we can see, on reflection, that although you appear to express only one idea here, you in fact have two ideas, each of which you'd better consider separately.

"What a bad thing he has done to me" (meaning, "He has seriously frustrated my plans, and his actions have greatly inconvenienced me"). The observation that I have done a "bad thing" to you seems accurate.

Second, you tell yourself, "How terrible of him to treat me in such a shoddy and inconsiderate manner." Here you see what I have done as "terrible," and you wind up with an Irrational Belief. As we shall see later, this idea of thinking of an action or event as "terrible" or "horrible" is unhealthy and irrational because it may lead you to do a good deal of damage to your goals and happiness.

By allowing your IBs to take precedence over your RBs, you do not give sufficient attention to the full reality behind your Activating Experience. Your neglecting to contemplate, in advance, the possible outgrowths of your response at C (Consequence), may make you react self-destructively and can lead to the same kind of problems that we saw with both the free-expression method and the "sit-on-your-anger" approach. Rational Emotive Behavior Therapy firmly holds that unless you are aware of your ability to change your Irrational Beliefs, you will have difficult problems in dealing with your anger. REBT also maintains the importance of changing your feelings at C when they are destructive. *It states that if you want to change your feelings and your actions in the quickest, most efficient and effective way, you'd better pay particular attention to changing your Belief System.*

At A you are sure that I have treated you unfairly by withdrawing from our agreement.

- At RB, your Rational Belief System, you believe, "I don't like that. I wish he hadn't treated me so shabbily."
- At HC, your Healthy Consequence, you experience feelings of disappointment, displeasure, and discomfort.
- *Rational Beliefs (don't like) and Healthy Consequences (disappointment)*

Yet we find that at UC, your Unhealthy Consequence or disturbed feeling, you are angry at me as well as disappointed with my behavior. You find your anger unmanageable and self-defeating, and therefore unhealthy. Using the REBT method, I help you seek the Irrational Beliefs (IBs) that led to your Unhealthy Consequence (raging at me).

- *Irrational Belief and Unhealthy Consequence (anger)*

To locate your IBs we use the method of logical, empirical checking, designed to discover any illogical or unempirical ideas you might hold at B. By putting the case into the REBT framework, a clinician can discover your RBs and IBs simply through a knowledge of your feelings and behavior at both points A and C. Logically, for example, your Irrational Belief isn't something like, "How obnoxious of Dr. Ellis to lead me on like that and then withdraw in that manner." This idea *does* make sense, as just about everyone would agree. Also, your viewing my behavior as merely obnoxious will likely lead you to feel not anger but rather disappointment. So, in continuing to look at your ideas about such behavior, we may discover that you have said or thought, "I think it's *awful* that Ellis acted in such an irresponsible manner. He *absolutely shouldn't* treat me that unfairly!" Although this may not at first glance appear very irrational or illogical, you have, in fact, made one of the four irrational statements that angry people often make:

You have told yourself that you find it *awful*, *horrible*, or *terrible* that I have treated you in this manner. You have equated unfairness or injustice with *horror* and failed to distinguish between the two.

As I have just indicated, REBT states that you can discover the nature of your Belief Systems by knowing the facts at points A and C. People experience a relatively limited number of emotions, which fall within a few major headings, and certain thoughts connect with certain emotions. People teach themselves to use these thoughts to evoke emotions. As we have stressed before, your Belief System makes it possible to apply value judgments such as good or bad, right or wrong, to any experience. Here again you can see a strong relationship or interaction between thinking and feeling.

In fact, one of the main REBT hypotheses states that you seem to feel what you think or expect to feel—and not what you actually do experience. You prejudice your feelings about something with your views of what you believe you should feel. Usually you can more quickly, easily, and importantly change your feelings as you change your thinking than you can change your thinking by modifying your feelings. But the reverse is also often true.

Just how much *do* your feelings about something cause you to change your thinking? You frequently know that you desire to act in a manner that you believe is highly undesirable. When such feelings become extremely strong or urgent, you may act in a manner contrary to your own beliefs. When you act this way, you often rationalize so as to alter, at least temporarily, certain beliefs. But once you gratify your feelings through actions, you frequently revert to your former beliefs, and feel guilty because you did not really change those beliefs but merely laid them aside temporarily to allow yourself to act in a certain way. Hence, we see that your thoughts may alter your feelings, yet we can also see that you often only temporarily alter them in specific situations.

The following four irrational statements represent some main beliefs that angry people generally hold:

1. "How *awful* for you to have treated me so unfairly."
2. "I *can't stand* your treating me in such an irresponsible and unjust manner."
3. "You absolutely *should not, must not* behave that way toward me."
4. "Because you have acted in that manner toward me, I see you as a *terrible person* who deserves nothing good in life, and who should be punished for treating me so badly."

A relationship exists between these four statements. Note that besides the negative views in each of the statements, they include another common factor—a tendency to merge the action with the person or to evaluate his negative action with the whole person.

This failure to separate a person from his action implies that only an (x) person can act (x) and that all (x) acts must be performed by (x) people. Further, and more specifically, any person who does anything that any other person deems bad or unjust must *be* a bad person. If a good person performs good acts, then he can *never* do anything bad, for he *is* a good person and capable of only good acts. If a bad person performs bad acts, he can *never* do anything good, for he *is* a bad person and can perform only bad acts.

This overgeneralizing seems logical, yet wisely we'd better remember that logical "truths" often do not accord with facts. We can see the logic of the above statements, yet we may just as easily see their irrationality. We know realistically that people who are seen as "good and respectable" often do gross injustices to others. Also, we have often seen people who have acted unjustly and unfairly a number of times labeled as "bad people." Thus, we know that "logical" thinking often is false to life, although it may hold true to the rules of logic.

In the case of your angering yourself at me and viewing *me* as rotten when I do a rotten act (unfairly break our apartment-sharing agreement), you had better try to find the primary or underlying irrationality that makes you feel anger at point C. Using what you have learned about the relationships existing between people and their actions, you can see your underlying irrationality consists of making a false association between your evaluation of me and your evaluation of my action. So although REBT holds that there seem no absolute laws or rules that will apply to all people in every situation, you may still use its simple rule of thumb for discerning the difference between RB and IB in your Belief System:

> Your beliefs are rational so long as they do not make an evaluation of the *action* into an evaluation of the *person*. And further: You remain rational so long as you view the action in a limited way: by the effect that it has upon you who experience it. The evaluation of a person can only legitimately arise from evaluating all his acts over an entire lifetime, and even then he would have to be dead. For if still living, you cannot evaluate what he will do in the future.

We cannot judge an individual's Belief System as *totally* irrational unless this person has either a most severe psychotic disorder or severe mental retardation. Even then every person alive holds an Irrational Belief about something from time to time, and psychotic and retarded people have *some* sensible ideas. People's Belief Systems largely determine their feelings and reactions. But remember that that Belief System can include RBs and IBs *simultaneously*.

If, at point A, you feel inconvenienced or disappointed by a situation, then you may have a healthy negative feeling. But your emotion of anger at the person causing your inconvenience shows (at C) disturbance because you had better separate the evaluation of the action and the evaluation of the person even though most people do not make this separation. By confusing a damnable act with a damnable person, you make yourself needlessly angry. You might expect to feel disappointed, inconvenienced, or discouraged at C by unfair actions. But when you feel angry and hostile, and assume that the perpetrator of these actions *is* a terrible person, you overgeneralize, as Alfred Korzybski has showed, and disturb yourself.

For the sake of clarity, we'd better look at the causal relationship between your IBs and your anger. Although we have no incontrovertible proof that these IBs are the most direct or only cause of anger, by looking at the intrinsic relationship between thought and feeling we find a very close connection between the two. We have seen that using the REBT model, we have been able to point out to people their own IBs and, further, to teach them how to reduce them. In the process, we discovered that their anger diminished or evaporated.

While I would find it of great interest to investigate the transactional relationship between thinking and feeling, the huge amount of data that I would have to consider in order to make this clear and complete would go beyond the scope of this book. Suffice it to say that although I only present REBT as a theory, I know from clinical experience and from many outcome studies—summarized in my books *How to Control Your Anger Before It Controls You* (cowritten with Chip Tafrate) and *Overcoming Destructive Beliefs, Feelings, and Behavior*—that REBT and Cognitive Behavior Therapy (CBT) are effective.

Having established two aspects to your individual Belief System—

rational and irrational—you confront another problem. If we indeed assume that humans are basically rational and constructive, why, then, should such rational animals have Irrational Beliefs and act in accordance with IBs that sabotage their goals?

The answer is that when people are merely frustrated, they usually feel annoyed at the frustration. But when they think someone *unfairly* frustrates them, they often make themselves angry at the frustrating *person*.

When I withdrew from our sharing arrangement, you experienced frustration. You did not get what you wanted. Now, if we had never reached an agreement and I had not unfairly broken this agreement in the first place, you would have felt frustrated with the situation and perhaps disappointed, but you would not have felt angry with me. You would have simply judged your situation as undesirable or bad. But now that I have "unfairly" withdrawn from our *agreement*, although you remain in the same position as you would have been had we never entered into an agreement and I changed my mind about living with you, you feel incensed with me, because of my *unfairness*.

What makes you disappointed in one instance and angry in another even though your situation in regard to sharing an apartment with me stays the same in both—we don't share an apartment? Your Irrational Beliefs that I *shouldn't* treat you unfairly and that I am a *bad person* for doing so.

By feeling angry with me, you can blame me for your situation, and you can also give yourself a false assurance that you are doing something to relieve yourself. By fighting me for treating you in a manner you consider unjust, you do not have to confront the original dissatisfaction; hence, you have an illusion that you actively do something about your situation.

You may get several secondary gains through anger, such as the one above. An understanding of secondary gains provides some explanation of why rational humans hold Irrational Beliefs, why all humans at times allow their IBs to influence them and hence act dysfunctionally.

If you derive some secondary gain from your anger, why should you make any attempt to rid yourself of it? Through our understanding of secondary gains, we can see that every action has its *intention*. Each action you carry through has a specific aim or goal. For instance, anger may lead to some secondary gain in that it relieves you from dealing with a difficult situation. Even though your anger may have a positive goal, you'd better critically evaluate its possible destructive qualities. So we'd better look closely at some of the realistic consequences of anger.

1. Anger stems from your belief that a person's action is *the same thing as* the person himself. Just as you evaluate his act as negative, you respond to his whole being as "bad." Your Irrational Belief thus results in your damning a whole person who will most probably in turn respond in a defensive manner in order to protect her own self-image. So long as you are angry, your openness vanishes, and your anger will inhibit a speedy and effective resolution of your problem.
2. Anger, a rather strong emotion, tends to overlap or extend into other areas of your life. Many people, when angry, feel hostile to others who have done slightly "wrong" things. This often creates unnecessary social tension and a counterproductive atmosphere.
3. Your depression and anxiety that may result from increased tensions stemming from anger reduce your effective performance in the various aspects of your life.
4. Points 2 and 3 may lead to the creation of negative responses from other people that may in turn cause you to feel highly critical of yourself. In many instances, this encourages self-downing and intensifies your anxiety.
5. Anger compounded with a combination of its above-mentioned side effects can create difficult tensions both within yourself and in your relationships with others. These may result in such complications that you have difficulty realizing that your original anger leads to other bad situations. Hence, any resolution of the original problem will still fail to resolve the new difficulties that that anger encourages.

As we view these points, we can easily see that the side effects of anger far outweigh the secondary gains that you may achieve. For the secondary "gains," *in the case of anger*, remain dysfunctional and have no real effect except perhaps camouflage upon the original situation. REBT theory concludes that anger has few *real* benefits.

In concluding this chapter, let us return to our REBT model and the illustration we have presented and use REBT methods to work through your problem of being angry at me.

You entered into an agreement with me whereby we would share an apartment. Your part consisted of your getting the place ready and furnishing it and mine with moving in with you. From that point we would share all expenses equally. At the last minute, and without sufficient notice or reason, I withdrew from my portion of the agreement—after you had fulfilled your part of the agreement. Your anger at me has these components:

A (Activating Event or Adversity): my withdrawal from our agreement, which you consider an "unfair act."
RB (Rational Belief): "What a bad action! I don't like it!"
IB (Irrational Belief): "How *awful*, I just *can't stand* Albert Ellis treating me in that manner! He *should not*, *must not* behave that way toward me, and I think that he is a *horrible person* for doing so and that he *should be punished!*"
HC (Healthy Consequence): disappointment, feelings of rejection, sense of loss of a good opportunity.
UC (Unhealthy Consequence): anger, feelings of hostility, a strong urge for revenge or punishment.

Because you have judged my conduct as obnoxious and because my withdrawal from our agreement has greatly disappointed and inconvenienced you, you would act wisely if you decided not to enter into any further agreement with me. If by my withdrawal I had put you to an extreme financial expense, you might possibly seek legal counsel if you could not get proper satisfaction from me directly. By minimally associating with me, you can avoid the hassle of my unfairly treating you again.

Yet by not making yourself feel angry, you leave open the possibility of reestablishing good relations with me, for you still acknowledge my good qualities. I discover that I cannot take advantage of you, for you guard against that. Because you do not totally reject me for acting unfairly, you respect me as a person in spite of my behavior, and you tend to respect yourself as a person in spite of your ineffective anger.

Although you have other alternatives with the REBT solution, you can see from this example that it not only deals with the disadvantages of anger but also provides the groundwork for reestablishing relationships on the basis of mutual respect.

We have thus far explained the basic principles of the REBT theory. The next chapter will examine various methods you can use to help you detect the Irrational Beliefs that create your anger.

4

Looking for Self-Angering Philosophies

I hope I have succeeded in explaining the general dynamic of the REBT theory as it applies to anger and other healthy and unhealthy emotions. However, as I remarked earlier, much more than a mere understanding of a problem or a knowledge of its underlying cause is required to solve that problem.

REBT gives you important insights into your present situation rather than mainly into your past problems. Psychoanalytic methods that attempt to reveal insights about your childhood are of little use in facilitating adequate "working through" of your present problems. Still, we had better make a distinction between REBT insights and classical psychoanalytic insights.

Granted that the influences of your parents, teachers, religious leaders, and environment may greatly contribute to your "personality," but your personality is by no means fixed and unchangeable. Take, for example, the condition of animal phobia, a common problem for many mature adults. Classical psychotherapy would attempt to trace your life back to early childhood in an attempt to discover what associations you have to the particular animal that you fear. It would then attempt to enlighten you with an interpretation of your fear.

My experience has shown me that such insights bring little help to you today. In fact, they may often dwell so much on such explanations of your problem that they reinforce your phobia by "helping" you see that you do have something to fear today. Your fears may thus increase!

The REBT approach would locate any IBs that you may hold at present and show you exactly how you can change these beliefs in order to overcome your problems. True, your insights about the past may have importance; but an insight that you can use to help solve a real present-day problem will prove more immediately useful. What happened ten or twenty years ago has little or no value now. It happened. The past remains fixed and unchangeable, while you may affect the present and future by your present thoughts and actions.

Those responsible for the upbringing of children have them more or less at their mercy. Youngsters have little or no choice in their somewhat helpless situation; and because their minds are in a formative stage, they have little ability to choose better alternatives. Children also lack the knowledge and critical evaluations so important in making the best decisions. Their inability independently to meet their own needs, such as obtaining food, clothing, and shelter, places them in a state of genuine dependency. Parents work hard to influence their children's behavior and beliefs. Once we reach adulthood we have aquired the knowledge, exposure, and independence to enable us to choose more wisely and rationally for ourselves. I don't know of any adults who haven't substantially changed their views of what their parents have told them, and the vast majority has managed to accomplish this without the aid of classical psychoanalysis.

REBT stresses the important idea that as adult human beings we consciously have choices; we make choices every day, and *we—not* our parents or others—direct these choices. As a mature adult you had better recognize that you control your ideas, attitudes, and actions; that you largely arrange your life according to your own dictates. Changing your life involves your willingness to separate yourself from the childish concept that your parents still can make you act and think today. It also involves your attending to your present and future situations, not to your infantile ones. Many of my clients, when they become aware of their irrational ideas, tell me they got these ideas from their parents or elders as children. Yes, but they stem from children's and adults' *own* creative talent for inventing crooked ways of thinking!

Let us now return to our REBT model and show you how to use the insights we have thus far acquired to locate and rid yourself of destructive, goal-inhibiting IBs and dysfunctional behaviors. In the last chapter we discussed what represents a clear understanding of how our Belief System interacts with our experience at point A and our reactions at point C. At this point we ask, "What does B consist of?" We seek to know both what RBs and also, more important, what IBs you hold.

You can use two more or less overlapping approaches to locate and differentiate your RBs and your IBs. First you ask, "What do I actually appear to believe at B just before I experience my Consequences at C?" If you cannot immediately answer that, you can see that you know both A and C. If C seems unhealthy—such as severe anger, anxiety, or depression—you may well assume that some type of IB influenced your feeling. We have already listed the four Irrational Beliefs that most people hold with regard to anger. But once again:

1. "How *awful* or *terrible* that you treat me like this!"
2. "I *can't stand* your irresponsible behavior!"
3. "You *absolutely should not* act in that bad manner toward me!"
4. "Because you behave as you should not and must not, you are a *rotten person* who deserves to be punished!"

Although these statements hold for anger, they often seem not to apply when you experience severe anxiety or depression at C.

Severe anxiety is more or less an internal danger signal activated when for some reason, either conscious or unconscious, you feel something will happen that will prevent you from getting what you want or will really harm you. Anxiety often stems from sets of Irrational Beliefs that you hold about yourself, while anger stems from Irrational Beliefs that you hold about others. Using our illustration, let us say that for some reason or other you suspected that you received a signal or message from me that I would withdraw from our agreement before I directly expressed my plans to do so. Let us suppose that you heard me speaking to a friend about some future plan of mine that would not work out if our agreement still held. You do not yet know for certain what exact plans I have. You feel it inappropriate to honestly confront me on the issue. You feel you have no choice but to keep this information to yourself. These circumstances may represent A, while your feeling of anxiety may represent C. Because anxiety, like anger, constitutes an Unhealthy Consequence (UC), let us begin to use REBT to question those beliefs that you might hold at point A. Using what you have learned about the ideas we consider irrational in relation to anger and understanding that anxiety differs from anger in that you direct it inward rather than toward a person or object, you may look for a set of irrational ideas that overlap with anger in many respects.

When you experience anxiety as in the above-mentioned situation where I reneged on our apartment-sharing agreement, you may say or think to yourself the following:

1. "How *awful* if I can't manage things if you act irresponsibly toward me with regard to our agreement."
2. "I couldn't, under such conditions, *bear* the inconvenience you would foist upon me. I *couldn't stand* my own poor methods of coping with you or the situation."
3. "If I don't cope as well as I *must* cope, I am *inferior* and I deserve what I get for not handling the situation."

As you can easily see, the above IBs that apply to anxiety are almost identical to those that relate to anger. The only difference: You hold these ideas or beliefs in relation to yourself rather to another person.

Another illustration demonstrates how you may create unhealthy feelings of depression. Let us say that instead of withdrawing from our agreement, I got transferred to another location and had to move out of town. You realize that I had relatively little choice in the matter because the transfer included a promotion I really wanted, and you understand and support my decision. Yet although not angry with me, you discover that you feel extremely depressed at point C. You may perhaps think something like:

1. "How *awful* that things have turned out so badly for me!"
2. "I *can't stand* things turning out this way!"
3. "Things *absolutely shouldn't* happen this way, and terribly inconvenience me!"
4. "Nothing ever works out the way I want it to. Life is *always unfair* to me—as it *shouldn't* be!"

Obviously the above beliefs are irrational, yet just about all of us have thoughts like these when we depress ourselves. The general character of the IBs that relate to anger, anxiety, and depression are, as we can see, almost identical. The difference is where you direct IBs. Together these three constitute the three basic ways in which people upset themselves: putting others down, putting themselves down, and putting down the conditions of the world in which they live. Throughout the years my associates and I have encountered numerous Irrational Beliefs that people hold to make themselves angry, anxious, and depressed. Yet upon close examination I have found that I can place just about every IB people keep using under one of four major headings. Because of this, I formulated the following simple, yet descriptive names that cover these ideas:

Awfulizing
Can't-Stand-It-itis
Shoulding and Musting
Undeservingness or Damnation

In later chapters we will examine each separately and in greater detail. For the present these descriptive headings can serve as a general idea of the overall *tone* of Irrational Beliefs.

Throughout my long and rewarding career as a clinician, I have had the opportunity to work with and assist numerous people whose problems extended beyond the emotional difficulties that we have considered thus far. I particularly refer to persons who unfortunately have to cope with physiological as well as emotional problems—those, for instance, afflicted with certain handicaps such as epilepsy, dyslexia, encephalitis, attention deficit disorder, mental retardation, and severe personality disorders. Life presents them with extraordinary obstacles that make it almost impossible for many of them to live consistently happy and productive lives.

These handicapped individuals need not damn themselves or the world. Naturally when they realize the difference between themselves and others around them—as many of them do—they often develop severe feelings of inferiority and lack of self-worth. Children, in particular, who suffer handicaps and who associate with children who have less severe handicaps often hate themselves.

REBT practitioners have some wonderfully helpful aids to teach many sorely put-upon people how to live as happily and productively as their particular condition will permit. They often have a problem, such as endogenous depression, that may have biological or neurological origins. We sometimes cannot correct the handicap itself, but we can help people who make themselves disturbed about their handicaps. REBT contends that Irrational Beliefs serve as perhaps the main contributors to disturbance about disturbance, and that these IBs can be corrected so that people do not have secondary disturbances about their primary problems.

I find it almost impossible to overstress the disastrous results of what I call *Shoulding*. Should be? What *should* a person *be?* Who can judge and by what criteria? This irrational idea of *should* comprises perhaps the most destructive and counterproductive of all the irrational ideas I know. An absolutistic *should* can make people devalue themselves in their own eyes and lead to great despondency. Similarly, the idea of *should* can lead many to devalue other people and not merely object to their behavior.

Rational Emotive Behavior Therapy holds that you *absolutely should do* nothing. You have only to exist as you do and to live your life as best you can. If you can learn to accept yourself unconditionally

ally, with your handicaps and other problems, and if you can learn how to live with these difficulties when you cannot improve them, you may consider yourself well adjusted in spite of these handicaps.

REBT recognizes three major forms of irrational thinking. All come under the general heading of *musturbation* and may arise individually or in combination with each other.

Years ago I referred in my writings, talks, and in my work with clients to the *demandingness* or *commandingness* of humans who feel disturbed. I indicated that if you desire, wish, or prefer to do well in life or to have others approve of you, such desiring alone rarely gets you into any kind of emotional difficulty. You may feel distinctly sorry and frustrated when you do not get what you want, but you do not feel angry, anxious, or depressed. To create these disturbances, you almost always escalate your desires into assumed needs, your preferences into demands and insistences, your normal wishes into absolute dictates.

Whenever you feel truly disturbed emotionally, it seems almost inconceivable that you have not resorted to one, two, or all three of the forms of musturbation. Many human problems exist that have little or nothing to do with musturbation, but emotional problems virtually always relate to these forms of thinking and behaving. After talking with thousands of people with varying degrees of emotional upsets, I still haven't found any who do not themselves, with their own self-verbalizing hatchets, create their unnecessary emotional turbulence.

Men and women probably have literally hundreds of important Irrational Beliefs (IBs), any one of which can contribute to upsetting them. As I mentioned earlier, all these IBs seem to fit into only a score of major headings. We shall now outline the main IBs that contribute to or "cause" emotional disturbances.

IRRATIONAL IDEA 1

"I must do well and win the approval of others for my performances or else I am a *rotten, unlovable person!*"

Once you believe this idea, as almost all people in all parts of the world often seem to, you may then somewhat "logically" conclude: "If I am a rotten or inferior person, my life is *awful* and I am too incompetent to change it." This, of course, leads to strong feelings of depression, anxiety, and overall worthlessness.

Irrational Idea 1 primarily produces intense emotions of self-hatred and/or self-downing.

Some of the main corollaries of this Irrational Belief include:

1a. "I must have sincere love and approval almost all the time from virtually all the people whom I find significant or important in my life."

1b. "I must be a thoroughly competent achiever or at least have an outstanding skill or talent in something important to me."

1c. "I must succeed in avoiding noxious or unpleasant situations. My emotional misery comes almost completely from external pressures that I have little ability to change or control. Unless these pressures change, I cannot help making myself feel anything but anxious, depressed, self-downing, or hostile."

1d. "I must never encounter events that put me in real danger or that threaten my life, as I would have to make myself totally preoccupied with and upset about them."

1e. "I must continue to think, feel, and behave as I have in the past. My past life influenced me immensely and remains important today because if something once strongly affected me, it continues to determine and affect my present feelings and behavior. My early-childhood gullibility and conditioning still remain, and I cannot conquer my suggestibility and think for myself."

1f. "I must find a high degree of order, certainty, or predictability in the universe in order to feel comfortable and to perform adequately."

1g. "I must continue to rely and depend on other people. Because I remain weak in this respect, I shall also continue to need and rely on certain sets of superstitious and magical ideas in order to survive times of real stress."

1h. "I must fully understand the nature and secrets of the universe to live happily in it."

1i. "I can and should give myself a global rating as a human, and

I can rate myself as good and worthy *only* if I perform well, do worthwhile things, and have people generally approve of me."

1j. "I must never make myself depressed, anxious, ashamed, or angry, for if I give in to these feelings of disturbance, I am a thoroughly weak and rotten person."

1k. "I must never question the beliefs, attitudes, or opinions held by respected authorities or by my society, family, or peer group because they might be correct. If I do question them, people should rightly condemn and punish me."

IRRATIONAL IDEA 2

"Other people must treat me considerately and kindly and in precisely the way I want them to treat me. If they don't, society and the universe should severely blame, damn, and punish them for their inconsideration!"

2a. "Other people must treat everyone, but especially me, in a fair and considerate manner. If they act unfairly and inconsiderately, they are *rotten people* who deserve punishment and damnation, which society should see that they get."

2b. "Other people *must not* behave incompetently or stupidly. If they do, I justifiably can see and label them as thorough idiots who ought to feel ashamed of themselves and should expect none of the good things in life."

2c. "People who have the ability to perform well must not choose to shirk or avoid their responsibilities. They *absolutely ought* to accept and carry out their duties. They are rotten people and should feel utterly ashamed of themselves if they don't. People must achieve their potential for a happy and worthwhile life, or else they have little or no value as humans."

2d. "Other people *must* not unjustly criticize me. If they do, they are rotten people who deserve practically nothing good in life!"

IRRATIONAL IDEA 3

"The world (and the people in it) must include conditions that enable me to get everything that I want when I want it. Conditions must be arranged so that I don't ever get what I don't want. Moreover, I usually must get what I want quickly and easily."

3a. "Things must go the way I would like them to go because I *need* what I want and life is *awful*, *horrible*, and *terrible* when I do not get it!"

3b. "I must continually preoccupy myself with dangers and upset myself about them. In that way I increase my power to control or change them. And I *must* control or change them."

3c. "I must avoid, rather than face and deal with, many of life's difficulties and responsibilities since I need or must have immediate comfort and can't discipline myself or go through present pain to achieve future gains."

3d. "People *absolutely should* act better than they do, and if they act badly or create needless hassles for me, they are totally bad! I *can't stand* the difficulties they create by their horrible conduct!"

3e. "I must continue to suffer endlessly if handicaps plague me, no matter how I acquired these handicaps. I can do practically nothing to change them, and I find that so horrible that life is hardly worth living."

3f. "I must not find it difficult to change obnoxious or handicapping elements in my life. Such difficulties *absolutely ought* not exist! I find it *too hard* to do anything about them, and I might as well make no effort to change them since the situation is more or less hopeless."

3g. "Things like justice, fairness, equality, and democracy must prevail, and when they don't, I *can't stand it* and life seems *too unbearable* to continue."

3h. "I must find the correct and perfect solutions to my problems and to those of other people whom I care for. If I don't, catastrophe and horror will surely result."

3i. "I must remain a helpless victim of anxiety, depression, feelings of inadequacy, and hostility unless the conditions that cause my unhappiness change and allow me to stop feeling disturbed."

3j. "Since I managed to come into this world and still remain alive, my life must continue forever or just as long as I want it to continue. I find it completely unfair and horrible to think about the possibility of dying and of no longer having any existence. I also find it horrible to think about the death of those whom I love. Death, except for my enemies, must not exist."

3k. "As long as I remain alive, my life must have some unusual or special meaning or purpose, and if I cannot create this meaning or purpose for myself, I am hopelessly lost!"

3l. "I *can't stand* the discomfort of feeling anxious, depressed, guilty, ashamed, or otherwise emotionally upset, and if I really went crazy and found myself in an institution, I could never stand that horror or make the adjustment back to normal life."

3m. "When things really have gone badly for me for a reasonably long period of time and there exist no guarantees that they will change or that anyone will take the responsibility to make things better for me, I simply can't bear the thought of living any longer and may seriously contemplate suicide."

These corollaries—outgrowths of the three major Irrational Beliefs—represent a sampling of the dysfunctional ideas many people hold and that play a part in their everyday thoughts. Holding them, people condemn themselves, others, and the world around them. We can easily see that all these ideas contain elements of what *should* or *must be*, of how terrible a situation or person *is* if this demand isn't fulfilled. Each of them also contains the elements of your feeling hopeless and helpless. This idea of your making yourself powerless or at the mercy of "horrible" life conditions is one of your greatest irrationalities.

Let us now review each irrational idea separately so that we may gain a clearer understanding of the content, origin, and effect of each idea.

IRRATIONAL IDEA 1 deals mainly with your expectations of personal achievement. In addition, it involves the importance you place on other people's opinions of you. You set expectations for yourself and, if you do not live up to them, see yourself as inferior in your own eyes and in the eyes of others. Hence you feel that the only measure of your self-worth is the degree to which you can perform in a near-perfect manner. You feel that other people will condemn and reject you if you do not do as you *should*, as you *must*.

Naturally, as humans we sometimes have a tendency either to overevaluate our own potential or to set goals for ourselves that people whom we respect or admire have either achieved themselves or would like to see us achieve. In many instances these specific goals go beyond the realm of our capacity. It seems healthy that you may feel disappointed if you do not reach certain achievements. Yet I can see no real reason for you to make yourself depressed, anxious, or angry at the realization that such goals at the moment remain beyond your reach.

Viewing **Irrational Idea 2**, we see the same negativeness and dogmatism as exist in Irrational Idea 1. Here, however, you direct these evaluations toward other people instead of yourself, and you place unrealistic expectations on others.

Often humans like to feel or think that we are the center of the universe and that all other people *should, must* cater to our needs and whims. Naturally, when two or more persons interact, a distinct possibility exists that each of them will have this attitude. If so, conflicts can easily arise since each person has her own interest as a primary concern. You can healthily consider other people as well as yourself. However, you—and they!—may not do the same. You had better therefore prepare to cope with people who may treat you harshly and unfairly and to make yourself accept, though not like, that fact.

Irrational Idea 3 has the same basic components of the two previous dysfunctional ideas, and you may find it perhaps the most troublesome of the three. We mostly recognize the irrationality of demanding that the conditions of our environment personally suit us. Yet many people actually do upset themselves frequently and unnecessarily when these forces refuse to "comply." How many times have you met people who view it as "unbearable" when the weather does not suit their taste?

Most people at one time or another hold this and other Irrational Beliefs. This is hardly criminal. We all have IBs. But we'd better keep in mind that we would act wiser and feel a lot happier if we looked for and found these IBs and changed them. No magic cure here, nor any formula for eternal happiness, but an effective step that you can take to assist you in stubbornly refusing to upset yourself when your strong desires are thwarted. This has now been shown by many REBT and cognitive-behavior therapists, such as John Blackburn, Elizabeth Brondolo, Jerry Deffenbacher, Raymond DiGiuseppe, Christopher Eckhardt, Raymond Novaco, Mark Terjesen and Raphael Rose, Raymond Chip Tafrate, and Janet Wolfe.

5

Understanding Your Self-Angering Philosophies

Having examined some of the irrational ideas that accompany anger and other Unhealthy Consequences, we will now attempt to gain some insights into how you hold and can change beliefs. For no matter how faithfully you may have followed REBT theory, the system won't work for you unless you learn how to dispute and reduce your IBs once you find them. So turn your attention to three major insights that will help you Dispute Irrational Beliefs.

Insights we try to help REBT clients acquire are hardly the same as those that other therapies emphasize. Psychoanalysis, as we have already noted, stresses insight into what happened to you in the past and how this led to your present difficulties. Transactional Analysis, somewhat similarly, stresses insight into your childhood and your past and, like psychoanalytic insights, insists that you understand these past experiences before you can effectively change them and let yourself become a healthy adult.

Reichian, primal, and other abreactive or cathartic types of therapies contend that you have to have insight into the enormous pain inflicted on you during your early childhood and, further, that you must relive these early traumas before you can rid yourself of the effects that they continue to have upon your present life. Gestalt therapy demands that you must attain insight into every nuance of your present feelings and that this complete awareness of the here-and-now will change your attitudes and actions.

Rational Emotive Behavior Therapy holds that your present disturbance is not directly caused by your past life. **INSIGHT 1** stresses the extremely strong influence that your Belief System (B) has upon your reaction (C) to your past and present Adversities (A's). A does not really cause (though it significantly contributes to) C; B constitutes a more direct "cause" of C. It follows that if your Belief System constitutes a major influence on your Emotional Consequence, your previous Adversities may have even less influence on C than present Adversities.

REBT does not say that your past experiences have absolutely *no* effect on your present behavior. For instance, researchers have found that children who are severely punished by their parents may develop a tendency to feel more anger and act more violently toward others throughout their lives than will children who are less severely treated. While this tends to indicate that there exists a relationship between people's early training and their conduct, there are also other factors to consider.

Genetic factors may also encourage anger, as we shall discuss in detail later in this book. The violent characteristic of those raised in hostile and aggressive atmospheres may stem both from an inherited and from an acquired disposition. For if either one or both of a child's parents has innate hostile tendencies, they may well pass them on to their child. In addition, parents may react to their child's inherited aggressive tendencies with violent and aggressive disciplinary measures. This may then reinforce their children's violent dispositions, which may then be passed on biologically and environmentally to their own children. Here we see a somewhat vicious circle of violence, including innate and learned factors.

INSIGHT 1 stresses the fundamental point of the importance of the beliefs you hold today. The teachings you received from your parents and social group during your childhood may, in fact, have a great deal of influence upon these beliefs. Yet, as stated, you can change these beliefs, despite the way in which you may have acquired them.

Here you have the difference between an REBT insight and the insights of various schools of psychoanalysis. Insight into the *origins* of your Belief System may help you very little. It may merely serve to sidetrack you from the much more important insight: "I clearly see that right now I make myself angry by my Irrational Beliefs at B. Now let me see what I can do to zero in on these beliefs, understand their specifics, and *change* them."

Many kinds of therapies, especially psychoanalytic methods, cater to people's search for meaning and satisfy them with brilliant interpretations of why they got the way they now are. These interpretations, even if correct, often do not help them to change. Even when REBT shows them their IBs that lead to their disturbed reactions, this *meaningful* explanation may not get them to change. More is required!

Now let us examine REBT **INSIGHT 2**: *However you may have originally acquired your Belief System, particularly your Irrational Beliefs (IBs) with which you create your emotional disturbances*, you *keep these beliefs alive by repeating them to yourself, reinforcing them in various ways, acting on them, and refusing to challenge them.* Others may have helped you acquire your Irrational Beliefs, but the primary reason you still subscribe to them is because you continually indoctrinate yourself with them today.

You *actively* keep reindoctrinating yourself with Irrational Beliefs. Your Unhealthy Emotional and Behavioral Consequences exist *because* you continue to maintain irrational philosophies or beliefs from which they stem. Although it "seems" or "feels" as if your anger "naturally" persists once you make yourself hate someone, you actually and actively *keep it alive* by constantly telling yourself that this person *should not* have acted badly and *is* damnable for acting that way.

As a child, I contend, you subscribed to the rational and irrational teachings of your parents because you had a limited ability to recognize the difference between them. When your elders told you that a person was *totally damnable* if he broke a promise or agreement, you naturally believed them. If, as you grew older, you had given some critical thought to these views, you might have noticed that many people who go back on their agreements actually are *not* completely *bad people*. In fact, if you had given the idea of "terrible people" consideration, you might have discovered that your own parents, from time to time, went back on their word to you. Did that make them totally rotten and worthless? Hardly! You probably then would have realized that your anger stemmed from your belief that people who treat you unjustly are worthless.

REBT shows you how you can use the principles of reinforcement and penalization to work *for* you rather than against you. It shows you how you can *change* your ideas about your elders' teachings regarding how people *should* act toward you. REBT methods, used properly and conscientiously, help you minimize your Irrational Beliefs, unhealthy feelings, and dysfunctional actions.

In his social-reinforcement theory Albert Bandura makes a similar point. Bandura, a devotee of social-learning theories of human behavior, also acknowledges the highly cognitive element in human reactions and behaviors. Although his social-reinforcement theory is similar to our REBT theory, there remain some important differences. Bandura implies that if I should act in an asocial manner toward you, you still have a number of alternatives—any one of which may fit into the framework of the sentiments of the social group. You would therefore have a choice of any one of a number of responses. You could hate me or take me to court. The social rules of your community inform you that I had better not act unfairly toward you and that I may risk a penalty if I do so.

As a human you tend to accept this communication and these rules. Thus, to some extent you learn to feel displeased about my act. You have a tendency to think about whether the rule I broke had little or no importance, whether I inconvenienced you mildly or greatly, and whether you can or cannot get away with your anger against me. In other words, you might use social standards to determine how much active aggression your society would sanction, and you may choose to act according to those guidelines. All human emotions, Bandura concludes, have a pronounced element of cognition and social learning. REBT takes this same combined cognitive-conditioning outlook, but it especially stresses self-conditioning, as well as conditioning resulting from external social influences.

A second aspect of **INSIGHT 2** deals with sustained emotions about anything that happens to you at point A. This applies particularly to feelings of anger. REBT hypothesizes that *the frustration or injustice you originally experience doesn't in itself make you hold on to your hostile feelings for me for prolonged periods of time. Your ongoing, or sustained,* view *of that original frustration—rather than the frustrating conditions themselves—makes and keeps you angry with me.*

If I treated you inconsiderately, you could easily make yourself upset with me for a day or two—or for many weeks. Every time someone mentioned my name, for instance, your original feelings of animosity could reassert themselves.

What of the times when you might continue to harbor feelings of raging at me for weeks, months, or even years? Here, every time you refer to me and my unfairness to you, you repeat the Irrational Beliefs that originally created and provoked your angry feelings. For unless you continually repeat to yourself these IBs and vigorously throw yourself into holding on to them, *your ongoing, or sustained, view of your original view of how unfairly I treated you, rather than the injustice itself, keeps you angry.*

INSIGHT 3 states that *in order to change your disturbed feelings and behaviors and the Irrational Beliefs that lead you to have them, you almost always have to resort to a great deal of work and practice.* For no matter how aware you become of the self-defeating nature of your dysfunctional attitudes and actions, your awareness does not help you unless you effectively Dispute your ideas. That normally requires much practice and work.

All our beliefs, whether rational or irrational, vary in intensity and effect. For instance, many people hold certain superstitious beliefs, but their intensity may from time to time increase or lessen. Although most people thoughtfully agree that such things as black cats and broken mirrors are meaningless, these same people may avoid certain situations because their unconscious superstitions have gained an overpowering influence over their actions. The primary point to understand in relation to **INSIGHT 3**: A considerable difference exists between *telling* yourself something and really *convincing* yourself about the rationality or irrationality of a belief.

Because Irrational Beliefs are often held intensely, you'd better *strongly* Dispute them at point D (Disputing). No matter how aware you are of the irrationality of a belief, that insight will help you little unless you develop skill at questioning and Disputing it. Unless you Dispute your IBs powerfully, they may still control you. As we have stressed in this chapter, insight and knowledge alone are not enough. Emotional insight, as well as action, are required.

The more powerfully and emotionally you Dispute (at point D) your anxiety-creating or anger-producing IBs, the better you will dispel them. The next chapter will outline ways of Detecting your Irrational Beliefs, Discriminating between them and your more Rational Beliefs, and then Debating your IBs.

6

Disputing Your Self-Angering Philosophies

In REBT theory D represents Disputing. It means that after you have found the Activating Event or Adversity (A) that precedes your disturbed Emotional or Behavioral Consequences (C), after you have ferreted out your Rational Beliefs (RBs) and Irrational Beliefs (IBs) about A, and after you have clearly acknowledged that your IBs directly help create your Unhealthy Consequences (UCs), you vigorously and persistently Dispute your IBs.

Kishor Phadke, a brilliant associate of mine in Bumbai, India, gave some special thought to point D, or Disputing, and decided to break it down into three main components:

Detection
Discriminating
Debating

I find his distinctions useful, since Disputing largely consists of detecting your main Irrational Beliefs, discriminating them clearly from your Rational Beliefs, and then debating these Irrational Beliefs actively and vigorously. So far, I have outlined the ABCs of anger and have tried to show how you can detect your IBs with the help of three major REBT insights. Now I will show you in detail how you can persistently and strongly *debate* your IBs.

To begin your debating, we shall repeat the four major kinds of Irrational Beliefs you tend to hold when you make yourself angry and show what you can do actively to debate or Dispute them until you minimize them.

Using our apartment-sharing illustration, your first Irrational Belief may be:

"How *awful* that you made me go to so much trouble and then withdrew from our agreement."

Assuming that you devoutly believe this IB and that you want to challenge it, you first ask yourself, "What makes Ellis's withdrawal *awful*?"

Now, if you answer the question about the awfulness of the situation by describing the inconvenience and expense my behavior caused, you will find yourself in some difficulty. For as stated earlier, my injustice to you may only lead to disappointment—not anger. Anger stems from carrying things farther and viewing my betrayal as awful, terrible, and horrible. You may have a tendency to equate unfair, inconvenient, or disadvantageous with *awful* behavior. But are they really *awful*?

One dictionary definition of *awful* begins as follows: "1. inspiring awe. 2. terrifying; appalling. 3. worthy of reverence and solemn respect." It goes on to the colloquial meaning of the term: "very bad, ugly, disagreeable, unpleasant, etc.: as, an *awful* joke." The problem with both these definitions is that you tend to attach an emotional feeling to the word *awful* that goes beyond its practical meaning.

Perhaps it would be easier to clarify the difference between the practical and the emotional aspects of the word *awful* by examining your view, "How awful that Ellis made me go to so much trouble and then withdrew from our agreement." At first, you probably feel disappointment and then feel anger. Thus, you hold two different ideas about my behavior, one rational and the other irrational. Rationally you think that I have treated you rather unfairly and that you find that treatment, as the dictionary states, "very bad, ugly, disagreeable, unpleasant, etc." We may term your feelings rational or healthy because they aid your basic goals. When you and I made our agreement, you thought it would have advantages for you. My withdrawal has now frustrated that goal, so you rationally evaluate my actions as disagreeable and unpleasant.

Rational merely means that your appraisal of my breaking our agreement leads to *healthy* negative feelings at point C. Considering the circumstances, you might feel exceptionally sorry, displeased, and disappointed because my unfairness has inconvenienced you enormously. You would then have strong healthy feelings at C. But your Rational Belief would *not* lead you to feeling *un*healthily angry. You create your anger by your IB, "Ellis *must not* treat me unfairly!" This powerful *must* adds an unhealthy emotional quality to your awfulizing.

Awfulizing is one of the main creators of irrationality and disturbed emotions and behaviors. It goes beyond the feeling of unpleasantness and includes *additional* badness to existing badness. By calling my injustice to you *awful*, you state or imply that it is badder than it *must* be—is practically *more* than bad. By awfulizing about my behavior, you imply several dubious things:

1. "Dr. Ellis treats me totally or 100 percent badly."
2. "He seems to treat me worse than he ever treats anyone."
3. "He *should not, must not* treat me that badly!"
4. "He *must not* treat me badly at all but *should* only treat me well."

Assuming that you irrationally believe my unfairness to you is awful, let us take the next step in disputing your Irrational Beliefs. You can ask, "What makes Ellis's breaking the agreement *awful?*" You can then probably see that:

1. It wasn't 100 percent bad—and certainly not *more* than bad.
2. I could have acted *worse* in several ways. For instance, I could have moved into the apartment with you and refused to pay my part of the rent.
3. I *should* have treated you badly, if that is what I actually *did*. I

have to have done what I *did*—though I don't have to do it in the future.

4. There is no reason why I *must* always treat you well.

Although you can justifiably see the treatment you received as *very* bad, inconvenient, and disappointing, you cannot find it *more* than this, and yet you do irrationally think it so when you define it as *awful*.

Dr. Donald Meichenbaum, an outstanding cognitive-behavior therapist who has done many important research studies of Cognitive Behavior Therapy, refers to REBT as a semantic therapy, and I agree with him. It helps people discriminate between their generalizations and their overgeneralizations and between their reality-oriented thinking and their unrealistic thinking. In the case of the term *awful*, people often think that they mean *bad* or *very bad*, while their actual emotional meaning seems to include *totally bad* or *worse than it must be*. REBT helps people see what they really mean when they use the term.

REBT does not say that you only emote through the use of words and language in overgeneralized ways. Obviously animals and very young children have emotions, and neither has the use of language. But animals and children have limited emotional repertoires and, even more significantly, they tend to emote in an unsustained, quickly dissipated manner. When children get old enough to use language effectively, they then acquire the ability to sustain their feelings and, unfortunately, also to make and keep themselves emotionally upset.

Moreover, as humans we invariably seem to talk to ourselves about our emotional reactions. When we feel highly emotional about something, we observe that state and evaluate how good or bad it is. We do this partly because we have learned from others that some emotions are "good" and some are "bad," that some have advantages and some have disadvantages. But we also do it because humans seem to observe their emotional reactions. We can view our emotional state and think about the possibilities of living with or changing it, or we can "awfulize" and say many negative things about it to ourselves. We have this choice.

When you see me treating you in a certain manner and you think my behavior unfair, you tell yourself something about my unfairness. By doing this, you create a pronounced emotional feeling in your gut, either healthy sorrow or irritation or unhealthy rage. You then observe your emotional reactions (which you may not realize you partly have chosen for yourself), and you evaluate them. You feel emotional about your emotions.

You use certain words to create emotional reactions. The words you use affect you according to the meanings you give them. Words such as *awful* and *terrible* usually create disturbed emotions. Other words, such as *bad* and *obnoxious*, tend to create healthy or undisturbed reactions. Not always, of course. You can say to yourself, "How obnoxious! I find Dr. Ellis's treatment unfair!" and mean that you find it *more than* obnoxious. Or you can say to yourself, "How awful I find that treatment," and mean that you merely find it obnoxious and that you strongly wish I would treat you more fairly.

Do not think that every time you see something as *bad* or *unfortunate* you stay within social reality and that every time you see something as *awful* or *horrible* you depart from social reality. Again, you control the meaning that you impose on words and, thus, the power that you give to them. In general, REBT has found that when you use words like *awful*, *terrible*, and *horrible*, you give them exaggerated meaning. If you see and can change this tendency, you will significantly decrease your disturbed feelings.

Many people have a difficult time understanding that when they say something like, "How *awful* that so-and-so treated me unfairly," they go beyond the facts of the "awful" situation and imply that:

1. Someone has treated them *totally* unfairly.
2. They have been treated as unfairly as anyone could possibly treat anyone.
3. They can no longer enjoy life because this unfair treatment has taken place.

4. The person who has treated them unfairly is *completely* bad and hardly deserves to live.
5. The unfair treatment was so bad that it *absolutely should not* have been that bad.

Many people do not understand that the use of the term *awful* unrealistically implies these things. By continuing to use the term, they continue to upset themselves about it.

"*How awful that I have been treated in that way*" often means "*when they should have, must have treated me fairly.*" For you to say that something should or must not exist demands that people at *all times* treat you in the way in which you wish they would. You demand something of other people that they can never fulfill. How obviously irrational!—for you expect others to treat you in accordance with your personal wishes at all times.

If you say to yourself that someone *absolutely should not* act unfairly toward you, you imply that you do not merely see his action as wrong but also view the (entire) person who committed the action as bad. You feel that this person is capable of acting justly, and you feel it is essential to you that he do so. He *must* always act fairly, and *must never* act otherwise. This unrealistic demand that others must always act fairly in every situation makes you feel enraged when they (of course!) don't. You can more rationally realize that many decent people—including yourself—sometimes do unfair or unjust deeds. You can more sanely feel keen disappointment and annoyance at the unfairness you encounter and not at the *people* who behave "unfairly."

By looking closely at your own *awfuls*, *shoulds*, and *musts*, you can examine and rid yourself of many of the irrational ideas that lead to unhealthy emotional feelings at C. Once you learn to master the REBT technique of finding, disputing, and debating your Irrational Beliefs, you can use it for the rest of your life.

Windy Dryden and Jane Walker devised an REBT Self-Help Form that you can use to understand the ABCDEs of Anger and to keep actively Disputing your Irrational Beliefs. I revised their form, and we routinely use it at the psychological clinic at the Albert Ellis Institute in New York to give to our clients. See pages 50–53.

Other methods that you can use to Dispute your Irrational Beliefs that help create your feelings of rage are presented in the later chapters of this book and in the writings of many other practitioners of Rational Emotive Behavior Therapy and Cognitive Behavior Therapy. These include articles and books that you can find in the references at the end of this book, especially those of Aaron Beck, Jerry Deffenbacher, Raymond DiGiuseppe, Windy Dryden, Paul Hauck, and Raymond Novaco. Particularly helpful ways of Disputing your Irrational Beliefs that create several kinds of disturbances in addition to severe anger can be found in my books; in Michael Bernard and Janet Wolfe, *The REBT Source Book for Practitioners;* and in Susan Walen, Ray DiGiuseppe, and Windy Dryden, *A Practitioner's Guide to Rational Emotive Therapy*.

Let me stress again that when you Dispute your Irrational Beliefs leading to disturbances, you do this Disputing quite forcefully and *emotionally*, and that you do it *behaviorally*—that is, see that it includes *actions* that contradict and help minimize your dysfunctional beliefs.

REBT Self-

A (ACTIVATING EVENT)

- Briefly summarize the situation you are disturbed about (what would a camera see?)
- An *A* can be *internal* or *external, real* or *imagined.*
- An *A* can be an event in the *past, present,* or *future.*

IB's (IRRATIONAL BELIEFS)

To identify IB's, look for:

- DOGMATIC DEMANDS (musts, absolutes, shoulds)
- AWFULIZING (It's awful, terrible, horrible)
- LOW FRUSTRATION TOLERANCE (I can't stand it)
- SELF/OTHER RATING (I'm / he / she is bad, worthless)

D (DISPUTING IB'S)

To dispute ask yourself:

- Where is holding this belief getting me? Is it *helpful* or *self-defeating*?
- Where is the evidence to support the existence of my irrational belief? Is it *consistent with reality*?
- Is my belief *logical*? Does it follow from my preferences?
- Is it really *awful* (as bad as it could be?)
- Can I really not *stand* it?

Help Form

C (CONSEQUENCES)

Major unhealthy negative **emotions:**

Major self-defeating **behaviors:**

Unhealthy negative emotions include:

- Anxiety
- Depression
- Rage
- Low Frustration Tolerance
- Shame/Embarassment
- Hurt
- Jealousy
- Guilt

RB's (RATIONAL BELIEFS)

To think more rationally, strive for:

- NON-DOGMATIC PREFERENCES (wishes, wants, desires)
- EVALUATING BADNESS (it's bad, unfortunate)
- HIGH FRUSTRATION TOLERANCE (I don't like it, but I can stand it)
- NOT GLOBALLY RATING SELF OR OTHERS (I—and others—are fallible human beings)

E (NEW EFFECT)

New healthy **negative emotions:**

New constructive **behaviors:**

Healthy negative emotions include:

- Disappointment
- Concern
- Annoyance
- Sadness
- Regret
- Frustration

REBT Self-

A (ACTIVATING EVENT)

My boss criticized me in front of others.
He didn't give me the raise I worked hard for and deserve.

- Briefly summarize the situation you are disturbed about (what would a camera see?)
- An *A* can be *internal* or *external, real* or *imagined.*
- An *A* can be an event in the *past, present,* or *future.*

IB's (IRRATIONAL BELIEFS)

He must not criticize me, especially in front of others.
He has been very unfair to me, as he absolutely should not be.
He is a totally unfair and lousy person!

D (DISPUTING IB'S)

Why must he not be so critical?
Where is it written that he has to be fair?
He acted unfairly, but that doesn't make him a totally unfair and rotten person.

To identify IB's, look for:

- DOGMATIC DEMANDS (musts, absolutes, shoulds)
- AWFULIZING (It's awful, terrible, horrible)
- LOW FRUSTRATION TOLERANCE (I can't stand it)
- SELF/OTHER RATING (I'm / he / she is bad, worthless)

To dispute ask yourself:

- Where is holding this belief getting me? Is it *helpful* or *self-defeating*?
- Where is the evidence to support the existence of my irrational belief? Is it *consistent with reality*?
- Is my belief *logical*? Does it follow from my preferences?
- Is it really *awful* (as bad as it could be?)
- Can I really not *stand* it?

Help Form

C (CONSEQUENCES)

Major unhealthy negative **emotions:** *Rage, Depression*

Major self-defeating **behaviors:** *Doing poor work to spite boss. Telling others what a louse my boss is.*

Unhealthy negative emotions include:

- Anxiety
- Depression
- Rage
- Low Frustration Tolerance
- Shame/Embarassment
- Hurt
- Jealousy
- Guilt

RB's (RATIONAL BELIEFS)

I wish he would not be so critical, but he has every right to be.

Obviously, it is only written in my head. He can easily be unfair.

No matter how unfairly he and other people act, he also does many good things and cannot be totally unfair and rotten as a person.

E (NEW EFFECT)

New healthy **negative emotions:**

Frustration
Disappointment

New constructive **behaviors:**

Having unangry discussion with boss.
Making effort to do better at work.

To think more rationally, strive for:

- NON-DOGMATIC PREFERENCES (wishes, wants, desires)
- EVALUATING BADNESS (it's bad, unfortunate)
- HIGH FRUSTRATION TOLERANCE (I don't like it, but I can stand it)
- NOT GLOBALLY RATING SELF OR OTHERS (I—and others—are fallible human beings)

Healthy negative emotions include:

- Disappointment
- Concern
- Annoyance
- Sadness
- Regret
- Frustration

7

Some Methods of Thinking Your Way out of Anger

Antiawfulizing and antimusturbation form a core of rational thinking to uproot your feelings of anger, rage, resentment, and fury. You awfulize and resort to musturbation in four major ways, and once you tell yourself that you find something *awful*, that it *must* not exist the way it does, you also frequently convince yourself of other related Irrational Beliefs. Let us now look at these common irrationalities and at how you can work on them.

REBT refers to one of your beliefs as *I-Can't-Stand-It-itis*. We frequently find this type of awfulizing or musturbation in statements like: "I *can't stand* being treated so unfairly and being put to such great inconveniences by your unfair treatment!"

What we call Debating, as part of Disputing, in REBT, merely means asking yourself questions that will challenge your Irrational Beliefs. The obvious challenges consist of "Why?" "How?" "In what manner?" "What evidence exists for this?" "Where can I find the proof?" Thus, you ask yourself, "Why or in what manner can't I stand such unfair treatment?"

If your answer to this turns out to be something like "I *can* stand it because it doesn't really seem that terrible," you would seem on the right track, but in fact, your answer doesn't quite suffice. First of all, by using the word *terrible*, you will have, as we have noted earlier, a difficult time defining the term itself. Even if you yourself don't find the situation so terrible, a friend or some outsider might judge it as terrible. Others could then sway you into irrational modes of thinking, even if you had already successfully debated the idea of terribleness yourself. Agreeing with someone else's concept of terribleness most likely will encourage you into believing that you *can't* stand it and that Ellis *shouldn't* act in that terrible way. For, as I have stressed before, the four basic kinds of IBs people tell themselves to create their emotional upsets tend to interact so that one leads to the other:

1. "It is *terrible* for Ellis to treat me that way" seems also to mean—
2. "I *can't stand* his behaving in that terrible manner!"
3. "Therefore, he *absolutely shouldn't* act in that terrible way."
4. "He *is* a terrible person to treat anyone, especially me, that way."

In one way these seem like four different Irrational Beliefs. But terribleness, I-Can't-Stand-It-itis, musturbation, and damning oneself or others all represent different forms of the same basic proposition. If we start with one of these forms, we often imply or overtly end up with the other forms as well.

REBT hypothesizes that if you can stop believing—really and thoroughly stop believing—in one of these forms of irrationality, you will then tend to stop believing in the others. No certainty about this, but you have the tendency to do so.

We return now to debating I-Can't-Stand-It-itis. If we forget, then, about terribleness, my unfair treatment of you leads to an evaluation such as, "Because Ellis has treated me exceptionally unfairly and has caused me great amounts of unnecessary harm, I *can't stand* his doing that to me!" You can now ask yourself the question: "*Why* can't I stand it?" With the idea of terribleness omitted, it appears that you see the situation as intolerable because you think you have experienced *too much* pain; *too much* suffering has resulted from my unfair action. You have somehow escalated much pain and trouble into *too much* pain and trouble. The term *too*, as used here, has a highly exaggerated, surplus implication. You use it to demand that I (and others) must create only so much inconvenience and *no more* for you. After that point you consider the pain *too much*.

Thus, whenever you have the idea that you can't stand the degree of unpleasantness that you experience with my unfair treatment, you suffer not only frustration but low frustration tolerance (LFT) as well. We can loosely describe LFT as the tendency to rant and rave at, rather than merely dislike, frustration. The ranting and raving makes you feel much *more* frustrated than you would otherwise feel. If you Debate, and keep Debating, your I-Can't-Stand-It-itis, you will arrive at a more practical attitude for dealing with frustration and a new philosophy or cognitive Effect (E), which we can call I'll-Never-Like-It-But-I-Can-Stand-It-itis.

The question of whether you will make this basic change in attitude still remains. Anything you believe you can also definitely *refuse* to believe. You cannot control to any great degree what actually exists, but you do control—almost completely—what you *think about* what exists. While you have very little control over how I treat you (fairly or unfairly, well or badly), you do have many choices over the manner in which you *view* my unfair behavior. Thus, even if you judge my actions toward you as unfair and others agree that you have really been treated unfairly, you still can choose to:

1. Believe that you *can't stand* this unfairness or that you can.
2. Define the unfairness as *awful* or to define it as merely bad.
3. Think I *must not* treat you in an unfair manner or to think it *preferable* that I not treat you this way;
4. Judge me as a thoroughly horrible person or to judge me as a person who has acted unfairly toward you in this particular respect.

If you will challenge and debate your hypotheses that you have little or no choice but to feel that you *can't stand* my treating you badly and that you *can't stand* it because you find it *too* bad and that it *shouldn't* be so bad—if you will challenge this, then you will do something effective about surrendering these Irrational Beliefs.

Let us now go on to debate your next IB: "Dr. Ellis *should not, must not* treat me unfairly!" You can Dispute this IB as follows: "Granted that Ellis has dealt with me unfairly and that most people in our society would agree that he has, why *must* he not abuse me in this unfair manner?" If we approach this question from the point of social morality, one might say that if the people in general ignored the *oughts* and *shoulds* of its social, moral, and ethical standards, their society could not survive as a civilized unit. Yet morality doesn't actually determine what *ought* or *should* exist; it merely establishes guidelines with regard to either right or wrong. In other words, civilized morality states that one *had better* act "properly" rather than "improperly" and goes on to say that otherwise bad results will accrue. If bad results occur by someone's actions, the members of a society may feel impelled—because of civilized morality—to penalize the transgressor in order to encourage him to act otherwise in the future.

To avoid quibbling, let us clearly define the difference between "had better" act as opposed to "ought to" act in a certain manner. The statement "You *had better* act in a certain manner in order to bring about good social results" has as its follow-up statement, "If you do not act in such a manner, your community, members of your society, will decide that poor results have occurred and that you and their society will suffer." This statement seems realistic since we can observe right and wrong acts and discover whether they really do lead to good or bad results for you and your community. We can check this by consulting impartial observers.

However, the statement, "You *ought to* act rightly to get good results," implies the following hypotheses: "If you do not do what you *ought* to do . . .

1. " . . . poor results must occur for you and for everyone in your society."
2. " . . . some universal law commands that you deserve to get bad results and necessitates that dire things will happen."
3. " . . . you are a totally bad person."
4. " . . . you cannot possibly accept yourself and strive for real happiness in life."

The first of these propositions ("If you do not do what you ought to do, poor results must occur for you and for everyone in your society") seems highly exaggerated, for if you act wrongly, it would seem most unlikely that you and everyone in your society would suffer. The second and third propositions are overgeneralizations and unfalsifiable and unverifiable. And the fourth proposition again is false, since some people manage to accept themselves and to strive for (and gain) a good deal of happiness in spite of the fact they behave wrongly or immorally.

Thus, we see that two somewhat similar, yet contradictory, ideas exist here. For when you hold the idea that "People *ought* to treat me, *must* treat me better," you really imply:

1. "I would find it highly preferable if they did treat me better"
and
2. "Because I would find it preferable, they have to treat me better."

Although the first belief is rational, the second one seems highly irrational. We hold, in REBT, that if you stick with the Rational Belief ("I would find it highly preferable if they did treat me better"), you would merely feel sorry and displeased with the poor treatment you actually received. Yet if you persist, as many people have a tendency to do, in the Irrational Belief ("Because I would find it preferable, they have to treat me better"), you would in all probability end up feeling very angry. Therefore, to minimize your anger, you'd better ask: "Why *must* I (or anyone) be treated fairly at all times?" The rational answer: "Although it would be desirable to be treated fairly at all times and although social rules declare it advisable for people to act fairly to me, no universal law exists that I *must* get treated fairly."

If you agree with the above, you will find that you will feel sorry and disappointed when others treat you unfairly, but you won't feel dysfunctional anger and rage.

Let us once again review the main REBT formula that we have discussed up to this point.

Activating Experience or Adversity (A): I have treated you unfairly by withdrawing from an agreement we have made.
Rational Belief (RB): "I find Dr. Ellis's action deplorable and unfortunate."
Healthy Consequence (HC): feelings of frustration and displeasure.
Irrational Belief (IB): "How awful! He should not, must not treat me in that manner."
Unhealthy Consequence (UC): anger and rage.
Disputing and Debating (D): You detect your IBs and Dispute and Debate them by asking yourself questions that challenge your interpretations or beliefs regarding my treatment of you.
Effective New Philosophy (E): "I can see no reason why Ellis *must* treat me fairly even though I would definitely prefer it. He can treat me any way he wants, however wrong he may be."
Behavioral Effect (BE): loss of anger, relief, and return to the Healthy Consequence (HC): feelings of sorrow and disappointment.

Until you go through these ABCs and DEs many, many times, until you do them vigorously, strongly, and powerfully, and until you act on them over and over again, you will tend to sink back into your Irrational Beliefs and into your Unhealthy Consequences. Only with continual practice will you minimize your IBs and, even then, never for all time to come. You will often tend to regress into your former habits—as all humans do. You will hardly attain perfection at all times, yet by using the REBT methods you can often use your ability to recognize your IBs and UCs by using the process of Debating and Disputing them as they recur.

In most situations where you feel enraged, you have a human tendency to equate the particular anger-producing action with the person responsible for it. ("He *is* a terrible person to treat me that way!") You give global ratings to individuals because of their actions. We have already discussed this type of reasoning in chapter 3.

Yet because of its importance and because it constitutes one of the most difficult of your Irrational Beliefs to debate, we will now briefly review it again.

Your globally rating people and their actions implies that only a *rotten person* can act in a rotten *manner* and that all rotten acts are done by rotten people. Further, and more specifically, it implies that any person who does anything you deem bad or unjust must be a *bad person*. If a good person performs good acts, then he can *never* do anything bad, for he *is* a good person and capable of only good acts. If a bad person performs bad acts, he can *never* do anything good, for he *is* a bad person and can perform only bad acts. This was clearly pointed out in 1933 by Alfred Korzybski in *Science and Sanity*. He called your tendency to make this illogical jump "the *is* of identity" and said that virtually all humans follow it. As noted in chapter 3, Rational Beliefs start with chosen desires or preferences—for instance, "I want to remain alive and achieve happiness"—and they evaluate acts or traits as "good" or "bad" according to how people's behaviors aid or block their chosen desires or goals. They evaluate behaviors as helpful or unhelpful to *people;* but they do not evaluate or judge people *themselves*, in their "essence" or their "totality." For by making such a global evaluation of *humans*, you overgeneralize and tend to sabotage your survival and happiness.

Is there, then, no such thing as a bad person? REBT holds that no, there are no bad people and, similarly, there are no good people. Although some do more "good" and others do more "bad" deeds, all people do some of both. A human is a *process*, not a *thing* or an *activity*. Your expectation that people act in a certain manner at all times is irrational, for as humans we can never be all good or all bad at all times and in every situation. Keep in mind the multidimensionality of people. Their many acts may make considerable contributions to humanity, and at the same time they may also have many deficiencies. For instance, a man might be a great scientist and his work may be of great benefit, yet in his personal life he may consistently treat others unfairly and unjustly. By avoiding rating people globally, you allow yourself to see their many aspects even though they may on occasion treat you unfairly.

Back to our apartment-sharing illustration. My withdrawal from our agreement may have unfairly harmed you, but if you rate me globally for this, if you make yourself angry with me for this action, you no longer allow yourself to enjoy my qualities that induced you to want to share an apartment with me in the first place. Thus, with your anger, you may cut yourself off from rewarding personal experiences with me (and others) in the future.

Giving global ratings to other people also encourages your human tendency to rate yourself globally, to place the same unrealistic expectations on yourself as you place on others. In this way you seek to gain self-esteem or self-confidence—frequently called ego strength—by living up to these expectations. But even though you may act fairly or justly in many situations, you may also fail to do so from time to time. When this occurs, you tend to feel depressed and self-downing because you have failed to live up to your expectations of yourself. Self-confidence includes and always leaves you on the brink of self-deprecation. Self-esteem leads to self-downing. Ego strength involves incipient loss of ego. You don't normally have self-esteem without self-disesteem. Just as you begin to like yourself because you do the right, good, or fine thing, you also begin to hate or deprecate yourself because you do the wrong, bad, or even ordinary thing. Self-esteem, if you feel it, requires continual booster shots, and the only real and effective booster seems to consist of more good deeds, more high ratings for your traits. If you give global ratings to yourself or others, you will feel forced to change your estimations of you and them continually. However, if you stick to rating only your behaviors, you will remain far less confused and more consistent in your rating the effectiveness of what you think, feel, and do.

In REBT we consider virtually all *anger at a person* unhealthy. If you feel angry about my act of unfairness, you at worst consider it very bad and think that *I'd better* change it for the trait of fairness. That seems rational because as long as I act unfairly, I will needlessly hurt you and others, and you, they, and even I would find it preferable to avoid that. You could, of course, consider my unfairness *awful*, meaning totally—or 100 percent—bad, but that would be irrational since you would then exaggerate. As long as you stick to thinking of my unfairness as highly undesirable and as long as you stick to hating *it*, we can call you healthfully or rationally angry. We can define rational anger as extreme annoyance, irritation, frustration, pique, or displeasure at my unfair acts. Your rational anger leads to determination to stay away from me because of my misdeeds, and possibly your *attempt* to get me to change, to act more fairly. All these reactions seem quite sensible. But if you view my unfairness as awful or totally bad, and you also view *me* as bad for acting unfairly, you exaggerate or create unrealistic thinking—and may feel anger, resentment, rage, fury, and wrath about me *and* my behavior.

Theoretically, you could acknowledge your anger and feel healthily angry with me for my unfairness. But the vast majority of the time that you feel angry, you think that because you don't like my behavior, it absolutely *must not* exist, that I who created it *should not* have acted the way I did, that you find it awful that I acted unfairly, and that I am a *bad person*.

You can feel extremely annoyed and displeased and may call those feelings rational anger. The trouble with doing so arises from your tendency to refuse to face your feelings of "real" or dysfunctional anger and to insist that you merely feel annoyed when you truly feel very angry. So I personally prefer to think of practically all emotions of anger as unhealthy and self-defeating, even though I acknowledge that you may prefer to label some of them as "healthy." I fully acknowledge that whenever I honestly feel "angry" I not only *want* people to act well but also *demand* or *command* that they do so. If you can feel "angry" without such a demand or command, fine—you can then say that you feel "rational anger." But for the sake of clarity and finer discrimination, I would prefer to label your "rational anger" as "strong annoyance" or "profound irritation" at other people's *behaviors*.

I have said that if you rate my deeds, such as my fairness to you and others, as good, this may be accurate and rational, but that if you rate *me* as good for acting well, you are being inaccurate and irrational. You tend to help me raise my self-esteem by rating me as "good." But then I also will tend to put myself down when you rate my traits and me as "bad." Global rating rarely works, since all humans possess a number of faults no matter how many good qualities they may have. For even if I always acted fairly to you and others, I wouldn't always do everything else well. No human does. So your esteeming me as *a person* because I act good is not practical in this world of exceptionally fallible humans.

You and I had better avoid the idea of self-esteem and self-confidence. If I esteem myself and see myself as a person who almost invariably does good and wins the plaudits of others, I also will strongly tend to castigate myself when I do bad. As we agreed, I will do bad on many occasions. Moreover, when I feel self-disrespect, lack of confidence, or low self-esteem, I almost automatically will assume not merely that I have certain disabilities and deficiencies, but that I *have* to continue to have them. For if I am no good or worthless for treating you and others unfairly, then how can a rotten me, an individual whose essence consists of worthlessness, change and behave better in the future? If I see myself as an unfair person, won't I predict that I will keep acting unfairly and probably fulfill my own prophecy? Self-esteem and its concomitant, self-downing, practically never steadily work. Therefore, using self-esteem to help myself feel better about my acts won't produce very good or lasting results. If this seems true, for what purpose should I rate myself?

When I say of myself, "I am a good person, and I really like my goodness. I would be a worthless person without it," I mean that I like myself *because* I act good and would dislike or down myself if I acted bad. Besides the disadvantages already mentioned, this type of good–bad self-rating has the great disadvantage of keeping me anxious if I do not always live up to the expectations I have imposed on myself. And I imply something still more by the idea of self-esteem: Because I do such good things, act exceptionally good in many respects, I can legitimately see myself as a *better person* than anyone else. You may do good, too, and I view that as fine. But I tend to feel that I can do better, outstandingly better, and qualify as a *really* good person. I have to show everyone, including myself, that I am a *better* human. What we call self-esteem, then, often amounts to grandiosity, when we think of ourselves as better or more worthy than other people.

One of our primary purposes in self-rating is that we try to show not only that we are human (which is true, no matter what we do) but also that we are superhuman, or superior to all other humans. When we say, "I have self-esteem," we really say that we are nearly perfect, godlike, and noble. We don't merely mean that our *traits* are superior to those of others; we actually mean that our essence is better than that of others. We may also mean that if we don't excel over other humans and become universally acknowledged as superior, we have little or no value.

I have always found it interesting that when people do something poorly, they not only see themselves as pretty worthless individuals, but also tend to accept and forgive others, very often, for exactly the same deficiency. For example, if someone writes a poor essay, he may often, upon realizing the poor quality of the work, view himself as a total failure who can never write well. Yet if someone else were to write something equally poor, he would tend to forgive the other person's deficiency. People tend to feel far more self-critical than critical of others because they demand almost perfect behavior of themselves.

If you encounter an excellent writer—far more skilled than yourself—you may feel so resentful and intimidated by the other's success that you can neither appreciate nor learn from his skills. For this would involve admitting that person's superiority insofar as writing. Having accepted your own inferior writing ability, you would most likely automatically surrender your total self-worth. For these and many other reasons, you'd better wisely avoid attempting to rate either yourself or others by any one of their good or bad traits. It can lead mainly to self-defeat.

I do not question here the idea of evaluating and judging specific traits and characteristics in yourself and others. You may passionately like or dislike anything you choose. I stress the idea of carrying your judgment of a trait into other areas of a person's total makeup. I would suggest that your wisest approach is evaluating each trait individually and comparing all these traits—both those that you find appealing and those that you find distasteful. With this overview, you can then decide whether you had better avoid or seek out a particular person. But not to damn or worship him or her!

If you see that person's bad as well as good traits, you can *accept* her with distasteful characteristics. In every individual you will find disagreeable acts and traits. You may, of course, attempt to help someone alter her "bad" traits, but you'd better not make that change necessary to continuing the relationship: for often you will find a person's deficiencies unchangeable. Until you readily accept that people have a combination of good and bad characteristics you will find it difficult and frustrating to enter into any kind of honest close relationship with another.

If we can accept fallibility in ourselves and in others, we will no longer demand that a person *should* or *must* act in a specific manner at all times. We will no longer insist on perfection and will no longer find imperfection intolerable. We will be more appreciative of our own qualities and those of others. This more realistic attitude will also better enable us to live happy and productive lives.

While you may often find it difficult to tolerate negative aspects of your intimates, you also do not want to live without those same people and their traits that you enjoy. The illustration of the apartment-sharing agreement serves as a good example of this situation, too, for you discover that you have to live without something that you wanted very much but that you could not have. If you would face your loss rationally—and not demand that I, who broke the agreement with you, feel guilty or inferior—you could perhaps at some time in the future again agree to carry out our agreement. Granted, a while may have to pass before this would occur, but if you act rationally during the difficult period of our relationship, we could have an excellent chance to resolve our difficulties.

In using the REBT approach to the problem of rage, you uniquely concentrate on changing yourself, rather than changing me. This frees you from the self-disturbing that accompanies anger, anxiety, and depression. Instead of expending time, thought, and energy on me and my "rottenness," you use your strength to get what you want from me as quickly and as easily as possible. Rage will only bring you further unpleasantness, such as feuding with me.

The REBT method encourages your independence and helps you realize your potential as a human while teaching you to accept your shortcomings without creating feelings of worthlessness. By reducing unhealthy attitudes about yourself and others, you can come to realistic views. You live in a rough world; and if you expect to get the important things that you want, you had better prepare to deal with its situations and people in a hardheaded manner.

With REBT tools, you will find yourself well equipped to live happily and sanely—to unupsettedly confront the daily frustrations that often plague your life. You can also cope better with situations and people or conditions that block your goals. To achieve such an outlook seems well worth the effort that the REBT method requires.

8

Some Methods of Feeling Your Way out of Anger

In this chapter we shall discuss some of the emotive methods used in REBT to overcome your anger. By "emotive" I mean a forceful, hard-hitting, sometimes dramatic way of interrupting and changing your anger and a method that focuses on your "feelings" or "desires"—which invariably include "thoughts" and "actions" but which we can somewhat arbitrarily describe in their own right. "Behavioral" methods, which we consider in the next chapter, may overlap with "emotive" methods but tend to stress "actions" rather than "feelings."

The first and perhaps most important of the emotive methods of overcoming anger is unconditional self-acceptance or self-respect. This includes the strong resolve to accept yourself fully, no matter what you may do, including making yourself angry.

If you were to come to me, an REBT therapist, and tell me that you keep angering yourself, I would try to show you—by my attitudes and behavior toward you—a model of what REBT calls unconditional other-acceptance (UOA). I would agree with you about the disadvantages of your anger, but I would accept you as a human *with* your wrong behavior and would not in any way put you down for having it. My unconditionally accepting you, as Carl Rogers pointed out, with bad behavior may well enable you to accept yourself and to have more time and energy available to change that behavior. Of course, others don't always accept you. But even if almost everyone tends to severely criticize you for your feelings and behavior, you can still accept yourself fully. For if you take the criticisms of others to heart, if you *agree* with them that you are a worthless person because of your poor actions, you *choose* to agree with their notions. You could, instead, listen to these people, fully acknowledge their negative opinions about you and your actions, and then only see your *behavior* as inappropriate, but not that you are a *bad person* for having such behavior. You then would *decide* to disagree with them. (If you can decide to *agree* with others' globally downing you for your anger, you can also decide to *disagree* with them.) If you already tend to down yourself without much influence from others for your unhealthy feelings and actions, you can decide not to agree with your own self-downing attitudes. You can decide to accept yourself with your anger while acknowledging it as a fault that you would like to amend. This strong decision amounts to an emotive method of self-choosing.

The more decisively, the more strongly and firmly you determine to accept yourself and to refuse to down yourself *at all*, no matter what you do in life, the more you will *feel* self-accepting. You accept yourself, as George Herbert Mead and Harry Stack Sullivan pointed out, by hearing other people's positive appraisals of you and adopting them as your own. You can also be self-accepting by figuring out for yourself that you can have that feeling, no matter what, and by firmly deciding, *choosing* to accept yourself even though you may hold some emotions (such as anger) that you wish to alter. The next step involves your working continually at *maintaining* your feeling of self-acceptance. We believe an idea strongly not merely because certain people keep repeating it to us but also because we consciously or unconsciously repeat it to ourselves over and over.

Even if you have a physiologically biased idea—such as the notion that cake tastes good and meat tastes bad—you keep repeating this idea to yourself many times. Especially when you eat cake, you tell yourself how good it is and how much better it is than steak.

Unaware or semiconsciously, we put a good deal of effort into endorsing one idea ("Cake tastes great!") and "verifying" an opposing idea ("Steak tastes rotten!"). Out of this kind of perpetual work and practice comes your strong—and highly emotive—conviction about the relative merits of cake and steak.

Similarly, you can practice fully accepting yourself with your anger, and the more often and more strongly you work toward this acceptance, the better you will feel about yourself. In REBT we assume that anger does you more harm than good and that knowing this, you would prefer to minimize it. We view surrendering your IBs as an important part of minimizing anger and enjoying a happier life. At the same time we stress the importance of fully accepting yourself and of repeating to yourself unconditional acceptance.

Another emotive technique consists of Rational Emotive Imagery (REI), formulated in 1971 by Dr. Maxie C. Maultsby Jr., a rational-behavior psychiatrist. I have adapted it as follows: First, you imagine a negative event that normally leads to your feeling angry. Vividly and intensely imagine, for example, that I not only refuse to share the apartment with you and unjustly withdraw from our agreement, but that I also deny I ever made such an agreement with you. I strongly assert that you fabricated the whole story in an attempt to make me into a bad guy.

Now imagine this negative experience and let it evoke intense feelings of anger and rage. Let yourself feel enraged at me, both for going back on my word and for denying we had ever made such an apartment-sharing agreement. Rather than avoid these angry feelings, let them erupt with their fullest intensity; let yourself fully experience them for a few minutes.

After you have really and truly experienced your rage for a while, push yourself—really try to push yourself—to change these feelings. Use what you have learned from REBT and work through the ABCs step by step. If you feel anger, don't think that you can't change this feeling by talking to yourself. You can. You can change it at almost any time by working at doing so: by getting in touch with your gut-level feeling of anger and by pushing yourself to change so that you experience different and more healthy feelings, such as keen disappointment and irritation at my behavior. You definitely have the ability to make this emotional change. So give it a sincere try; concentrate and do it.

After you have pushed yourself to feel the Healthy Consequences of keen disappointment and irritation rather than your dysfunctional feelings of anger, take a careful look at what you have done to make these changes and try to retrace or recapture the exact steps of your mental process. You will note that you have in some manner changed your Belief System at point B, and thereby changed your Emotional Consequences at C. You may produce this change by telling yourself, "Oh, well, I'll never like Ellis's denying we ever had our agreement, but he definitely has the right, as a fallible human being, to act in that obnoxious manner." Or, "He really has inconvenienced me greatly by his unfair behavior, but my world won't come to an end because of that inconvenience. How annoying! But I don't have to view it as all that bad."

Let yourself clearly see what you have done by carefully and closely examining what important changes in your Belief System you have made. Make yourself fully aware of the new Rational Beliefs (RBs) that create your new Healthy Consequences (HCs) regarding the unpleasant A—my acting unfairly to you and then denying my unfairness.

If your angry feelings do not change as you attempt to change them, don't give up. Keep fantasizing the same unpleasant experiences or events and keep working at your emotions until you do change them from unhealthy to healthy negative feelings. You create and control your feelings, and you *can* change them.

Once you succeed in feeling disappointed or irritated rather than angry and once you see exactly what beliefs you have changed in your head to make yourself feel disappointed but not emotionally disturbed, keep repeating the process. Make yourself feel angry; then make yourself feel disappointed and annoyed but not angry; then look again at exactly what you did to bring about these changes. Keep practicing by doing this over and over again until the process becomes familiar and increasingly less difficult to carry out.

If you keep practicing Rational Emotive Imagery (REI) for a few minutes every day for several weeks, you will reach a point where whenever you think of an event about which you would normally make yourself angry, you will tend automatically to feel disappointed and annoyed rather than enraged.

If you have trouble practicing REI every day, you can reinforce or motivate yourself by rewarding yourself after you use it with some personal indulgence that you particularly enjoy. On days when you fail to do your REI exercise, you can deny yourself something you like or penalize yourself by doing some task you find distasteful.

I have rarely met an individual who could not keep practicing REI to reduce anger. Over the past years I have taught hundreds of people this method, and those who actually and sincerely worked at it have in most cases been able significantly to reduce their tendencies to anger themselves at many situations.

You can also employ REI methods to create pleasurable feelings about someone, which will distract you and overcome your hostile feelings. R. W. Ramsay, a cognitive-behavior therapist at the University of Amsterdam, has done some experiments and has worked with a technique he calls emotional training. As applied to anger, you can adapt his emotional training as follows:

Think of an intensely pleasant experience you have had with the person with whom you now feel angry. When you have fantasized such a pleasant experience and have actually given yourself unusually intensely warm feelings toward that person, continue the process. Recall pleasant experiences and good feelings, and use them to overcome your angry feelings.

Rational Emotive Imagery and pleasurable self-training use the same principle of anger indoctrination that originally contributed to the formation of your IBs. Left to your own devices, you not only create anger toward others but also keep practicing and practicing these feelings until they "naturally" arise again. You may not be consciously aware of it, but you do this kind of practicing with regard to your unhealthy negative emotions. By the same token, then, you can deliberately practice achieving healthy negative emotions, as you do in REI, or you can deliberately practice positive or pleasurable emotions, as in Ramsay's emotional training technique. If you actively use these methods, they can help you achieve feelings other than anger.

REBT uses my famous *shame-attacking* and *risk-taking exercises* to help you overcome feelings of self-downing, but you can employ them to reduce anger as well. When I invented these exercises, I realized that most people upset themselves by making themselves feel ashamed: ashamed of doing something wrong and ashamed of others' witnessing their wrongdoing and thinking badly of them. In the shame-attacking exercise I try to get my clients to do things that they consider "risky," "shameful," "embarrassing," or "humiliating," such as telling strangers that they have just been released from a mental institution, yelling out the time of day in public, or wearing outlandish clothing. They then can see that these "shameful" acts really don't make them feel embarrassed or lead to self-downing unless they themselves decide to feel that way. They can also see that the shameful acts do not cause as much concern in the minds of others as the potentially "shamed" think they will; that others quickly forget about these acts, rarely concern themselves much with them. If you feel terribly ashamed or embarrassed by various harmless acts—like singing in public—you, too, can try a few of them until you see that not only can you bear to do them, but you can also learn much by performing them and can even come to enjoy them.

At times we cover up feelings of shame or embarrassment with those of anger. You can use the same method described above to practice feeling neither shame nor anger. For example, suppose a waiter in a high-class restaurant gives you poor service and you feel ashamed to bring it to his attention or to complain about it—for fear he will treat you with disdain or, perhaps, make some disparaging remarks about you. Force yourself, under such conditions, to speak to the waiter about the poor service and even ask him to do something you normally wouldn't: replace your soup, for instance, which you find too cold, with warmer soup. By doing this, you will see that your "shameful" act really has no intrinsic "shamefulness." As you do it, also try to get yourself to feel that the waiter has his own human fallibility and that once you express your displeasure with his behavior, you do not have to condemn him for behaving badly.

Similarly, if you tend to feel hostile toward people who act unfriendly to you, go out of your way "shamefully" to encounter some of them: Horn in on a conversation they are having with someone else, or insist that you have met them before when you really haven't. By working against your shame in this connection, you will probably see that you may invent some of people's unfriendliness as a protection against your "shamefully" encountering them and that, in reality, they don't feel very hostile or unfriendly toward you.

Risk-taking and shame-attacking exercises are assertive behaviors. This brings us to regular assertion training, which REBT has used since its inception and which is an excellent way to tone down feelings of anger. For just as anger frequently covers up feelings of shame, it also stems from deep-seated feelings of unassertiveness. You would like, for example, to say no to a friend's request that you have no desire to fulfill, yet you don't feel comfortable about asserting yourself. Perhaps you fear being rejected if you say no, so you withhold your feelings and go along with your friend's wishes. Because you act unassertively, you can easily begin to hate yourself for acting so weakly and to hate your friend for manipulating you into doing something you don't want to do.

If unassertiveness leads to hostility, you may often resolve your anger by training yourself to act more assertively. Thus, if you firmly keep refusing to "go along" with individuals who try to get you to do so, you will not act weakly, you will have no reason to condemn your behavior or yourself for it, and you will not condemn others for "forcing" you to do what you do not want to do.

Assertion training, though it falls under behavioral methods of combating anger (which we will consider in the next chapter), also can be done emotively when you strongly desire to act assertively and fail to do so. If you sincerely want to say no to someone but hesitate because you fear rejection, you might try forcing yourself to say it until you "naturally" feel good saying it and can easily say it again and again. Your practicing such assertiveness training is an evocative-emotive procedure.

Forcing yourself to behave differently from the way you usually do comprises the main emotive element here. As I keep noting, "emotional" thinking and "emotional" activity are strong, forceful behaviors. When emotional, you very much want (or "need") things to go or not go in a certain way, and you feel highly motivated to get what you want. Emotionally, you move *powerfully* toward or away from various people and conditions. Forcing yourself to change your behavior (especially when you have trouble doing so) is an emotive, dramatic way of self-modification. Assertion training frequently is this kind of forcing.

In REBT we have always employed some of the role-playing and behavioral-rehearsal techniques originally created by J. L. Moreno and then adapted by Fritz Perls and other Gestalt therapists. Whereas Moreno, Perls, and others tend to use these techniques largely for abreactive purposes—that is, for the reliving of early emotional experiences and for cathartic release—we tend to use them in more behavioral ways, as espoused by behavior therapists.

Suppose, for example, that you want to tell someone off about something you dislike without raging, and you have trouble doing so. As your therapist, I might get you to try to express the feelings you have about this situation. You might then role play yourself, and another person (or myself) might role play the part of the individual whom you wish to confront. You would first tell exactly how you feel about the circumstances, perhaps trying to express yourself as honestly as possible. Then I and other onlookers (such as the members of your therapy group) would give a critique of your presentation, commenting on whether you spoke (1) too hesitantly; (2) too angrily instead of assertively; (3) quite appropriately. If you did well, we might ask you to repeat the performance several times, merely to rehearse it and get you used to it. If you did poorly, we might ask you to try doing it again in different ways, until you seemed to express yourself not only the way you felt but also in the way that would most likely bring you the results you wanted.

When alone, you can do this kind of role playing or emotive acting out in your head, in front of a mirror, or with the use of a tape recorder. Or you can do it with the help of a friend or a group of friends. It does not require a therapist or a therapy group, though often you will find such a setting useful.

You can employ REBT-type role playing, either with yourself or with others, not merely to express yourself and your feelings or to let off steam, but also to show yourself that you really create your own angry feelings and that you have much better choices. Many kinds of psychotherapies believe that if you feel angry at someone, you have to let out this anger before you can deal with the situation sensibly. They encourage you to scream or yell loudly at someone, pound pillows (which may represent the person you wish to strike), or otherwise "let yourself feel" your anger.

Considerable clinical evidence indicates, however, that the more you take out your anger this way, the angrier you tend to become. REBT offers a good explanation for this occurrence. If you, for example, deliberately insult someone who has done something "wrong" to you or if you pound on a pillow that represents that person, you in all probability tell yourself something like, "He really did treat me unfairly and I hate him. He *absolutely should not* have acted that way toward me, and I really hope that he gets punished for treating me so badly!"

As you release your feelings in this way, you will "confirm" your Irrational Beliefs about the person you think has abused you. He has acted 100 percent wrongly; he had no right whatsoever to make such mistakes; he is a *rotten person* for acting in that way; he deserves to be punished. Perhaps after you release your hostility in this active manner, you will go back and review what actually happened and somewhat forgive the other person for his "awful" acts. More than likely, however, your expressed hostility will serve only to help you exacerbate the "terribleness" of these acts and make you feel, for the present and the future, even angrier.

Some people, after physically or verbally expressing their hostility to others (or to the world), see how much they keep making a mountain out of a molehill, and then calm down and feel only disappointed and sorry about the way others treat them. But the majority of people seem to "confirm" their irrational view that others *shouldn't* act badly toward them and that bad acts mean the entire person is bad. Ironically, the more these people "release," "ventilate," or "abreact" their anger, the angrier they feel, and the more likely they will tend to make themselves angry again at other unfairness. So although occasionally in REBT we help some people express their pent-up feelings of anger (for example, by encouraging them to tell someone off in one of our group therapy sessions), and although we help them show their feelings of annoyance or displeasure at the behavior of other people, we almost always try to help them see that they really create their own feelings of anger and that they have much better choices.

REBT emphasizes that when you feel others treat you unfairly, you had better acknowledge your feelings of anger, if you have them, admit that you largely create these feelings, and surrender the shoulds and musts with which you create these unhealthy feelings. In this way you can end up feeling very disappointed and sorry rather than angry, and you can perhaps choose to express these healthy feelings instead of choosing to express your unhealthy hostile feelings. Many research and clinical studies have been done reviewing the psychoanalytic hypothesis that letting your anger directly out, either verbally or actively, will reduce your rage. Almost all these studies show that this idea is largely a myth. Among scholars who have reviewed the results of these studies are B. J. Bushman and R. F. Baumeister, *Harvard Mental Health Newsletter*, Howard Kassinove, and Carol Tavris.

REBT by no means objects to your having intense feelings, including negative ones, but it encourages you fully to acknowledge, get in touch with, and stop denying such feelings. It shows you how to discriminate healthy feelings of annoyance and displeasure from unhealthy feelings of rage. REBT teaches you how to keep the former and how to change the latter. It gives you a choice about whether—and how—you express your feelings to others. No matter how you feel, you'd better honestly recognize your feelings. But recognize doesn't necessarily mean endorse. Nor does it mean express. Some of your authentic feelings you can fully endorse and had better express. But not all of them!

9

Some Methods of Acting Your Way out of Anger

Like enjoyment or pleasure, emotional disturbance—as noted long before modern psychotherapy came into existence—has a strong habituating component. This habituating tendency works more or less automatically and unconsciously and plays a large and important part in disturbed thinking, emoting, and behaving. We can explain this compulsion to repeat your anger as follows: People probably first began to treat you unfairly during your early childhood when you almost completely depended on others for the gratification of your urges. You probably thought something like: "They must not treat me that unfairly!" Having made this statement to yourself, you might have made yourself feel angry and lashed back at unjust people. But over a period of time, as you "practiced" this irrational belief, you swiftly, easily, and automatically began to make this idea—that you must receive only "fair" treatment and that others must not treat you in any other manner—part of your basic philosophy. So now, as this thought habitually and automatically occurs, you "practice" feeling very angry and lash back at people whom you think angered you.

Your thinking, your feeling, and your activity—the whole complex of your anger—therefore are immediate, reflexive, habituated responses. After a while you began merely to perceive that as soon as anyone treated you unfairly, you instantaneously felt angry and you then lashed back at an unfair person. Then you probably concluded—mistakenly—"The act of this individual's treating me unjustly automatically makes me angry." Actually, you habitually made *yourself angry*.

Although we allow our unconscious habituation tendencies to take over many of our originally conscious activities, we never entirely eliminate the cognitive elements directing our thinking and behavior. When we do well at something, we normally have an underlying philosophy, "I want to do well at this activity and will try to do it as well as I can." When we have poor responses to something, such as quickly and instantly making ourselves enraged at another's unfair behavior, we also seem to have an underlying philosophy, this time an absolutistic *should* or *must* attitude that sabotages our desire to do well and creates our self-defeating behavior.

Perhaps uniquely among major psychotherapies and self-help procedures, REBT fully recognizes that we can and do have conscious and unconscious ideas behind our "automatic" or habituated feelings and actions. It shows you how to look for and identify and then dispute and significantly change your philosophies that do not seem to work best for you—notably, your irrational philosophies. But it also acknowledges the enormous influence and power that habituated, "practiced" behavior has on thoughts and feelings. REBT's behavioral homework assignments try to harness and use that power constructively.

For instance, if you keep having a difficult time learning to play tennis because you feel inferior and put yourself down for not making any progress at mastering the game, you can—in spite of your negative attitudes—force yourself to play daily. Although your self-defeating views and self-downing feelings will interfere with your learning to play well quickly, they may not interfere with your learning to the point where you won't be able to play the game at all.

Despite your feelings and your inhibiting tendencies, you can persist at practicing playing. As you do so, you ultimately play tennis better, and finally you begin to play well. At that point in your progression you realize: "I thought I could never play tennis even adequately, but I now see that I can play fairly well. I still will not always play perfectly, but I see that I can play well enough."

By forcing yourself—in spite of your self-downing attitudes and your inhibitory behavior—to keep practicing tennis, you can actually affect your negative attitudes and thereby give up your self-downing about playing tennis. You can probably do this more swiftly and thoroughly if you also look at and dispute your Irrational Beliefs. But just as your beliefs influence your behavior, your behavior also influences your beliefs. You therefore have a choice of working on changing both your beliefs and your behavior or of changing either one to help you change the other. REBT encourages you to make both these choices. It not only uses highly cognitive and emotive methods (that largely involve changing attitudes and feelings), but also tries to get you to employ a number of active-directive, behavioral methods (that mainly involve changing overt actions). An important form of treatment, one in which REBT has pioneered extensively, consists of active, *in vivo* (in your own life) homework assignments. This means that we give almost all our regular clients—and we can teach people like you to give yourself—steady homework assignments to assist them in overcoming various emotional problems.

Using our illustration, let us assume that you feel angry with me for withdrawing from our agreement and that you seek help from an REBT therapist. Your first homework assignment might consist of your maintaining contact with me while you keep working through your problems of anger. For if you immediately break off this contact because you are angry toward me, your withdrawal is something of a cop-out.

Your goal need not merely include your efficiently stopping me from treating you unfairly again—which you could nicely do if you discontinued your relationship with me—but also can include getting yourself to feel only healthily disappointed or annoyed with my unfairness. If you stop contacting me, you may decrease your anger at me for the wrong reasons—because you are not around me. You will have done little to improve your own behavior and feelings. Thus, if you cease to feel angry at me because you forget about me and what I have done, what kind of change have you made? You will still, presumably, maintain the same philosophy as before. You merely won't activate that philosophy because you don't presently have any Activating Event in which you will employ it. This amounts to something like your angering yourself immensely because a man steals from you and your then feeling little anger toward him because he does not have the opportunity to steal from you again.

Avoidance of persons and situations does little to alter your anger-creating philosophy. You still have it, and you will continue to use it to enrage yourself whenever unfair experience occurs again. If, however, you take the homework assignment of continuing to stay in some kind of relationship with a man who has treated you unjustly and even perhaps give him an opportunity to repeat his poor treatment, and if you maintain this ongoing contact and *still* don't anger yourself about what he has done to you, then it would appear that you've really worked on, and to a considerable degree changed, some of your irrational, anger-creating beliefs.

Your homework assignment or behavioral project can consist of two parts: first, your behavioral activity itself *(maintaining the contact with an unjust person)*; second, your cognitive activity *(working on your ideas about people and their treatment of you while you continue to participate with them)*. I favor homework assignments with both behavioral and cognitive components, because by using this dual approach my clients can personally work through their emotional and behavioral problems simultaneously and use their own thoughts and actions to gain a clearer understanding of the connections among the factors we have been discussing.

In many situations anxiety accompanies anger. You may make yourself angry because you feel anxious about confronting others about their poor and unfair behavior, and by angering yourself you cover up the feeling of helplessness that accompanies anxiety. Thus, you use anger to create the false sense that you are working at doing something about your anxiety.

In vivo homework assignments can help you work out your compound difficulties of anger, anxiety, and depression in several ways. As mentioned, one way involves staying in an unpleasant or obnoxious situation and working through your disturbed feelings about it. For example, if you felt anxious about confronting me about my unfair treatment, you could force yourself to confront me about a number of my lesser faults. You might mention such things as my failure to meet or call you when I had said that I would or my speaking nastily to you.

You can try another approach to dealing with your feelings of anxiety or self-downing about having your anger. You can force yourself to realize that you have a right, as a human, to have feelings of anger. By acknowledging this shortcoming and deploring your anger but not damning *yourself* for having it, you would gain self-acceptance. In accepting yourself, you would also feel less intimidated about your other feelings, such as anxiety in anger-producing situations. You would then find it far easier to dispute your Irrational Beliefs, for you would allow yourself awareness of them.

Behavioral homework assignments can help you habituate yourself to face "disturbing" experiences and deal with them rationally. You see that you can survive happily in spite of your frustrations. In acquiring the discipline these assignments demand, you tend to increase your frustration tolerance. This greatly helps, since emotional disturbances—anger, anxiety, depression—in part result from low frustration tolerance (LFT). We often remain anxious about confronting people because we refuse to bear the discomfort that we would temporarily feel if we confronted them. We sometimes make ourselves angry because we refuse to acknowledge the reality of frustrating situations and passively accept them when we cannot easily and quickly remove them. By refusing to tolerate the difficult situations, we may sustain our anger, for through our inability to work through disappointing problems we do not give ourselves the opportunity to change the Irrational Beliefs that they should not exist.

Good activity homework assignments therefore help you stay with and tolerate unpleasant situations until you can effectively change them. The more you do this kind of homework, the more you tend to increase your tolerance for frustration and thereby minimize your tendencies to make yourself angry and depressed.

Joseph Wolpe, a famous behavior therapist, pioneered an effective *systematic desensitization* exercise that you apply through thinking and relaxing rather than through live *(in vivo)* action: Let yourself think of some situation in which you normally would feel very angry. As you picture it, let yourself relax by using any one of a number of techniques, such as yoga, or thinking of pleasant relaxing scenes. As you relax, your rage tends to dissipate. After you have practiced interrupting your anger with relaxing exercises over a period of time, you may well get to a point where you no longer feel anger in these situations.

Or you can use a hierarchy of "anger-creating" scenes, as Wolpe would again suggest. Write down a series of such scenes, ranging from mildly angering to greatly angering. Begin by picturing the milder type of situation and immediately interrupt your feelings of anger by letting yourself relax. After you no longer feel angry at this situation, go on to picture a more provoking situation and interrupt that one, again by relaxing. By continuing this process of training yourself to interrupt your anger, you establish a gradual sequence of desensitization to these situations. After you have gone through your own hierarchy of mildly, moderately, and intensely angering scenes and have succeeded in relaxing instead of feeling enraged, you will tend to feel desensitized to many kinds of frustrating situations.

Further details of using systematic desensitization combined with relaxation techniques are given in my book *How to Control Your Anger Before It Controls You*, which I authored with Chip Tafrate.

You will find systematic desensitization (SD) somewhat similar to Rational Emotive Imagery (REI), although it has an important difference. SD advocates that you begin with the least provoking situation and gradually work your way up to a more dramatic experience. You have to relax every time you go through the hierarchy of anxiety-creating or anger-inciting scenes that you imagine. REI, on the other hand, asks that you *begin with* the worst possible situation and let it flood your senses. Thus, you actively *force yourself* to change your feeling from an unhealthy one, such as anger, to a healthy one, such as disappointment. You may find both these methods effective.

REBT also makes use of B. F. Skinner's technique of *operant conditioning*. This self-management technique uses the principles of reward and penalization. You reward yourself with a prize (such as food, approval, or a much-sought-after privilege) when you perform a desired behavior; and use a penalty when you do not perform it.

Using penalties, as well as reinforcements or rewards, does not amount to the same thing as damning and putting yourself down for your poor behavior. Let us make a clear distinction between a *penalty* and a *punishment*. If you keep having temper tantrums and you wish to stop having them, for instance, you can legitimately deprive or fine yourself with some kind of penalty. In this case the term *penalize* simply means to deprive yourself of something you consider beneficial or enjoyable in order to help you change your undesirable behavior. To punish yourself, on the other hand, means (1) to penalize yourself in the sense just noted *and* (2) to denigrate yourself as a person for meriting the penalty.

Skinner's work has led to considerable criticism because with operant conditioning you can subtly manipulate people by using reinforcing principles to get them to do many things they don't really want to do. The technique can be abused, especially in controlled environments, such as schools, hospitals, and prisons. As used in REBT and most other forms of behavior therapy, however, operant conditioning mainly takes the form of contingency management or self-control applications. Clients who wish to change their self-defeating behaviors and, particularly, to discipline themselves when they normally have great trouble doing so, agree to carry out assignments and to accept pleasant reinforcements only if they complete their assignments satisfactorily. They also may agree to accept certain penalties if they do not carry out their assignments.

Self-management can also be used by individuals who make contracts with themselves. Writers and artists have for many centuries helped themselves work at their crafts for a minimum period of time each day by allowing themselves to eat, read, or talk to their friends only after they have put in this allotted amount of time. Millions of people have induced themselves to diet, exercise, or do other unpleasant tasks by imposing some stiff penalty on themselves if they do not live up to the contracts they make with themselves.

To apply this principle to our REBT theory, let us say that you have trouble spending time every day working on disputing your Irrational Beliefs and working on your other homework assignments. You know that you can use REBT theory effectively by working amply at it. You can make a contract with yourself, and to make your commitment more formal, you can write your agreement down in very clear terms. As a reward (or reinforcer) for having carried out your homework, you can select any activity or indulgence you particularly enjoy. Each day that you spend the required time disputing and debating your IBs, you can reward yourself. Failure to meet the requirements of your contract will result in a penalty (some activity or thing you find highly distasteful). You may sometimes find it preferable to seek the help of another person to assist you in enforcing this contract. A close friend or associate will often happily assist you, for when people care for you, they enjoy seeing you improve. Also, arranging with a friend to monitor you helps ensure that penalties and rewards are faithfully enforced.

Because people have such a wide range of likes and dislikes, I will not outline specific rewards and penalties. In general, rewards had better be desirable. I would also suggest you select rewards that you can receive immediately upon completing your daily assignments since they will then tend to work more effectively.

Like rewards, devise penalties within reason. Too severe or hard-to-enforce penalties will not be carried out. Penalties can consist of (1) not getting a reward and (2) depriving yourself of, or interrupting a part of, your daily routine that you enjoy. For instance, if you eat ice cream daily, you can deprive yourself of it on days when you earn a penalty. A penalty can also consist of a burden you impose on yourself in addition to the two mentioned above. Let us say that you generally take a cab or drive yourself to work because of your hatred of public transportation. As a good penalty you can force yourself to use this hated and inconvenient method. This is an effective penalty since you force yourself to put up with it twice: on your way to work and on your way home. A penalty can also add a burden to your daily routine, such as mowing your lawn.

If you wish, you can institute a special reward and penalty system. If you do your homework every day of the week, for instance, you can give yourself a super reward on the weekend—such as going to dinner at a special place. If you haven't kept your agreement, you can impose a special penalty like getting up early on a weekend morning to do some bothersome chore.

Let me reiterate the difference between penalty and punishment. As I tell my clients, you may decide to penalize laboratory animals for going down the wrong pathways in a maze in order to help them discover the right pathways. But you certainly wouldn't scream at or brutalize them if they hadn't responded correctly. You do this essentially, however, when you punish (rather than merely penalize) yourself for inefficient behavior—you put yourself down as a human.

So long as you stay with the idea "I want *to give up my anger*," you can logically follow it with: "and since I find it so hard to give it up and so difficult to train myself to work against it, I want to find a penalty that will help me work at giving up this anger." If you use this kind of formula, your desire to accept the penalty outweighs your desire to avoid the difficult task of disciplining yourself against your anger. You willingly impose a penalty on yourself in order to overcome your unwillingness to accept the pain of changing your behavior.

When you punish yourself, rather than penalize yourself, however, you really tell yourself, "I *must* give up my anger and make myself more disciplined; if I don't do what I *must* do, I not only will penalize myself, but will also put myself down for not keeping my agreement with myself." The punishing equation includes an absolutistic *must* and a self-downing consequence of that *must*. Many people find it difficult to make the necessary distinction between these two ideas, for they feel that some force in the universe degrades them when they have promised themselves to do something sensible and then have failed to follow through with that promise. REBT tries to help people stop this type of self-flagellation.

REBT also employs a good deal of assertion training (AT), strongly geared to help people act assertively rather than aggressively. When you assert yourself, you merely seek what you want and avoid what you don't want. However, when you act aggressively, you also add a hostile component to your feelings and behavior: Your belief that others have no right to block you from getting what you want leads you to feeling contemptuous toward them for refusing to give it to you. REBT teaches you how to distinguish assertion and how firmly and persistently to strive for the things you want without hating others, unnecessarily antagonizing them, refusing to compromise, and demanding or commanding that they *must* give you everything you desire.

REBT sets the stage philosophically for your trying to act assertively rather than aggressively and in this respect differs significantly from less discriminating therapies. Once you understand the key REBT principle and fully accept the fact that others do not make you angry but that you have the responsibility for creating your own rage, you can much more effectively perform many assertion training exercises that will help you overcome a good deal of your fury.

Self-assertion involves considerable risk taking: doing what you really want to do; refraining from doing what you really don't want to do. Naturally, other people may feel annoyed by or think disparagingly of you for your assertiveness. Assertiveness therefore entails possible penalties, and you had better consider these before you assert yourself, particularly in some instances where you assert yourself with a supervisor or boss. You may deem the risks you take too high, and thus you may decide not to assert yourself. Deliberately holding back on asserting yourself may at times constitute very rational behavior.

Many of the times when you behave passively, however, you view normal risk taking as being *too* risky because you are overconcerned about gaining the approval of other people. Rational Emotive Behavior Therapy shows you how to risk the disapproval of others in order to allow yourself the freedom of asking for what you want. It helps you first break down your avoidance of risk and then make more overt and assertive moves.

Some common assertive homework assignments that we would encourage you to try if you are using REBT include the following:

Take specific risks

Think of a few things you would like to do but have felt extremely afraid to do and have therefore avoided. Like sending back a poorly cooked dish in a restaurant. Or wearing an article of clothing that looks garish. Or eating a sandwich when riding a bus or subway train. Or raising your hand in a large audience to ask what the other people in the audience think is a foolish question. Or telling someone important to you that you dislike his behavior, while trying not to put him down for performing badly.

Risk rejection by asking for something

Think of something you really want—such as sex, a special food, a back rub, or going to a movie—something you think will result in refusal if you ask for it. Risk this refusal by specifically asking one of your associates, friends, or relatives for this favor. When refusal has occurred, try to talk the other person into rescinding this refusal. If you don't succeed, try on some other occasion to get what you want.

Risk saying no or refusing something yourself

Pick something that you don't usually want to do but that you often do in order to please others—such as going out to eat, having sex in a certain way, or carrying on a conversation for a long period of time—and deliberately take the risk of refusing to do this. You can at times forcefully refuse, just to make the risk of saying no greater. Or you can nicely but firmly refuse, and persist at refusing, even though the other person keeps trying to get you to do it.

Do something ridiculous or "shameful"

As noted in the previous chapter, you can do some shame-attacking exercises. Think of something you and most other people would think foolish for you to do in public and deliberately do this "shameful" or "embarrassing" thing. Like singing at the top of your lungs in the street. Or walking a banana, as if walking a dog or a cat on a leash. Or wearing a headband with a large yellow feather stuck in it. Or stopping a little old lady and asking if she would help you cross the street.

Deliberately fail at an important task—or act as if you had

Make yourself fail at a task that you normally would not want to let people see you fail at, and make sure they know about your failure. While playing in a baseball game, for example, deliberately drop a fly ball that practically falls into your hands. During a public speech make yourself stutter for a while. Tell people that you have failed an examination when you have really passed it.

Assert yourself coolly

Many of the proponents of assertion training who swear by the fight-'em-and-assert-yourself school forget that playing it cool often is a better way of getting what you want. Coolly assert that you live for your own enjoyment, and not for helping others. You feel determined to have your way prevail.

As Lois Bird correctly points out in regard to a mate who would get along better with a partner, "I don't care what you feel on a gut level; you don't have to spread it all over the verbal landscape. You can turn it off and talk to (your mate) with your cool intact." She doesn't quite note that this cool behavior makes you more assertive, in many instances, than overtly telling your partner off.

Rehearse resistance to giving in

George Bach and Herb Goldberg advocate a form of rehearsing resistance that consists of your getting together with a partner who makes a request of you and then giving him a reason why you don't want to fulfill this request. Your partner keeps coming up with reasons why you should fill the request, and you keep saying no—giving good reasons for your refusal. This rehearsal continues until you say, "You've convinced me," or your partner says, "I see that I won't succeed in convincing you, so I think we'd better stop."

Courageous confrontation

As noted above, hostility and violence often stem from lack of courage. You refuse to go after what you want and then, hating yourself for your own weakness, you feel angry and combative toward those with whom you have acted weakly. Especially in males, as Sherwyn Woods notes, "violence is a restorative act, attempting to restore masculine self-esteem via aggressive demonstrations of power and strength." When you are violent, you often deny feelings of passivity and dependency that in our society are deemed feminine.

One antidote to this kind of unassertiveness is courageously confronting those with whom you disagree. Certainly, overt conflict may then result, but at least you will get things out in the open, and may resolve them. If, therefore, you will courageously confront those with whom you seriously disagree, your confrontation may well show others that you have relatively little fear, will try to have your side prevail, and deserve consideration and perhaps compromise.

How do you perform this kind of direct confrontation? By showing yourself that you can stand opposition and rudeness and that if others dislike you, you need not dislike yourself. While so doing, you often had better force yourself—yes, force yourself!—to verbally confront your opponents. No matter what the initial pain of so doing, remember that the pain of nonconfrontation generally is much worse—and more prolonged!

Feedback

Robert E. Alberti and Michael E. Emmons, in *Your Perfect Right*, explain in detail how therapists can help their clients, especially their marital counseling clients, by rehearsing with and modeling for them assertive rather than aggressive behavior. You can do this kind of rehearsal by having one of your friends witness and "referee" a mock fight between you and, say, your mate or your boss. Set up a specific scene of conflict; decide with your onlooker exactly what you and your antagonist will do; have your witness critique your role playing; then replay the "drama," getting more feedback and coaching by your onlooker. Do the same role play several times, until you perfect it.

Without an onlooker, you can use a tape recorder or video recorder to "observe" you and your partner during your role playing and can get feedback from the recorded scene to see how you have done and how you can improve. Sometimes you can use the recorder, and sometimes you can use a live witness. At still other times you can have live verbal differences with your partner and then ask one or more onlookers to report back to you what they heard and how they felt about your own and your partner's assertiveness.

Prior preparation

Assertion often consists of preparing yourself in advance to deal with passive aggressors or procrastinators. One of your friends may not ask you to do things you don't want to do but may promise to meet you for appointments and never show up or consistently turn up late. If so, you then set very precise and active rules, such as "If you don't show up by ten-thirty and I haven't heard from you by phone, I shall go to the movies by myself." In making these rules, make sure that you don't make them idly and that you stick to them.

Clearly distinguish assertion from aggression

Alberti and Emmons make a fine point of clearly distinguishing assertive from aggressive behavior, following some prior leads by Arnold Lazarus and my own writings. As Lazarus and Allen Fay note, "Assertion involves taking a stand, resisting unreasonable demands, or asking for what you want. Aggression involves putting another person down. Assertion is positive, aggression negative." The main differences among unassertive, assertive, and aggressive behavior include the following:

- *Unassertive behavior:* You want something and do not honestly express your want or make any effort to obtain it. You resort to indirect, passive, somewhat dishonest actions. You frequently do not admit to yourself what you really want and don't want. You needlessly inhibit yourself and even deny some of your basic desires. You tend to feel anxious, hurt, and angry.

• *Assertive behavior:* You want something, honestly acknowledge to yourself that you want it, and for the most part try to get it. You act openly with others, but strongly and persistently try to get what you want for yourself. You feel self-interested and self-enhancing. You value other people's values and goals but often prefer your own somewhat to theirs. You are active and expressive.

• *Aggressive behavior:* You feel angry toward others for blocking your goals and often try to do them in rather than to get what you want. You strongly believe that they should not, must not thwart you. You are emotionally honest, but act in an all-for-me and me-for-all way. You express yourself fully—and frequently overdo it. You often feel righteous and superior to others and tend to damn them. You may later feel—or not feel—guilty about your hostility.

If you will see the differences among these three kinds of behavior, and not only think you have a choice between unassertiveness and aggression, you can train yourself, along the lines outlined in this book, to act truly assertively, with responsibility toward yourself and others—as Arthur Lange and Patricia Jakubowski and other REBT-oriented therapists advocate.

Acting assertively

Some of the elements of acting assertively, as outlined by Lange and Jakubowski and by Janet L. Wolfe, include these behaviors:

- When expressing disapproval of, or your desire not to do, something, use a decided no. Don't hedge or leave the decision up to the other person. Don't make yourself defensive or apologetic.
- Speak in an audible, firm voice. Avoid whining and making harsh and accusatory statements.
- Give as prompt and brief a reply as possible, without using long pauses or interruptions.

- Try to have others treat you with fairness and justice and point out when they don't. But don't insist or command!
- When asked to do something you consider unreasonable, ask for an explanation and listen to it carefully. Where appropriate, suggest an alternative act or solution you would prefer.
- Honestly express your feelings without using evasion, attacking the other person, or trying to justify yourself in a defensive manner.
- When expressing displeasure or annoyance, try to tell the other person the aspects of the behavior that you don't like. Don't attack, name-call, or imply that the person deserves damnation!
- Recognize the usefulness of I-messages instead of you-messages, but also note that the former provide no panacea. Joseph Wolpe, one of the pioneers in assertion training, tends to advocate I-messages and the use of anger in the learning of assertiveness. But therapists like Arnold Lazarus and David D. Hewes point out that I-messages, too, can include a great deal of self-defeating rage while appropriate you-messages may not. Thus, if you object to the way a salesman deals with you, you can angrily say, with an I-message, "I get miffed in this kind of setup, when I try to buy a shirt from you and you behave the way you do to me." Or you can nonangrily, with a you-message, say, "You really seem to feel uptight today. No wonder you act this way." Lazarus, thus, with his you-message, includes an understanding of the other person and even a positive reinforcement. So use but don't overvalue I-messages.

Degrees of assertiveness. Marlowe H. Smaby and Armas W. Tamminen note that there are various degrees of assertiveness and that some are appropriate for different kinds of situations or with different partners. Using minimal assertiveness, you merely hold your ground and refuse to let another control you, as when someone tries to horn in on a line ahead of you and you merely point to the back of the line and indicate that he had better head for it.

Using the next level of being assertive, you recognize another's side of the issue and feelings about it; but without vindictiveness, you solidly hold your ground. Thus, if a friend wants you to lie for him, you say, "I can see how you feel about this and why you want me to do it and how disappointed you will feel if I don't. But I also have strong feelings that I don't want to do this and will possibly get into some kind of trouble. So I wish you wouldn't ask me to do it. In fact, I feel somewhat uneasy about it now that you have asked."

Using a higher-level, bargaining assertiveness, you still firmly hold your ground but also go out of your way to see the other's point of view and find some sort of compromise solution. Thus, you may say to the friend who wants you to lie, "I can see how you feel about this and why you want me to do what you want and how disappointed you will feel if I don't. But I also have strong feelings that I don't want to do this and will possibly get into some kind of trouble, so you can see how I feel about it and why I won't do it. Still, I think I can see another way to help you. I will stick pretty much to the truth but will really go out of my way to get that person to give you a job so that he can see how capable you are. I will recommend that he give it to you even though you may lack the experience he desires."

If you practice these different levels of assertion and use them discriminatingly, you can act the way you want to act and still remain on good terms—even very friendly terms—with others.

If you take these assertive risks within the context of Rational Emotive Behavior Therapy, you won't feel terribly ashamed by them and you won't down yourself for acting in a way that seems at times foolish. Your goal in REBT doesn't consist of taking social risks or of bucking conventions simply for the sake of doing so. REBT stresses the gains you can make by the mere act of taking these risks. In taking them without worrying too much what other people might think of you, you assert yourself while, at the same time, convincing yourself that nothing *horrible* will happen. Also, you keep learning that you can tolerate the disapproval of others although you may not particularly like it. This enables you to feel that no person, including yourself, can legitimately put you down globally or evaluate you as a rotten person when you perform an unpopular act.

I don't claim that you will automatically surrender all your angry feelings and actions and turn into an individual who feels healthily displeased but never unhealthily enraged when unpleasant things occur. For even if you act appropriately assertive on practically all occasions, you may still remain an injustice collector who not only finds things wrong with others and with the world, but also whines and screams when such unfair things happen. I do hold that one of the main instigators of your anger lies in your acting passively and unassertively. But I contend that if you practice acting more assertively—while realizing that you do not need the approval of other people who may see you as *too* assertive—you will tend to feel less anger with less frequency than you do presently.

REBT stresses education and, consequently, employs all types of psychoeducational methods, including reading materials, audiovisual aids, charts and diagrams, slogans, and *modeling*. If you saw me as a therapist and presented to me your problem of often angering yourself at people who treat you unfairly or inconsiderately, I would try to act as a model of REBT's antianger philosophy for you. Thus, if you came late to therapy sessions, failed to listen—for whatever reasons—to what I kept saying to you, refused to do your homework assignments, or otherwise showed resistance to changing, I would attempt to *show you that I definitely disliked your behavior but that I did not angrily condemn you for displaying that behavior.*

Not that I would necessarily show complete calm or indifference to such actions. I most probably wouldn't! I take my work as a therapist very seriously, and if you failed to listen, for instance, I would still emphatically try to get you to see your self-defeating philosophies (your IBs) and would try to teach you how to uproot them. I would not angrily condemn you for your inattentiveness.

I would not want you to develop an emotional dependence on me and to change yourself because *I* wanted you to do so. This brings to mind something I discussed earlier in this book. I pointed out that when you openly criticize others for their "outrageous" behavior, you risk their urge to *defend* that same behavior. They would probably not feel the need to hold on to their "outrageous" behavior if you allowed them to reach critical conclusions about it on their own. So with my getting you to change authentically, I would attempt to get you to do so for your own benefit and only incidentally for mine.

To do this, I would act as a good model for you to follow: as someone who could show you more about your irrational behavior (anger) through modeling displeasure at your *behavior* but not anger at *you*.

Assuming, then, that it would be helpful to you for someone to serve as a rational model, the question remains: How could you get this kind of benefit for yourself without actually seeing an REBT therapist? The answer: Find good models in your own life.

Unfortunately, most people whom we encounter hardly fall into this category. In fact, they tend to anger themselves just as often about trivial unfairnesses or injustices as they do important ones. Exceptions, however, do exist—an unusual friend or teacher, an occasional relative, an associate—people who feel determined to overcome life's unniceties and who actively keep working at doing so.

Talk to these people.

Try to learn from them how they manage to keep reasonably cool in the face of life's annoyances.

Observe them in action. See if you can model some of your own feelings and behaviors after theirs.

Find them in books and other biographical materials, for literature is full of figures who often suffered great frustrations without making themselves unduly angry or upset.

Seek out these rational models and learn about their lives.

Other behavioral methods of working against anger that REBT finds effective follow:

Exposure to hostility

If you have the help of a therapist or therapy group or if you know REBT and attempt to use it with yourself, exposure to hostility, in the course of group therapy or in the course of your regular life, may help you. This does not mean that the hostility *itself* changes you, for it frequently serves as a bad model. But your practicing *coping* with this hostility, especially under therapeutic supervision, may help you handle yourself more effectively as you begin to look closer at and understand the nature of your hostility. As mentioned earlier, taking yourself out of a situation merely leaves the problem in a latent state, unsolved.

Constructive activities

As Andrew S. Wachtel and Martha Penn Davis and other researchers have indicated, individuals tend to feel alienated, anonymous, and impersonal. If such individuals can experience devotion to some highly constructive group or cause, they may divert themselves from, first, their sense of alienation and anonymity, and then some of their anger.

Early conditioning

Victor H. Denenberg and M. J. Zarrow did a series of fascinating experiments involving newborn mice, raised in one group by rats, in another—control—group by mice. They found "the mice reared by rats were heavier than the mouse-raised control mice; they also were less active in the open field and preferred to spend time near a rat instead of near a mouse. Our most dramatic finding was that the rat-reared mice would *not* fight when placed in a standard fighting-box situation . . ." This contrasted with the occurrence of a great many fights among control mice reared by mouse mothers, thus showing that the "natural" tendency of mice to fight can be significantly altered when they are "unnaturally" reared.

Other experimenters have found that mice raised in close proximity to dogs or cats will not later be attacked by these natural "enemies," while mice raised without this contact will suffer attack. Denenberg and Zarrow note that "we must therefore reject any hypothesis that states that aggression is a genetically determined, instinctive response that cannot be modified by experience. . . . This is not to suggest that genetic factors are not important. It is obvious that they are. What we are saying is that *both the genetic background and the environment in which those genes grow and develop must be considered* jointly *if we are to advance our understanding of behavior patterns.*"

If we apply this information to the human condition, people subjected to early conditioning designed to lessen their anger may decrease some of their biological tendencies to act angry and violent. Naturally, you can now do little about your own childhood, but you can give some thought, if you have children, to helping condition them to act less hostile.

Diversionary measures

As noted above, constructive action may serve as a good diversion to hostility, and so may less constructive behaviors. Norman Zinberg, following the ideas of William James and Sigmund Freud, wonders whether some kinds of competitive and semidestructive activities, such as organized sports and politics, can successfully help to sublimate anger more than other kinds of activities, such as private enterprise. No one as yet truly knows, but the *REBT position assumes that highly aggressive pursuits, such as dog-eat-dog industrial competition and prizefighting, help make humans more rather than less hostile.*

Robert Barton and Paul Bell found that mild degrees of sexual arousal served to inhibit subsequent physical aggression in experimental subjects. The use of reciprocal inhibition as a diversionary measure also tends to reduce feelings of anger. From the evidence available, *it would appear that all kinds of enjoyable, constructive, and even neutral diversions can serve to interfere with and at least temporarily to ease hostility.* Consequently, if you want to control your own angry feelings, you can consider using such distractions to help train yourself so that ultimately you will permanently tend to feel less enraged when confronted with obnoxious stimuli. As diversions, you can use thoughts, fantasies, games, activities, emotional involvements, pleasures, or any number of other activities. Discover what particularly works for you in this regard.

Coping procedures

One of the main factors that seems to help almost all disturbed emotional reactions consists of your engaging, and knowing full well that you engage, in effective coping procedures. Richard Pisano and Stuart P. Taylor, for example, found that forty individuals who had records as high aggressors against others reduced their aggressiveness not when they received punishment for aggressing or when given money for not aggressing, but when allowed to give equal punishment to those who attacked them.

When the aggressors realized they could cope effectively and capably with their opponents, they felt more secure and less hostile and punitive. And a good many other experiments similarly show that *when people feel that they definitely can cope effectively with some situation, they handle it better and upset themselves less about it.* I would therefore recommend that you try to develop a good set of coping measures that you can employ when faced with obnoxious events and badly behaving people. If you know that you can deal adequately with someone who treats you unfairly, you will have less of a likelihood of angering yourself at the person. This does not constitute an ideal solution—since you may see that you do not cope effectively with an aggressor. But it will help in many instances.

Cognitive awareness and desensitization

Ray Novaco conducted an experiment that involved showing people how to manage their anger through relaxation methods alone, through REBT alone, and through relaxation combined with REBT. He found that REBT worked better than relaxation and that both methods combined worked better still. We find the same thing in regular sessions of Rational Emotive Behavior Therapy: If we first show clients how they philosophically create their feelings of anger—by whining about injustices and frustrations and demanding that these absolutely must not exist—we then can best show them how to relax, how to instruct themselves in anger-coping methods, and how otherwise to live with and finally to remove their rage.

By using REBT, you can do the same thing for yourself. Acknowledge fully that you create your own feelings of ire and see how you do so—by insisting and commanding that something exist when it doesn't or that something must not exist when it indubitably does. As you understand this and work to modify your commands on others and on the universe, you will find yourself more able to employ the various behavioral methods that I have outlined in this chapter.

Let me emphasize once again that although REBT has a distinct theory of human nature, of emotional trauma, and of effective psychotherapy and although it uses many eclectic techniques, it is not an eclectic theory. It covers, in some respects, perhaps thirty or forty different methods, many of which vary greatly, but it employs them in the framework of the general REBT theory.

Its behavioral methods, for example, do not consist merely of symptom removal. If REBT therapists persuade you to practice several behavioral techniques—such as activity homework assignments, operant conditioning, and assertion training—to help decrease your feelings of anger, they will not do so merely to get you to stop feeling angry right now, while you remain in therapy. They will try to see that you leave therapy with a good understanding of how you incite yourself to anger and how you can stop this in the future as well as in the present—to stop it under very difficult conditions that might later arise in your life.

By giving you theoretical understanding and practical techniques that you can employ yourself, REBT attempts to provide you with a treatment methodology that will enable you not only to *feel* better, but to *get* better—for the rest of your life.

10

More Rethinking About Your Anger

REBT, though strongly cognitive in its approach, includes powerful and integral emotive and behavioral components. I have only thus far presented one basic cognitive procedure for reducing angry thoughts and feelings. That is D, or Disputing, in the ABCDE method of understanding and minimizing anger, and although Disputing has many complexities and includes such things as Debating and Discriminating, it nevertheless represents only one philosophic or cognitive approach to the problem.

If you really work at Disputing your Irrational Beliefs strongly, intensively, and persistently, you can also use several different methods to help examine and reject irrational thinking. Let me outline some important and helpful variations.

First of all, you can use the technique we call DIBS—Disputing Irrational Beliefs—which gives you a more systematic way of taking your absolutistic ideas and "ripping them up" many times until you no longer tend to subscribe to them. Like several other REBT methods, you do DIBS for a minimum of, say, ten minutes a day for about twenty or thirty days in a row. I have outlined the general DIBS technique in the last chapter of the revised edition of *How to Live With a "Neurotic,"* in *A Guide to Rational Living*, and in a separate pamphlet published by the Albert Ellis Institute. Let me present it here as well, to apply it specifically to problems with your anger.

Let us suppose, once more, that I have promised to share an apartment with you, have persuaded you to go to considerable expense to fix it up, and then have unfairly and irresponsibly backed out on our deal and refused either to move in with you or to reimburse you for your trouble and expense. You feel extremely angry at me, especially when we meet or when someone mentions my name, and you soon see—in the ABC model of REBT—that the primary Irrational Belief (IB) that makes you feel angry is "He *should not* have treated me that unfair way!"

You can now use DIBS—Disputing Irrational Beliefs—to question and challenge that thought. In using DIBS, you ask yourself the following questions, and preferably, write down each one and also write down your answers, so that you can review, add to, change, and consolidate them.

Question 1: *What Irrational Belief do I want to Dispute and surrender?*
Illustrative answer: "He should not have treated me that unfair way!"

Question 2: *Can I rationally support this belief?*
Illustrative answer: "No, I don't think that I can."

Question 3: *What is the evidence for the falseness of this belief?*
Illustrative answers:

a. "Perhaps he didn't even act that unfairly to me. True, I see his action as completely wrong and irresponsible. But he may have, and others may have, a different view of this matter. And their view may have some validity. So I don't even know that I have 100 percent certainty of his wrongness and irresponsibility."

b. "Assuming that I can prove that he did behave wrongly and unfairly to me, what law of the universe says that he *should not* or *must not* behave that way—that he *has to* act fairly? None! Although I and other people would find it right and proper for him to act fairly to me, he definitely doesn't *have to* do so."

c. "If he *should have* or *must have* treated me fairly instead of unfairly, he would have done so, for how could he avoid doing what he *must* do? The fact that he *didn't* treat me fairly seems to show that no reason exists why he *must have* done so."

d. "When I tell myself, 'He should not have treated me that way!' I really seem to mean that (a) the conditions that existed at the time he treated me that way should not have existed and (b) he should not have followed them if they did exist. But of course, the conditions of his life, his history, his personality, his biological makeup, and so forth, did exist at the time he treated me unfairly. And if these conditions did exist, how could he *not* have gone along with them, as I seem to demand? Suppose, let us say, his mother strongly objected to the very thing that I wanted him to do and suppose that he, because of his undue attachment to her, went along with her objections and decided to cop out of our arrangement. By my statement 'He should not have treated me that unfair way!' I actually insist that his mother must not have her objections and/or that he should not go along with them. But how can I *make* her give up her objections or *make* him ignore them? Naturally, I can't!"

e. "By demanding that he not treat me unfairly, I actually seem to believe the statement, 'Because he theoretically could have not acted in that unfair manner, he therefore *should not* have acted that way!' But this statement clearly represents a non sequitur: Its conclusion doesn't logically follow from its premise. No matter how true it may be that he theoretically could have chosen not to have treated me unfairly, that never means that he therefore *must* choose to act fairly."

f. "In demanding that he treat me fairly, I really devoutly believe the proposition, 'Because I strongly want him to act that way, he has to give me what I want!' But how accurate is that proposition? Clearly inaccurate!"

g. "I also seem to believe the idea that 'Because I have treated him quite fairly throughout our dealings, he *should* and *must* treat me with equal fairness!' Another nutty idea!"

h. "I see him as a complete louse for treating me lousily. But even if I can prove to virtually everyone's satisfaction that he did treat me unfairly and shabbily, I carelessly overgeneralize when I label *him*, his entire *person*, as a louse for treating me in this vile manner. He almost certainly has some good traits and performances, too. How, therefore, can I legitimately define *him* as a worm?"

i. "When I say, 'He should not have treated me that unfair way!' I really mean, by using this *should*, an absolutistic *must*. I don't say, 'He *preferably* should treat me fairly,' or 'He *most probably* would get better results for himself and society if he treated me and others fairly.' I dogmatize and absolutize that 'He *must* treat me fairly!' But as far as I know, I can prove no absolutes, and positing them and feeling completely convinced of their truth is futile."

j. "While I cannot prove the truth of my belief 'He *should not* have treated me unfairly,' I *can* show that if I continue to subscribe to this belief, I will in all probability feel very angry at him and could continue to feel angry for months or years to come, thus interfering with my chances of dealing with him effectively. Although my anger-creating statements seem unprovable, the poor results of my devoutly believing them appear eminently provable! Therefore, I had better give them up!"

k. "By demanding that he must treat me fairly, I imply that I *can't stand* his unfair treatment of me and that I can only survive and lead a happy existence if some force in the universe makes him rectify his erroneous ways and begin to treat me fairly. Obviously, my ideas in this respect are hokum. For although I'll never *like* the unfair treatment, I can certainly stand it and, if I stop foolishly making myself enraged at him, I can also arrange to have a long and reasonably happy life in spite of his unfairness."

Question 4: *Is my belief about him accurate—that he should not have treated me unfairly and that he is a louse for doing what he should not have done?*

Illustrative answer: "No, it is not accurate. I can probably obtain empirical data showing he treated me unfairly, and most probably get a consensus from many other people that he did. I could therefore accurately contend that his *behavior* seems lousy. But I don't seem to have any evidence whatever that *he is* a louse for acting that way. At most, my belief about him is only partially accurate, and significant aspects of it appear highly exaggerated and quite false."

Question 5: *What worst things could actually happen to me if he continued to treat me unfairly?*

Illustrative answers:

a. "I would not get reimbursed for the time, trouble, and money I have spent in fixing up the apartment he agreed to share with me and would therefore continue to suffer real inconvenience as a result of his withdrawing from the agreement."

b. "He might possibly give people a false impression of our differences, thus convincing them that he acted correctly and that I acted wrongly. This would blacken my name and reputation."

c. "As a result of his disliking me and perhaps inducing others to dislike me, too, I would suffer more inconveniences."

d. "Living in my new apartment by myself or having to share it with someone else, as a result of his reneging on his agreement to share it with me, might well prove highly annoying."

e. "I might continue to have hassles with him, particularly if we remain in contact. Even if we somehow resolve our differences, we both will tend to have a bad taste in our mouths and will lose out on our previous feeling of trust and friendship."

Question 6: *What good things could happen or could I make happen if he continues to treat me unfairly or refuses to change his ways?*

Illustrative answers:

a. "I could gain in assertiveness by confronting him with his unfairness and by trying to get him, even though unsuccessfully, to change his attitude and behavior toward me."

b. "I might well enjoy living by myself or finding another person to share my new apartment."

c. "The time and energy that I now expend in maintaining a friendship with him I might well put toward doing friendly things with others or to enjoying myself in other ways."

d. "I could practice my discussing and arguing skills through my attempt to get him to see things differently and to redress his unfair actions toward me."

e. "I could use this unfair situation with him as a challenge to work on my own attitudes, to acknowledge fully that I create my own feelings of anger when others mistreat me, to change my own anger-creating philosophy of life, and to prepare myself for more constructive action and less destructive rage and temper tantrums in the future when other people treat me unfairly."

The DIBS technique simply formalizes some of the more important aspects of disputing Irrational Beliefs when obnoxious and unwanted conditions occur. It consists of a systematic approach to D, Disputing, through a particular set of questions that you keep using whenever you feel emotionally upset at C. You can apply DIBS, of course, to feelings of anxiety, depression, despair, self-pity, and low frustration tolerance. As you may have already noted, this technique encourages a concerted, methodical approach, aims at your using it regularly, and asks that you do it in writing or with the use of a tape recorder, so that you can keep reviewing your previous Disputing and solidify it.

Another cognitive method of uprooting Irrational Beliefs (IBs) consists of a technique invented by Joseph Danysh (and outlined in his book *Stop Without Quitting*). It uses the principles of general semantics—the science of language discrimination—originated by Alfred Korzybski. Korzybski noted that virtually all humans naturally and easily overgeneralize and make continual use of meaningless higher-order abstractions in their words and meanings. He pointed out that people consequently tend to defeat themselves and behave self-defeatingly and render themselves "unsane." Several of Korzybski's followers, such as Wendell Johnson, have applied his techniques to the field of emotional disturbance, and much of their thinking has been incorporated into Rational Emotive Behavior Therapy—which some authorities describe as one of the leading semantic therapies.

As stated, Joseph Danysh's theory embodies these principles of semantic overgeneralization, and part of his technique provides us with a practical, cognitive tool for bringing to our attention some of our most foolish ideas and gives us a hardheaded method of changing them.

As applied to the problem of anger, you can use his *Referenting Cost-Benefit Analysis* technique as follows: Suppose you feel exceptionally angry whenever you see or hear reference made to someone who has "made you" angry in the past, and suppose you now want to reduce your irate feelings toward that person. Telling yourself, "Don't feel angry. Don't feel angry," won't really work. If anything, you may only succeed in suppressing your anger. You will not undo it.

Your emotional problem here probably consists of your *referenting*—that is, confusing your ideas about the person's *behavior* with your ideas about the *person himself*—in a sloppy, bigoted, and overgeneralized manner. Thus, if someone asks you to give the associations that immediately pop into your head when you think of the person's behavior, or of the person specifically, you would probably say something like, "His behavior is no good, rotten, unfair, and horrible. He is a no-good individual, a rotten person who is always unfair. I particularly cannot tolerate him!"

This type of exclusive, one-sided, and overgeneralized confusing of a person's behavior with the person himself will often make you feel exceptionally hostile. As long as you insist on making this connection, you will find it almost impossible to forgo your feelings of anger and view his behavior in a more accurate light.

Danysh's technique of referenting forces you to go beyond your prejudiced one-sidedness regarding people's behavior and to bring to your mind many more accurate terms to describe them and their actions. Referenting consists of taking a relatively vague word, such as *behavior*, and forcing yourself to list the much more specific referents, or concrete descriptions, that comprise it. Danysh's method particularly encourages you to bring to your own attention many of the diverse meanings of a term, instead of a few limited (and prejudiced) meanings.

For example, while thinking specifically of someone's—say, a woman's—behavior, write down a list of negative and pejorative terms to describe that behavior—such as "rotten, no good, unfair, horrible, awful, evil, and lousy." Then, on the same sheet of paper, go out of your way to think of and write down any terms you might think of to describe the positive or good aspects of her behavior—such as "fair most of the time if not this time, probably fair from her own point of view if not mine, acts in her own self-interest as I do, forthright, determined, assertive, sometimes very nice and considerate of other people, and concerned with other people in general." Finally, write down some of the aspects of her behavior that are neutral—many of the things she does or says that might not be construed as "good" or "bad" but just as descriptions of her performances—such as "interested in many aspects of life, highly absorbed in music, not devoted to sports, and makes many public presentations."

By referenting, as accurately and completely as you can, all these different aspects of your concept of this woman's behavior, for instance, you force yourself to keep in mind a more holistic, more accurate, and less one-sided view of her. Thus, your highly prejudiced views about her behavior—"rotten, no good, unfair, horrible"—will tend to diminish. You will begin to see her behavior more accurately and not as you might tend to fictionalize and distort it in your own mind because of a *particular* instance. In doing this you also do a cost-benefit analysis—see the advantages *and* the disadvantages of your dealing with this woman.

Similarly, you could take her name—which you at first only referented negatively—and force yourself to referent it on a piece of paper or tape recording in more favorable terms, such as "a person who acts both rotten and good; an individual who has bad points and good points; a woman who sometimes acts unfairly but much of the time behaves quite fairly." You could also force yourself to referent that person in a more objective, neutral, merely descriptive way, such as "a woman who stands five feet five inches tall, who does a wide variety of things, who associates with a good many people, who has diabetes, who has written a good many books."

If you force yourself to use this referenting technique, especially when you feel very angry toward someone, you will almost invariably find that you can "deemphasize" the bad traits and thus start to acquire a more enlightened, accurate, and realistic view of that person. Referenting won't make you automatically forgiving and unangry with all people whom you encounter and all the nasty actions they perform against you. But it frequently will help. When you get into the habit of doing it, you will tend to find after a while that you stop making yourself as often or as intensely angry at people.

Another good method that you can use both cognitively and behaviorally consists of what Viktor Frankl calls paradoxical intention. Various other therapists use it in different ways and often call it different names. In REBT we sometimes refer to it as reducing irrational beliefs to absurdity. Using paradoxical intention, you can take any idea and reduce it to absurdity—by exaggerating in your mind the wildest implications of the original idea. For instance, if you want a man to do something for you and you make yourself angry because he refuses to cooperate with you, exaggerate your wish for power and control over him:

"Of course he has to do what I want him to do! I have absolute control over his behavior. If he tells me that he will jump through hoops to please me and then refuses to go through with this jumping, I can easily put him in chains and whip him until he jumps and jumps and jumps! In fact, if I want him to give me a million dollars or to grovel in the dust before me ten times a day, he has no choice but to do my bidding! Because I desire him to do anything whatever, he completely has to do it! And if he refuses, I can immediately send down thunderbolts and annihilate him."

If you take the idea of having control over a person to a ridiculous extreme such as this, you will soon see that you really have virtually little control over him and that he has a right to do whatever he wishes even when he unfairly inconveniences you by exercising this right. You will see that human nature does not exist in the manner that you command it to exist; thus, you will start interrupting your own foolish demandingness.

Just as you can use paradoxical intention cognitivly (in your mind) as described above, you can also practice it behaviorally through oppositional behavior. If people treat you unfairly and you feel exceptionally angry because of this treatment, instead of starting to plan to punish them in various ways for their iniquity, you can deliberately force yourself to take the opposite track and to act very nicely and *un*hostilely to them. You can, for example, keep befriending them in various ways: Invite them to interesting functions that you think they will enjoy; do them special favors; show unusual consideration and kindness toward them. By such paradoxical behavior, you will first of all practice feeling unangry instead of angry at them—and you may actually make yourself feel nice or at least neutral about their "abominable" behavior. Second, you will, by turning the other cheek in this manner, set them a good example and show them that their unfair treatment doesn't necessarily have to produce rage in you. Third, you may encourage them to look again at their behavior and to see how badly they treated you. Finally, you may help them act very nicely toward you and even make reparations for the wrongs they have already done you.

I do not contend, in this respect, that this kind of turning-the-other-cheek philosophy will always work or that it is wise for you to keep using it. But I do say that if you use it judiciously and realize that you do it for paradoxical reasons (and not routinely, in every instance where someone treats you unfairly), you may gain considerably and help reduce your feelings of rage.

Paradoxical intention also works against human stubbornness. If people treat you unfairly and you recognize that they have a problem doing so, you may *perversely* continue to feel and act angrily toward them in order to maintain your false integrity—to make yourself feel "stronger" when, in actuality, you keep acting weakly. This phenomenon occurs commonly between you and your parents, for instance, during your childhood. They advise you, mainly for your own good, to get up promptly when the alarm clock rings in the morning and to get yourself off in time for school. You don't like to get up that early, and you lazily (with your low frustration tolerance!) resist. But you also see that by resisting, you keep getting into trouble with the school authorities and sabotaging some of your own goals—for example, to get good marks in high school and therefore to be admitted to a good college of your own choice.

Perversely, you tell yourself something like: "I won't get up early to please my parents! Damned if I will! That would prove me a ninny who only goes along for their ride. I'll show them! I'll deliberately stay in bed late, indicate my strength, and follow my own integrity!" If you act that way as a child—or, for that matter, as an adult—you merely fool yourself. Because your parents advise you to get up early, you foolishly—and perversely—convince yourself that if you do so, you will follow their rules and do it for *them*. You consider that a kind of weakness, when actually it would be a strength. You "strongly" resist them and actually act weakly when you do.

Similarly, often, with anger. Often you feel furious and see your fury as self-defeating and perhaps as encouraging others to treat you even more unfairly. Yet instead of trying to change your musturbatory philosophy about people's behavior, you cling to that philosophy and convince yourself that you rationally feel enraged and that you'd *better* show offenders their faults. By convincing yourself that to do otherwise would make you weak and cause you to lose your own integrity, you choose to persist with your rage. Actually, to give up your anger while keeping a strong dislike about unfair acts would make you stronger and probably get better results. But if you see it differently, and perhaps deliberately make yourself even more enraged and go after the person who has wronged you, you will continue to feel angry.

When you interrupt your perversity with paradoxical intention and deliberately make yourself think nicely about and act kindly toward others in spite of their unfairness, you paradoxically fight your own irrationality. In terms of what you really want for yourself and for your relationships with others, you can get better results by acting good instead of bad to them.

Rachel T. Hare outlines another form of paradoxical intention that I have used to help my clients cut down their angry feelings and actions. Give yourself limiting conditions under which you allow yourself to have temper tantrums. One of my clients felt exceptionally irate and combative every time he imagined that someone on the street spit in his direction and "saw" some spit on his shoes. I persuaded him to contract with himself that he would only let himself feel angry when he could prove, with clear-cut evidence, that someone had actually spit on him. Since he could rarely prove this, his fits of anger subsided greatly.

To use the same paradoxical or limiting technique on yourself, pick a set of conditions where you feel you have been treated unfairly and where you frequently feel rage. Deliberately limit or hem in this set of conditions. Contract to allow yourself to feel and act angrily, for example, only when (1) everyone agrees that people have truly treated you unfairly, (2) everyone also agrees that the unfairness has caused you a considerable amount of harm, and (3) you can prove that you have been severely hurt by unfair treatment.

If you allow yourself, in this paradoxical manner, "freely" to feel your rage while deliberately restricting yourself, you may soon see that you can live with your own restrictions, that you do create your anger yourself, and that you have the power to limit and control it. Such paradoxical techniques work because they get you away from thinking, desperately, "I *must* feel angry" or "I *must not* feel angry." They give you a wider range of possible reactions and help you convince yourself that you can function with this wider range.

Other kinds of humor also dramatically interrupt your overly serious manner of looking at unpleasant events, thereby needlessly making yourself angry. Consequently, REBT therapists frequently use humor to help their clients poke fun at their own solemnity and learn to accept Adversities better. I gave a famous paper, "Fun as Psychotherapy," at an annual convention of the American Psychological Association in Washington, D.C., and made a great hit in giving it, since I sang—yes, sang—two of my rational humorous songs in the course of my presentation.

I pointed out in this paper that "if human disturbance largely consists of overseriousness and if, as in Rational Emotive Behavior Therapy, therapists had better make a hardheaded attack on some of their clients' fatuous thinking, what better vehicle for doing this uprooting than humor and fun? . . . Let me briefly mention here that my therapeutic brand of humor consists of practically every kind of drollery ever invented—such as taking things to extreme, reducing ideas to absurdity, paradoxical intention, puns, witticisms, irony, whimsy, evocative language, slang, deliberate use of sprightly obscenity, and various other kinds of jocularity."

Following this REBT lead, you can frequently laugh at yourself when you see yourself getting angry, look for your grossly exaggerating what others *must* do to satisfy you and how things *should* go right to make your life easier, and thereby cognitively and emotively attack such silly notions. When you demand good behavior in others, you can remind yourself, "Oh, yes, I always act perfectly well myself. I *never* treat others unfairly or go back on my promises to them. Well, hardly ever!" When you think that you absolutely need others' approval and that they amount to complete rats for not giving it to you, remind yourself what a love slob, a Mr. or Ms. Jehovah, you have made yourself into. When you inwardly or outwardly whine and scream because poor economic, artistic, or social conditions exist for you, tell yourself something like: "Oh, yes, I run the universe, and whatever I want has to, in fact *immediately* has to, come about. Everyone has to live with frustration and annoyance, but not *me!*"

Call to your mind, also, what I often tell my REBT clients: "Life, whether I like it or not, generally gets spelled H-A-S-S-L-E. Tough taffy!" When you command that you must have certainty and that you can't stand it when you don't have guarantees of success, love, fairness, and ease, show yourself: "I think I'll engrave a beautiful certificate that absolutely, with no shadow of a doubt, guarantees that I will always get exactly what I want at the very second that I want it. Then I'll get along wonderfully well and won't have to feel angry about anything!"

Keep using humor, directed against your nutty ideas but not, of course, against yourself as a person. If you want to sing to yourself (or others) some of my humorous songs, you can use these from the songbook *A Garland of Rational Songs* and from other REBT sources.

WHINE, WHINE, WHINE!

(To the tune of the Yale "Whiffenpoof Song," Composed by a Harvard Man in 1896!)

I cannot have all of my wishes filled—
Whine, whine, whine!
I cannot have every frustration stilled—
Whine, whine, whine!
Life really owes me the things that I miss,
Fate has to grant me eternal bliss!
And since I must settle for less than this—
Whine, whine, whine!

PERFECT RATIONALITY

(To the tune of Luigi Denza's "Funiculi, Funicula")

Some think the world must have a right direction—
And so do I, and so do I!
Some think that, with the slightest imperfection,
They can't get by—and so do I!
For I, I have to prove I'm superhuman,
And better far than people are!—
To show I have miraculous acumen—
And always rate among the Great!—

Perfect, perfect rationality
Is, of course, the only thing for me!
How can I ever think of being
If I must live fallibly?
Rationality must be a perfect thing for me!

I WISH I WERE NOT CRAZY

(To the tune of Dan Emmet's "Dixie")

Oh, I wish I were really put together—
Smooth and fine as patent leather!

Oh, how great to be mated
To this lovely state!
But I'm afraid that I was fated
To be rather aberrated—
Oh, how sad to be mad
As my Mom and my Dad!

Oh, I wish I were not crazy! Hooray, hooray!
I wish my mind were less inclined
To be the kind that's hazy!
I could, you see, decide to be less crazy;
But I, alas, am just too blasted lazy!

LOVE ME, LOVE ME, ONLY ME!
(*To the tune of "Yankee Doodle"*)

Just love me, love me, only me,
Or I will die without you!
Oh, make your love a guarantee,
So I can never doubt you!
Love me, love me totally
Really, really try, dear;
But if you demand love, too,
I'll hate you till I die, dear!

Love me, love me all the time,
Thoroughly and wholly;
Living turns to slush and slime,
Unless you love me solely.
Love me with great tenderness,
With no ifs and buts, dear;
If you love me somewhat less,
I'll hate your goddamned guts, dear!

Another of my rational humorous songs that you can use to interrupt and change your angry feelings is the next one:

POUND, POUND, POUND!

(To the tune of J. Pierpont's "Jingle Bells")

You will get release and let your anger out
If you blast the peace, scream and yell and shout.
Go to any length, show you can't be stilled,
And you will have enormous strength—until the time
you're killed!

Pound, pound, pound! Pound, pound, pound!
Pound your enemies!
Oh, what fun it is to stun
Anyone who does not please!
Sock, sock, sock! Knock, knock, knock!
Howl and whine and cry!
Everyone from you will run
And will hate you till you die!

Pout, pout, pout! Shout, shout, shout!
Make the biggest mess!
Rip, rip, rip! Slip, slip, slip
Into rabid craziness!
Think, think, think! Drink, drink, drink
Only of cruel fate!
Beat your breast and be obsessed
With just everyone you hate!

Since I have done marriage and family counseling for more than thirty years, people frequently ask me how they can check or control their anger at their spouses or at others with whom they have a close relationship. Well they might! As another well-known marriage counselor, Dr. David Mace, pointed out in an article in the *Journal of Marriage and Family Counseling*, overt or covert feelings of anger probably interfere with love and disrupt more intimate relationships than do any other causes. Dr. Mace rightly takes to task the "marital fighting" concepts of George Bach and his followers and points out that if you tend to argue and fight with your mate, you can use the REBT approach of dissolving your anger, rather than palliatively expressing it or diverting it.

More concretely, he outlines three main methods of doing this:

1. Acknowledge your anger. Tell your partner, "I feel angry at you," just as you would say, "I feel tired," or "I feel frightened."
2. Renounce your anger as unhealthy. Even though your mate has treated you badly or unfairly, face the fact that you create your own anger, that you need not do so, and that you usually harm your relationship by feeling it and by expressing it against your partner.
3. Ask your partner for help. Show her that you have a problem in dealing with your anger, and see if she can suggest some plans to help rid you of it and to make your relationship better.

David Mace has some wise suggestions, and I highly endorse them. In a follow-up article, also published in the *Journal of Marriage and Family Counseling*, I add these additional REBT methods to help you deal with your anger at anyone with whom you have a close relationship:

4. Acknowledge your anger to yourself. Don't merely inform your mate about your angry feelings, but frankly tell yourself, "Look: Let me face it. I really feel angry at my partner. Not merely displeased; not merely annoyed at his *behavior*. I feel angry at my mate as a person. I am condemning *him*." Unless you do something like this, you will not tend to feel in touch with your anger and will merely give it lip service. Once you acknowledge your rage to *yourself* and work at defusing it, you may then choose (or not choose) to express it to your mate—depending on his vulnerability.

5. Assume full responsibility for your anger. Do not hesitate to admit that you created it, that you angered yourself. Say to yourself something like: "Yes, my mate may have acted bad and treated me unfairly, but she only frustrated me, gave me what I didn't want. I made myself feel healthily annoyed and irritated about her bad behavior, because I honestly want her to act differently and feel sorry when she doesn't. But I also unhealthily *made myself* angry by commanding that she *must not* act that way; *has to do* what I want; makes my whole life terrible and awful when he or she doesn't; and conse-

quently is a thoroughly rotten *person. I* chose to think this way and thereby anger myself against my partner. And I can, if I want to do so, always choose to think differently and change my feelings of anger into healthier feelings of disappointment, sorrow, and annoyance." If you fully, in this manner, acknowledge your own responsibility for making yourself angry, you will by that very admission tend to reduce much of your angry feeling.

6. Accept yourself with your anger. As soon as you damn yourself for having neurotic symptoms—anger, panic, depression, or feelings of worthlessness—you tend to add to these symptoms. For if you see yourself as a worm for feeling, let us say, enraged at your mate, how can you picture a total worm like you acting unwormily in the future? While you are berating yourself for stupidly making yourself angry, how can you understand exactly what you told yourself to create your anger and to work at changing it?

Accept yourself, then, *with* your anger. This does not mean, as some psychological writings imply, that you had better view angry feelings as "good," "healthy," or "constructive." You can see them as "normal" in the sense of being part of the human condition—as an aspect of your human fallibility—and also, as David Mace points out, as a part that tends to harm your intimate relationships.

7. Stop making yourself anxious, depressed, and self-downing. As you learn to accept yourself, no matter how angry you feel or how foolishly you can act when angry, you can also learn to accept yourself with any of your other "wrong" or "bad" behavior, and if you do this, you will give up most of your vulnerability—the feelings of hurt and self-pity that often help you feel very angry.

8. Look for the philosophic source of your anger. After fully acknowledging your feelings of anger, refusing to down yourself for having these feelings, and eliminating some of the self-deprecating elements in your creating these feelings, you can look for the philosophic sources of your anger. Assume (as shown throughout this book) that just about every time you feel enraged in your gut, you have a profound philosophic assumption behind this feeling and that this assumption includes some *should, ought,* or *must.* Consequently, *cherchez le* should, *cherchez le* must! Look for the *should*, look for the

must! In anger at your mate, you frequently hold the *must* of resentment—"You *must* treat me kindly, considerately, lovingly, and approvingly!"—and the *must* of low frustration tolerance—"The conditions under which I live *must* turn out nicely and nonfrustratingly so that I easily get practically everything I want without too much effort."

More specifically, when angry at your mate, you usually tell yourself: (a) "My partner *must* treat me considerately and lovingly. He actually behaves unfairly and disapprovingly. I *can't stand* this behavior! I find it *awful*! What a total louse that makes him!" And (b) "I got together with this mate in order to feel great joy and happiness. Obnoxious economic, social, sexual, or child-rearing conditions exist in our relationship. They *must* not continue to exist this horrible way! How *terrible* that they do! I *can't bear* it! Mating therefore is an absolutely frightful state, and I hate the very thought of going on with it!"

So look—and keep looking until you find—your own *shoulds*, *oughts*, and *musts* about (a) your mate; (b) your children; (c) the conditions under which you live; (d) your in-laws; and (e) your sex relations with your mate. As soon as you really clearly understand these *musts*, you locate the most important sources of your hatred and rage—as Dr. Robert A. Harper and I point out in *How to Stop Destroying Your Relationships* and as Chip Tafrate and I show in *How to Control Your Anger Before It Controls You*.

9. Discriminate your wishes from your demands and commands. Try clearly to distinguish your wishes about your mate and your relationship from your musturbatory commands. You can very legitimately tell yourself, "I would much rather have my mate have sex with me twice a week than have it once every two weeks." But you can then unhealthily add, "And therefore, my partner *must* do so!" Just about every one of your absolutistic commands to your partner has a somewhat realistic and reasonable wish or preference behind it. Search in your head and your heart for *both* the wish *and* the escalating command that insists you *have* to fulfill or satisfy this wish. Separate the two very, very clearly!

10. Dispute and debate your absolutistic *musts*. Merely *under-*

standing your demands on your mate (and on the universe) will not solve your problem. For you can easily say to yourself, "Oh, yes, I see now that I feel terribly angry toward my partner because I keep commanding that she do exactly what I prefer. Well, maybe I'd better give up my demands and translate them back into wishes." Fine—but not enough!

Unless you very actively, persistently, and strongly dispute, question, and challenge your demands, you probably will never give them up. Only by arranging a thoroughgoing change in your philosophic assumptions, your absolutistic *shoulds*, will you reduce your angry feelings. And by reduce, I do not mean suppress, repress, avoid, or sweep under the rug. I mean actually *diminish* them! Also, make it much less likely that you will re-create them in the future.

11. Employ behavioral and emotive means of undermining your feelings of anger. As noted throughout this book, you not only manufacture your own angry feelings but then reinforce them by various emotive and behavioral acts. You therefore had better use evocative-emotive-dramatic and active-directive-behavioral methods to change your anger. Thus, emotively, you can deliberately act lovingly rather than angrily toward your mate. You can train yourself to empathize more effectively with your partner's point of view and feelings. You can practice what Carl Rogers calls unconditional positive regard or what in REBT we call unconditional acceptance. You can use nonblaming I-statements instead of condemning you-statements about your mate's behavior. You can express your hostile feelings about your partner to other people (such as friends) rather than directly. You can role play some of your angry reactions to your mate. You can use Rational Emotive Imagery to let yourself imagine your mate's acting very bad, allow yourself to feel very angry, and then practice changing your feelings to disappointment rather than anger.

As for behavioral methods, you can use several to help reinforce your attacking your feelings of anger. You can deliberately stay in anger-inciting situations to give yourself practice in coping with such conditions and in changing your hostility-creating philosophies as you deal with them. You can practice assertiveness instead of passivity, to ward off your building up unnecessary feelings of rage when you do not legitimately assert yourself with your mate. You can use operant conditioning or self-management methods and reward yourself when you react unangrily to your partner while penalizing (but not damning) yourself when you react angrily. You can employ behavior-rehearsal methods and train yourself (by working with a model or role-playing partner) to react healthily when your mate does some "upsetting" act. You can make written or oral contracts with your mate to do some things that he wishes to do, provided that he will also do other things that you would prefer. You can use relaxation, meditation, thought stopping, or other desensitizing and diverting methods to take yourself, at least temporarily, out of anger-arousing situations and to give yourself extra time to work against your musturbatory philosophies.

In many different ways, then, you can apply virtually all the anger-reducing methods outlined in this book to the problem of acknowledging your making yourself incensed at your love partner (or other person) and to giving up your angry feelings and enjoying more of the good feelings that this relationship may include.

REBT writings, such as my books *Feeling Better, Getting Better, and Staying Better* and *How to Stubbornly Refuse to Make Yourself Miserable About Anything—Yes, Anything!*, contain much antianger material, and tens of thousands of people have helped themselves become less irate by reading this material. In addition, the Albert Ellis Institute in New York City distributes a good deal of other materials, such as posters, buttons, tape recordings, wallet cards, videotapes, and films to help you work against angering yourself. I have frequently heard from many who have had little or no actual rational therapy but who have used these kinds of materials to good effect and have modified their angry behavior tremendously by persistently working with them.

At the Institute we also offer a great many talks, seminars, workshops, marathons, and other public presentations that help large numbers of people with their anger. At the Friday-night workshops, "Problems of Daily Living," that I have conducted almost every week for almost forty years, people either bring up their personal problems and receive direct help from me and members of the audience or else participate less actively and learn how to handle their problems mainly by observing how the audience and I work with other people.

REBT employs all types of psychoeducational methods to help people work against their self-defeating emotions like anger. And you can explore various methods yourself and use any or all of them to help see what you tell yourself to make yourself angry, understand how to dispute and challenge your own anger-creating irrationalities, and act and emote in antihostile ways.

11

Ripping Up Your Rationalizations for Remaining Angry

Since there exist many rational reasons for giving up our feelings of anger and such sensible ways of dealing with these feelings, why do we find it so easy, then, to ignore them? Why do we favor—even, at times, revel in—staying angry?

Probably, first of all, because anger has definite biological roots, which we will now consider.

As many ethologists, physiologists, sociologists, and other scientists have shown, a great deal of evidence indicates that you make yourself angry partly for biological reasons. Donald T. Lunde and David A. Hamburg, for example, have shown that in animals—as well as human children and adults—fighting behavior prevails in males much more than in females because of the influence of testosterone, the male hormone. Additionally, Yoram Jaffe and his associates have discovered that sexually aroused males and females are more aggressive than nonaroused subjects; and Edward Donnerstein and his research group have found that highly erotic stimuli tend to facilitate and maintain aggression in males.

R. C. Boelkins and J. F. Heiser, after examining research data from animal and human studies, conclude that we can view aggression "as an adaptive behavior having its origins in genetically coded neural mechanisms . . . acted upon by both hormonal and psychosocial factors." The famous psychologist Harry F. Harlow held that "aggression most likely remains in man as a solid component of his biological heritage as a primate." Sigmund Freud, considering a great amount of clinical and anthropological evidence, gave us this summary statement:

> The bit of truth behind all this—one so eagerly denied—is that men are not gentle, friendly creatures wishing for love, who simply defend themselves if they are attacked, but that a powerful measure of desire for aggression has to be reckoned on the part of their instinctual endowment. . . . Civilized society is perpetually menaced with disintegration through this primary hostility of men towards one another. . . . The tendency to aggression is an innate, independent, instinctual disposition in man . . . it constitutes the most powerful obstacle to culture.

Many outstanding social and physiological scientists have held that biological, hereditary, and chemical factors play a pronounced part in human aggression—along with psychological and sociological learning.

Other social thinkers, such as Ashley Montagu, hotly dispute this view. Montagu states that human "aggressiveness is a learned form of behavior. There is absolutely no evidence whatever; indeed, the evidence is entirely in the opposite direction, that man is in any way 'programmed' to behave aggressively."

Montagu seems partly right, for no *conclusive* evidence exists for the programming of aggression, anger, and violence in humans. But most authorities agree that we have innate tendencies to be easily self-programmed in such ways. For many reasons, our biological tendencies predispose us to react angrily.

In *The Psychology of Aggression*, K. E. Moyer notes that certain allergens can, in some people, lead to many types of irritability, including acute and chronic physical violence. Anthropologist Ralph Bolton, studying exceptionally hostile tribes like the Qolla of Peru, found that a higher protein intake tended to create opposite behavior. Sociologist Pierre L. van den Berghe summarizes his views on human aggression and available resource competition by saying that "... Homo sapiens rates high on territoriality, hierarchy and aggression, and that these forms of behavior are biologically predisposed ... an understanding of human behavior must necessarily be both biological and socio-cultural."

Many other scientists—especially ethologists such as Konrad Lorenz, Robert Ardrey, Desmond Morris, N. Tinbergen, and Lionel Tiger—have likewise beaten the drum in recent years to apprise us of the fact that hostility has fairly evident biological roots. And even those who have criticized their "findings," such as Edward C. Ryterband, have admitted that at least part of their argument appears valid. Ryterband, for instance, has noted: "No intelligent arguments can or should deny that environment has significant effects on all of man's behavior. Increasingly, evidence has accumulated not that there are instincts which control us, but that much of our behavior springs from both genetic and environmental sources."

Erich Fromm, in his *Anatomy of Human Destructiveness*, largely concerns himself with showing that we don't have specific or insurmountable instincts to destroy ourselves or to wage ceaseless feuds and wars. He stoutly opposes the instinctivist-hydraulic model of aggression that writers like Freud and Lorenz espouse—the model that says that we as humans have innate destructive or aggressive energies and that if we do not express and utilize them directly, they will force us into extreme forms of violence, such as war, genocide, and suicide. At the same time, Fromm admits that the data of the neurosciences that he reviews "have helped to establish the concept of one kind of aggression—life preserving, biologically adaptive, defensive aggression. They show that man is endowed with a potential aggression which is mobilized by threats to his vital interests."

So even Erich Fromm, obviously, does not completely oppose a biological basis to anger and aggression. He merely shows that this basis does not doom us to the worst forms of aggression, particularly mass murder, which some other theorists, including Freud, seem to think it does. Also, as Morton Deutsch points out in reviewing Fromm's book, his basic thesis holds that destructiveness (and, presumably, all other character traits) results from the interaction of various social conditions with human existential drives—such as our awareness of our powerlessness, our ignorance, and our death. But these existential drives themselves have a clear-cut biological basis, as I think Fromm admits. So his seeming antagonism to biological forces in our nature remains very partial.

In recent years much evidence has shown that human aggression has both strong biological *and* environmental (social-learning) elements. Granted that almost all contemporary theorists acknowledge anger's strong biological as well as sociological roots, don't mistakenly "use" the biological basis as a reason for not changing your own irate behavior. Granted that you have innate tendencies to enrage yourself at the real and imagined injustices of the world. Admitted that you have strong predispositions to condemn others as a whole for some of their behaviors and to wish them dead for doing "wrong" and "immoral" acts, I still ask: Why must you *go along* with those physiologically based tendencies? And what justifies your using its "historical" basis as an *excuse* for your rage?

Don't forget, in this connection, that you have numerous other biologically based urges that you nearly always control—and with good reason. You naturally and biologically spit, chew, defecate, and pass flatus. But do you do so unrestrainedly, without any controls on yourself?

No matter how strong are your inherited predispositions to scream at others, tell them how completely stupid they act, and pummel them into the ground when they seriously treat you unfairly, the fact still remains that you don't *have* to do any of these behaviors and you can usually (if not always) appreciably cut them down if you willingly work hard to do so. No evidence exists that you will necessarily end up with an ulcer or high blood pressure if you block or control your rage any more than it exists for your winding up diseased if you control several of your other biological functions.

As a member of society I personally squelch many of my biological, pleasure-oriented urges and I do so every day in the week, perhaps even every hour of the day. I eat less than I want, copulate on only limited occasions, frequently keep silent when I would thoroughly enjoy continuing to talk, go fully clothed in even the hottest of weather, and restrict my biological urges in countless other ways. Not only do I manage to get by with minimum or moderate discomfort as I limit myself in these ways, but I actually often feel pleased to do so. As a diabetic, for example, I *enjoy* curbing my diet and forcing myself away from sugary foods that I would relish but are also almost lethal for me. Curbing my anger does not unbearably frustrate me. In fact, in some ways, I manage to enjoy my self-curbing, too!

People also hold on to their anger because they do not realize their alternatives. Even downtrodden individuals, such as minority groups or women, whom our culture has sorely tried and abused, need not give vent to their anger, nor must they cravenly submit to exploitation and subjugation. They have more than the grim choice of: (1) passively submitting to their controllers, letting themselves get "walked over," or (2) angrily ranting, raving, or actually resorting to violence. Of these two choices, the first seems definitely the worse and includes unassertive subservience. So I definitely do not recommend that.

In REBT we seek a third path, one that exists *between* cravenly giving up what you want and nastily telling others off—fighting them to the death. We advocate, instead, *determined opposition*. If I, for example, lived as a woman in our still antifeminist society, I would realize how many injustices and handicaps I had to bear because of my femaleness, and I would fervently dislike, oppose, and even hate these needless barriers. But I would not (in much the same way that my male oppressors bigotedly scream and whine against female rights and privileges) idiotically convince myself that "Because social rules treat me unfairly, they *must* not exist! How *awful* that they do! I *can't stand* society's discriminations! The people who promulgate and sustain these rules are *totally rotten tyrants*, whom we have to annihilate entirely if we want these horrible customs changed!"

In other words, no matter how disappointed, frustrated, and determined I felt about antifeminist traditions, I would not waste my time and energy screaming and wailing about such prejudices. Instead, I would determinedly organize myself and my sympathetic cohorts to fight and change them. Claudeen Cline-Naffziger partly sees this third, nonangry, determined path toward social change when she notes: "Florynce Kennedy's analysis of action-oriented anger is educative for both women and their therapists. She suggests that instead of women putting down other women, husbands, family, or custodians as is wont to occur, women must be encouraged to put their anger energy on the sources of power. Anger energy is more potent when focused on those above rather than those around or below."

Previously, Ms. Cline-Naffsiger noted that "most women have such a reservoir of anger and so much energy stored up in tending it that they need screaming, kicking, yelling sessions to release the excess and get the burden down to a manageable size." She failed to see that this kind of screaming and kicking behavior carries with it a distinct *philosophy* of anger—namely, that things *must* not remain indubitably unpleasant even when they almost certainly *will*, at least for a while, remain that way. And she doesn't see that such tactics will mainly siphon off energies that women could put to constructively fighting to change the social system.

Moreover, as thousands of years of human history have proved, once a downtrodden group angrily and violently pits itself against a group of ruling oppressors, its childish demandingness frequently leads to equal irrationality and lack of rational judgment against its opponent. So either the original rulers get back into power and savagely annihilate the rebels or (as in the somewhat typical cases of the French and Russian Revolutions) an even more extreme group of rebels takes over from the original group—and a frightful and almost completely senseless bloodbath and suppression of human liberty ensues.

As a longtime revolutionary myself, particularly in the fields of sexual permissiveness and psychotherapy reform, I have frequently made angry outbursts against my "reactionary" opponents, and sometimes I still do. But I have almost always found that my anger does more harm than good for my own cause and that I work more effectively for what I want and against the stupidities I don't want when

I vigorously, forcefully, determinedly—and *non*angrily—keep fighting for what I consider just, good, and efficient.

Scores of psychologists such as George Bach and Herbert Goldberg point out the great harm that we do to ourselves by refusing to acknowledge and express our feelings of ire. In agreement with Freud, they insist that "when open aggressive expression or interpersonal encounters are suppressed, either for conscious reasons, such as the desire to be polite or 'nice,' or for deeper motivations, such as the fear of angry interchanges, these feelings are not lost. Rather they are driven underground, so to speak, and re-emerge transformed behind socially acceptable masks."

Such remarks require careful consideration. Bach and Goldberg seem to mean that you may sometimes have *disturbed* reasons for suppressing or repressing feelings of anger. Thus, if I treat you unfairly, you may first feel you have to act politely to me in order to show everyone, including me, how you rate as a "nice person." We can call this "disturbed" because you then tend to run your life mainly for others and not enough for yourself. You make yourself so concerned about my and others' opinions that you refuse to ask yourself what *you* really want—and you feel frustrated and unhappy for surrendering too easily to any opposition.

Your second disturbed reason for suppressing anger: your fear of possible rejection and anger if you risk telling me your feelings of displeasure. You would really like to show me my unfairness and try to get me to act better toward you, but you feel terribly afraid of such a confrontation because it might turn into an angry interchange. You again start worrying too much about what *I* might think of you and too little about what *you* really want. Once again, this means that you feel you have to make yourself into a totally "nice person" who rarely quarrels with anyone, seldom risks disapproval. Unassertion, or the giving up of what you really want in order to desperately win another's acceptance, means that you fail to live, that you give up much of your healthy desiring, and that you fail to ever let your own individuality emerge.

If wanting to be a "nice person" and fear of rejection are your motives for squelching your feelings of anger, you will drive underground some of your *other* feelings—especially your feeling that you have a right to exist in this world and to have others treat you fairly. Bach and Goldberg quite rightly point this out. But they also seem to forget that you could have quite different, *healthy* reasons for not feeling or expressing anger—namely, your wish to have more loving, cooperative, and friendly relations with me and others and your desire to have more of the things you want and less of the things that you do not want in life.

In other words, Bach and Goldberg fail to see that while you can (1) unhealthily need and insist on others liking you, you can also (2) healthily desire and want to get along better with them. If you have the first need, you then, peculiarly enough, tend to suppress the second set of feelings, and, perhaps more important, you also suppress your desires to get along with yourself and to try to achieve what *you* want to do in life. Since, however, you *do* want others to like you and you *also* want to get what you desire out of life, the overpolite demeanor that Bach and Goldberg deplore denies this—and especially denies your own wants and preferences. But Bach and Goldberg, unfortunately, forget that when you healthfully surrender your dire *need* for others' approval, you can still healthfully retain your *desire* for their affection. You can therefore consciously suppress (instead of consciously repress) some of your angry feelings—and thereby get along better with them and with yourself. Overpoliteness may unduly restrict you, but normal politeness may distinctly aid both your interpersonal and intrapersonal relations.

The various arguments in favor of anger often have a fairly sensible core, but this easily gets escalated out of proportion to the underlying half-truths it contains. Of course, anger has its good points! So do murder, tyranny, revolution, baby seal hunting, and cannibalism. All these expressions of the human spirit can be self-fulfilling and sometimes—though not too often!—do somewhat more good than harm. Moreover, if we completely removed them from the human condition, we would suffer a distinct loss.

So with anger. Many authorities have rightly pointed out its humanitarian elements. Israel Charny holds that "aggression is an omnipresent, instinctive force in all of life which we might best define as the purposeful, pulsating energy or strength for being that is one's life force." Albert Solnit indicates that "in children the aggressive behavior serves to make contact with the love object and gain libidinal satisfaction." Martin Roth points out that political, religious, and revolutionary wars have a pronounced altruistic element because they would not have occurred without the peculiarly human characteristic of self-sacrifice.

Edward Sagarin shows how suppressed people can acquire respect for themselves through hatred for others. W. W. Meissner contends that "human aggression has a positive and constructive role to play in the development of man's religious spirit." Edward D. Joseph sees aggression as including behavior and activities, mental and otherwise, that emerge as forceful and that involve a direct approach to the object. Nevitt Sanford indicates that we want children "to be angry about the right things (human exploitation for example) and to express their anger in ways that help to counter destructiveness." Chris Meadows designates anger as "the emotion which primes aggressive behavior in defense of life and integrity." Rolland S. Parker points out that expression of anger and aggression may help people confront and master difficult situations.

All these points make some sense. But they also may be considerably misleading. For they mainly confuse "anger" or "aggression" with assertiveness, the strong motivation to change obnoxious stimuli, and the determined effort to effect that kind of change. True, hostility contains such constructive elements. But even more true: You can keep these elements and still minimize what we normally call hatred and rage.

The apologists for anger and aggression apparently do not see this. They do not define their terms clearly enough, or they hopelessly think that you can only assert yourself—especially in the face of difficult or obnoxious conditions—through a childish demandingness or whining that things should not, must not exist the way they do, and through consequent feelings of anger. Wrong! You can keep your determination and your assertiveness without grandiose rage if you think clearly and act forcefully along the lines outlined in this book!

Anthony Storr whitewashes anger in this way: "Only when intense aggressiveness exists between two individuals . . . love can arise." True—if you train yourself to feel and act entirely unemotionally, with no passion whatever, you will knock out "bad" emotions like hostility—and "good" ones like love. But rational, as I keep emphasizing to my clients and to audiences all over the world, does *not* mean unemotional. It means *healthily* emotional. Storr, for example, seems to believe that you need aggressiveness in order to love, and I believe that you don't. But although both of us may be overgeneralizing, neither of us may be irrational—unless we also believe that our view *has to*, absolutely *must* prevail. Our passion doesn't make us irrational—but our dogma does!

"Constructive" aggression advocates believe that if people "do you in" and you let yourself have a brief or mild period of anger against them, you handle yourself well, while if they treat you just as badly and you let yourself intensely and prolongedly hate them, you handle yourself badly. This idea has some sense to it since long and extreme hatred usually makes for worse results than short and moderate hatred. But few, if any, of the abreaction-encouraging writers or therapists seem to realize that *all* anger, even one percent anger, tends to include *should*, *ought*, or *must*, and that even your one percent anger differs significantly from the 99 percent irritation that you would feel if you applied your irritation only to my *actions* rather than to me as a whole person.

If you limited your reaction in that healthy manner when I treated you unfairly, you could, for instance, strongly say to yourself, "I loathe Ellis's behavior! I thoroughly wish that he would not act that way! I feel very determined to get him to treat me better." In that way, you would tend to feel exceptionally irritated at my actions and would be unusually determined to get me to stop them rather than weakly and briefly telling yourself—or me—"I really hate him for treating me that way! He *absolutely should not* have done that!"

Remember, in this connection, the old joke about the woman who tells her highly conservative parents that she "is a little bit pregnant." Either her pregnancy exists—or it doesn't. Her statement that she is a "little bit" pregnant doesn't face the real issue: that she *really* is. If you make yourself act only a "little bit" angry for "a little while," you obscure the fact that you still take a mistaken position about people's unpleasant behavior and still *command* that they not act that way. In my view, murdering a hundred people definitely is worse than murdering one. But that hardly makes the single murder right or proper!

Dr. Robert I. Daugherty has stated that "sometimes, anger can be fun." Yes, once in a while, arguing gets your adrenaline excitedly going. It can be the highlight of your day.

Yet we had better not forget, in this connection, that Hitler *enjoyed* sending millions of Jews and Gypsies to the gas chambers. Stalin and other tyrants *felt great* about imprisoning, torturing, and finally managing to kill many of their political opponents. Many harmful human acts can seem fun, such as overeating, overdrinking, drug taking, and playing hooky from school. Most of these "fun" conditions, however, consist of short-range hedonism and in the long run lead you—and especially the people you feel angry at—into all sorts of difficulties. Although your *basic* goals in life had better be pleasure, happiness, and enjoyment, your going for certain *immediate* gains, such as those bestowed by rage and violence, hardly helps you achieve your main purposes.

Patti Hague expresses this idea: "Maybe by nurturing myself and having more faith in my lovableness and my relationships I'll not be so fearful of angry responses from others and I'll let my newfound freedom to express anger become powerful instead of dwarfing it with tears." As people frequently do, Ms. Hague seems to assume that displeasure results in anger or tears with no alternative available. And she also implies that if she has lovableness and can act well in relationships, she has the leeway to express her anger without disadvantage and thereby to gain honesty and self-respect.

Another half-truth! For if Ms. Hague looked at the situation more rationally, she could fully accept herself *with* her failings—including her unlovableness and her poor relationships. Making self-acceptance contingent on good acts is a risky procedure! Assuming that Ms. Hague could manage unconditionally to accept herself, she could then better afford to express her displeasure to others, to say to them, for example, "I really don't like the way you keep treating me and wish you would stop it!" *Anger*, however, would go far beyond this kind of displeasure and would stem from the idea, "Because I don't like the way you keep treating me, you *must* not continue to do so, and if you do, I see you as a rotten person!" No matter how much Ms. Hague might fully and unconditionally accept herself, making herself angry in this grandiose way still is damning others, and she would mainly replace self-condemnation with denigrating others. Still a mistake!

Various types of therapy, such as Reichian, primal, and bioenergetic therapy, claim that if people react violently and angrily in a therapy session or group, they actually lose their hostility and act less angrily in real-life situations. However, as far as I can see, many people who undertake these kinds of therapies end up by feeling more angry as the therapy "progresses." I have talked with hundreds of individuals who think they have "successfully" undergone Gestalt, psychoanalytic, and various kinds of "rage" and "fight" therapies, and the majority of them have felt and acted more hostilely than they did before their "cure." This substantiates the experimental work of Dr. Leonard Berkowitz and several other psychologists who consistently find in research studies that individuals who punish, curse at, and otherwise aggress against wrongdoers usually begin to feel more angry instead of simply blowing off steam and feeling less irate.

People who act out their anger and retaliate against those who act unfairly may, of course, *sometimes* wind up by feeling less angry. For a variety of reasons. (1) They temporarily run out of energy and get too exhausted to continue their rage. (2) They acknowledge and face their feelings of anger and thereby help desensitize themselves to such feelings. (3) By expressing their fury, they note their own asinine reactions and show themselves how foolishly they behave—and need not behave in the future. (4) They irrationally believe that now that they have told someone off for acting badly, that person "deserves" forgiveness. (5) They like the fact that they have asserted themselves, instead of fearfully bottling up their displeasure at the "wrongdoers." Liking themselves for this assertiveness, they feel more able to accept others with their "wrongdoing." (6) They once in a while, by expressing their anger (instead of more sensibly expressing their displeasure), induce "wrongdoers" to change their ways; they feel very good about this change and therefore surrender their anger. (7) They often get a lot of approval from anger-inciting therapists or therapy groups, feel good about this approval, and temporarily forget their anger.

For many reasons such as these, anger-inciting therapy may sometimes work. But even when it does, it tends to augment the *philosophy* of anger. While you keep screaming and cursing at people for acting badly, you keep reinforcing your notion that they *must* not do what they did and that they are lousy *individuals* for acting this *horrible* way. Consequently, even when your *current* anger at them subsides, you make yourself furious at them and other wrongdoers in the future. So while anger-inciting therapies "work," at least to some extent, they often end up by creating more harm than good.

Leslie Greenberg and Sandra Paivio advocate an "emotionally focused treatment of anger." But they note that their expressive approach "distinguishes between overcontrolled anger and unregulated anger." It assesses different anger processes and states "for the purposes of appropriate intervention." It is therefore emotive *and* cognitive.

Bach and Goldberg insist that "constructive aggression increases as hurtful hostility is reduced and informative impact is increased." They therefore advocate some "aggressive rituals," such as bataca fights, in the course of which angry people fight each other in limited ways and make sure that others do not get too badly mauled. The participants in these ritualistic fights know that they set definite limits, give themselves only a short time span in which to fight, set up various restrictive rules, use a good deal of playacting, and sometimes fight in a deliberately outlandish and extreme way. Thus, they add an element of absurdity and humor to what they do. Under such conditions, they not only allow themselves to let off steam, but also acknowledge and show themselves that a real fight, with no holds barred, has bad results and that they'd better not engage in *that* kind of a struggle.

On the other hand, fighting in a limited or playacting form also has its distinct limitations. While the fighters scream at each other or hit each other with harmless bataca bats, they usually tend to rethink that their enemy *does* act 100 percent wrongly and *must* stop doing so or will be a louse. Such controlled fighting may temporarily help the participants—but largely because they still think that they indubitably behave correctly and that the hated person behaves badly. They demand, as end result, that the other must unquestionably act better in the future. No real forgiveness or acceptance of human fallibility is present in such ritualistic fighting. So even when such techniques temporarily work, they have their serious limitations.

Yet another limited and dubious view of why we hold on to anger was expressed by William James: that since as humans we have innate tendencies toward violence, we'd better let ourselves have other intense emotional outlets and thereby provide ourselves with a moral equivalent of war. Erich Fromm cites the allegation that if Hitler's concentration camp guards had released their repressed urges toward sexual sadism in their sexual relations, they would have shown more kindness to the prisoners. Fromm takes a very skeptical view toward this theory.

I agree. Several studies have shown that people who get sexually aroused can act more sadistically and violently toward their victims than those who lack such arousal. True, some individuals, if they participate actively in situation A—such as picketing for a political cause or engaging in a sex orgy—will therefore feel diverted from participating in situation B—such as violently assaulting some of their peers or those over whom they have control. But other individuals will do exactly the opposite. They will perversely learn, from the first set of experiences, how to act more assertively and aggressively in the second set of experiences and will therefore behave more instead of less angrily.

People take different messages from the same experiences. One woman grows up with an alcoholic, badly behaving mother and therefore decides never to take a drink for the rest of her life. Her sister grows up with the same mother, decides that drinking seems a good way to get through life, and makes herself into a severe alcoholic. As we keep emphasizing in REBT, Activating Experiences, at point A, *do not* make you feel Emotional Consequences, at C. Your beliefs or interpretations *about* those experiences do. Consequently, out of one hundred people who have frustrating experiences at A, twenty may make themselves less hostile at the people who "anger" them—and eighty may make themselves more hostile.

The body therapies, such as Reichian and bioenergetic therapy, abreactively encourage people to give vent to their anger or to release the bodily armorings that block the expression of pent-up feelings of rage, and they do on occasion thereby lead to a catharsis of anger. By using these therapies for assertion rather than for anger, some people actually wind up less angry. But such therapies lead many people to do just the opposite. Mostly, these therapies tend to augment anger. The majority of body therapy clients seem to make themselves considerably more hostile as their therapy progresses.

Body therapists, of course, vary enormously, just as other therapists do. Alexander Lowen and his followers frequently incorporate considerable rational, anger-interrupting philosophies. Many years ago, before he became well known, Lowen told me that as he manipulated people's bodies, he also employed several modes of cognitive therapy—including Freudian, Jungian, and Adlerian techniques. If you read his works carefully, you will see that he still does, even though he primarily stresses psychomotor methods. Other body-oriented therapists seem to do likewise.

One of Lowen's followers, Dr. Alice Kahn Ladas, writes in this respect:

> Bioenergetic analysis is not primarily a ventilative therapy. The basic concept is not the ventilation of anger . . . but the capacity to stand on one's own two feet literally and psychologically. For many people, this involves becoming aware of anger, rage, or even hatred that has been repressed in the past or in the present. Anger that has been repressed in the past inevitably produces certain types of chronic muscular tension. One may pull one's punches until one has a widow's hump, or

> lead with one's chin until one has a stiff jaw. It is the job of a bioenergetic therapist to loosen such chronic postures and, when this is done, feelings of anger or rage may be experienced. At such a time, the person in therapy is encouraged to discharge them *in the therapy session*. A competent bioenergetic therapist definitely discourages the acting out of character problems outside of the therapeutic encounter. The analytic aspect of therapy involves the use of intellect to understand and integrate feelings that come up during the session. This is done through discussion.

As you can easily see, Dr. Ladas uses body material largely to *reveal* anger—and then uses rational discussion to discharge it. In REBT we similarly encourage people to *acknowledge* their feelings of hostility, to *understand* how they create them, and to *work* at giving them up. We do this more efficiently and with less danger of illegitimate conclusions on the client's part, than occurs in various body therapies.

A large amount of clinical and experiential data shows that expressing your anger may help to reduce your rage and to feel relieved. Some of this "evidence" seems partly correct, and some of it seems exaggerated. Naturally, you can temporarily feel better, and even less irate, if you directly or indirectly express your anger toward others. But you almost always temporarily release yourself, and in the long run you repeat your hostility-creating philosophies—that the people who hurt you *should not*, *must not* act the way they indubitably do—and also build up future angry reactions. Occasionally you let off steam—and then realize that you don't have to totally condemn your opponents. But usually, you see them as more contemptible than ever, and you tend to hate them more.

Many experiments have shown that when subjects let out their anger on others, they usually feel angrier. Leonard Berkowitz, James A. Green, and Jacqueline R. Macaulay allowed one group of frustrated subjects to strike the frustrator and another group not to do so. Those who did the striking proved just as apt to anger themselves about the same individual in the future. Berkowitz, Arnold

Buss, and Seymour Feshbach did separate experiments in which they inhibited their subjects' aggression, and all of them found that direct or indirect inhibition tended to reduce rather than to augment hostile behavior. Summarizing many such studies, Feshbach notes that "our own observations indicate that *acknowledging and labeling the affect [anger] provides a sufficient degree of expression in most instances of anger arousal [italics mine]*" and that *overt* expression of it therefore does *not* seem necessary.

Feshbach also significantly observes: "Most psychotherapists agree that the reduction in anger that occurs in patients for whom anger has been a major problem is primarily a result of insight and more refined discrimination rather than the cathartic expression of the affect. Cognitive reorganization may be a far more effective means of reducing violence than promoting its sublimated or free expression." Helene Papanek, a noted Adlerian therapist, also notes that for the expression of hostility to bring about therapeutic change, such expression had better result in a learning experience and help strengthen people's social feeling—for example, give them a better focus on learning to express and to experience themselves in new positive ways.

The view that if people, especially children, see angry and violent actions in books, on the movie screen, or on TV, they will experience a vicarious cathartic effect and will tend to release their own inner anger harmlessly has little sustaining evidence. Very little! Some children and adults, under some conditions, may view or read about violence and may thereby release their own anger, instead of giving vent to it. But as Dr. Leonard M. Liebert and his associates have shown, the reverse seems to hold in many more instances. In one of their reports, for instance, they conclude: "At least under some circumstances, repeated exposure to televised aggression can lead children to acknowledge what they have seen as a partial guide for their own actions. As a result, the present entertainment offerings of the television medium may be contributing, in some measure, to the aggressive behavior of many normal children. Such an effect has now been shown in a wide variety of situations."

The same thing happens in this respect as may happen with other kinds of disturbance. Most children or adults, when shown models of other people who behave in a disturbed manner sexually, socially, morally, or otherwise, decide that such behavior doesn't seem right for them and may strongly determine *not* to engage in it. But a certain minority of individuals, when witnessing self-defeating or antisocial acts, use them as "good" models. Such vulnerable individuals may take on some of the worst aspects of the models and may thereby harm themselves. The notion, therefore, that humans normally release their aggression harmlessly when they witness anger or violence does not fit the facts.

Studies of people's indirectly expressing themselves angrily by viewing films, reading violent stories, having hostile fantasies, or otherwise using indirect means of anger catharsis have shown even less evidence for the value of abreaction than have studies of overt hostility. Leonard Berkowitz, in a paper on "The Effects of Observing Violence," found that watching violence generates more violent reactions in many people.

The National Commission on the Causes and Prevention of Violence submitted a report indicating, according to *U.S. News and World Report*, that "television has been loaded with violence. It is teaching American children moral and social values 'inconsistent with a civilized society.'" The Surgeon General's Scientific Advisory Committee on Television and Social Behavior also did a special study of children's viewing television violence and concluded that there exists "fairly substantial experimental evidence for short-run causation of aggression among some children by viewing violence on the screen. . . . Extensive violence viewing precedes some long-run manifestations of aggressive behavior."

Many authors, including Victor B. Cline, Arnold Arnold, and Jacques-Philippe Leyens and his coworkers have shown that the witnessing of violent films by children and adults will help increase feelings and acts of aggression. Albert Bandura and Clarissa Wittenberg have summed up some of the data as follows:

> This body of research points up the fallacies in several popular ideas. One is that violence only affects those who are already

violent or deviant and involved in aggression. This has not been borne out. All viewers tend to be affected. Normal children also learn and are encouraged to perform aggressive acts by viewing them under certain circumstances. Another idea is that if parents instill in their children adequate standards of what is right or wrong, the violence they see will "wash over them." It was clearly demonstrated that even where children can label behavior as bad or wrong, they may imitate it if it was successful, and the conflicts would be resolved more often by a reevaluation downward of the worth or the role of the victim. Whether or not the observed aggressive acts are successful becomes more important than the moral value of these aggressive acts. Perhaps the most prominent idea which has been questioned is that of catharsis. There is no evidence that viewing violence, at least in most forms, dissipates aggressive drives and makes a person more healthy. In fact, it has been demonstrated that a frustrated viewer watching violence would become less inhibited and more likely to act on violent impulses.

Many other studies, such as that by Mary B. Harris and George Samerott, also present evidence against the hydraulic view of anger: the view that you have to vent your anger in some overt or fantasized form or else it flows out of you in violent or self-harming ways. Jack E. Hokanson summarizes many of the studies in this field by noting that "the results show clearly that overt aggression does not inevitably lead to either physiological tension reduction or a reduction in subsequent aggression." If anything, these studies indicate that in our culture "aggression will have at least a temporary arousal-reducing effect, and that the likelihood of future violence will be enhanced."

In another view of anger-inciting studies, Richard Walters concludes that "the series of studies reported above lend considerable support to the belief that the observation of violence in real life or on film or television can have harmful social consequences."

Which means? That the view that you'd better let out your anger and cathartically let others know how you feel, or at the very least let it out symbolically by viewing violent films or other representations, represents a nice theory—but one hardly borne out by the facts!

Rollo May theorizes that violence stems largely from naïveté or innocence and that if we have greater knowledge, accept the evils of the world, and work at achieving our own individuality while at the same time acknowledging our social responsibility, we will feel less hostile.

He makes some good points. Knowledge itself probably won't make us unangry at others. But if we accept ourselves and others *with* our and their evils, we will stop commanding that these evils not exist and will make ourselves less hostile. Acknowledging social responsibility in itself also does not eliminate hostility—and may actually increase it. If I acknowledge that I'd better treat you fairly and let you live and do your own thing, as long as it does not interfere too seriously with mine, I will tend to accept the reality of my living as a social person and will not hate you when you want me to treat you nicely or justly. So responsibility, in that sense, lets me have a higher frustration tolerance and therefore feel less angry at you and at the world.

At the same time, however, I can easily say, "Because *I* act responsibly, you should do so, too! And because you don't do what you *should*, you are a rotten person who hardly deserves a good existence!" With this kind of "responsible" thinking, I can easily make myself angry at you. Similarly, by striving for more individuality, I can either believe, "I want what I want, but if I don't get it, and you don't give it to me, tough!" Or: "I need what I want, and if I don't get it, and you block me from achieving it, how awful!" In the latter case, I may make myself hostile.

Innocence, in other words, does not merely include my seeing the world as a nonevil, marvelous place. More important, it may include my demandingness—my believing that the world *must* not have evil in it and that it *has to* work the way I want it to work. With this kind of absolutistic innocence, I will probably make myself angry.

Psychoanalytic and primal therapies hold that people have to get in touch with their past hostility toward their parents and the intense rage they felt when young in order to work through their hostility today. This is often a mistaken view: No good evidence exists for it and considerable facts are directly contradictory.

First, many children don't rage that badly when they feel frustrated. They certainly don't like it, but they fairly calmly persevere and do not act like little gods who *must* not get frustrated.

Second, when children do whine and scream, inwardly or outwardly, about their parents' frustrating behavior, their own tendencies to enrage themselves are the real issue, not merely the acts of their parents. To say that these acts made them angry is often false. *They* caused their own screaming *about* their frustrations. Similarly, if they have an allergy to, say, grapefruit and their parents keep feeding them grapefruit, we cannot conclude that their parents made them (except genetically) allergic or caused them to break out in a rash. Their parents *contributed* to their allergic reactions but didn't truly *cause* them.

Third, even some highly vulnerable children, once they get frustrated early in life and inwardly or outwardly scream about frustrations, manage to come to terms with, stop screaming about, and ultimately accept them. Only *some* children grow into adults who seem to remember the original frustration and screaming forever, plaguing themselves about it many years after it first occurred.

Finally, even when self-plaguing adults yell and scream today about what happened many years ago, they frequently make themselves more rather than less angry at their parents for frustrating them—and more angry about the "insults" and "horrors" that the world foists on them. Their "unrepressing" their anger usually helps them to escalate it rather than to give it up. Only if they stop believing, today, that their parents *should have* treated them better, and are total *worms* for not doing so, will they likely surrender their feelings of anger. Such a change in their Belief System is unlikely in various kinds of primal therapies.

Most people who feel very angry know quite well how they feel and only occasionally do not know it. Most of them seem *too much* in touch with their feelings—and consequently keep making themselves angry all the time.

Almost any therapist can, of course, bring out "hidden" anger by inducing clients to scream, to go through painful physical exercises, to beat pillows, or to remember "horrible" childhood incidents. How much of this anger represents unconscious or repressed hostility, however, and how much does the therapist *presently* incite? Answer: Much of it may fall in the latter rather than the former category.

Remember, in this connection, that according to REBT theory, we naturally and easily *make ourselves* angry; have an underlying biosocial *tendency* to do so. Consequently, if I as your therapist get you to playact anger toward me or a member of your group, forcibly restrain you so you cannot move, poke you in the gut, or imply that your mother really was a bitch for unduly restricting you, I will have no trouble in helping you make yourself angry *right now*. Having a talent for foolishly inciting yourself, you will usually follow my instigative lead and will make yourself just about as angry as I want you to feel. But this hardly proves that, all along, you really *did* violently hate me, or your mother, and that I now have merely made you conscious of this feeling. Probably, for the most part, you really like me, and your mother, but you *occasionally* feel hostility toward us. This hardly constitutes serious "unconscious" rage on your part.

Therapy-instigated anger, therefore, rarely represents your true or basic feeling, only occasionally reveals your general resentment, frequently exaggerates how angry you feel—and may *encourage* you to make yourself angrier than you usually would. It boosts the therapist's ego—and, often, hinders you. If you have a therapist who seems obsessed with your getting in touch with your angry feelings, rather than helping you acknowledge and *give them up*, you'd better suspect his own motivations—and run to another therapist as soon as possible!

Theodore Isaac Rubin holds that real anger leads to warmth and health and seems as necessary as eating or loving. He implies that if your anger takes the form of spontaneous, direct expression of feelings of displeasure, we can then call it "real" and look forward to cultivating rather than suppressing it.

This view has its dangers. To use a term like *real anger* amounts to using a term like *real love*. All love, as I have said in *The American*

Sexual Tragedy and other writings, is "real" love—whether short or enduring, mild or passionate, conjugal or romantic. *Real* mainly means existent—and not ideal. So with anger. Virtually all anger falls under the heading of "real," and it seems to consist of two fairly clear-cut factors: (1) sincere and sometimes profound disappointment when someone treats you unfairly or badly and (2) the Irrational Belief that this unfair or bad treatment should not, must not exist, and that its perpetrator is a totally rotten individual. The more sincerely, directly, authentically, and spontaneously you experience anger, the more it seems to include both these factors.

Rubin means that when people treat you unfairly, you can feel intense disappointment, sorrow, regret, and frustration, and that *this element* of anger often has a healthy quality because it helps you go after what you want and fight against the injustices of the world. Rubin fails to define anger very accurately and also believes it aids love. I believe it often does just the opposite. The more you express your sincere disappointment with people's bad behavior, the more they tend to feel turned off, less loving. Sometimes, of course, they agree that they have disappointed you in some ways, and they change those ways, thus helping create a warm and healthy relationship between the two of you. But often nothing of the sort happens!

Moreover, when you express downright anger—no matter how directly and spontaneously you give vent to it—you imply that others do not have the right to disappoint you and that they thus are no good. This almost always turns them off and leads them to return hatred rather than love. Occasionally, if you express great hostility toward someone for whom you truly care, you will make yourself so contrite that you will act much better after apologizing that your love for them and theirs for you may increase. Also, if they have sufficiently strong positive attitudes toward you to begin with, your anger may inspire them to go out of their way to make amends to you and to cement your relationship. Occasionally! But don't count on it. In most cases love begets love, and hate begets hate.

Jay Kuten, along with Theodore Rubin and George Bach, also develops the thesis that rewarding sexual love requires a joint recognition of individual integrity, which you and a partner can enhance by adaptive exchanges of anger. The first part of Kuten's thesis makes good sense since you will not likely love anyone else too much if you do not first accept yourself and strive for a goodly degree of individual integrity. But normally you would attain such integrity by assertiveness, not by hostility. If you show your partner that you want some degree of individuality and that you will, if necessary, break up the relationship if you don't get it, you will have a greater likelihood of ultimately forming a warm and lasting relationship than if you angrily insist that your mate not frustrate you. Assertiveness and good love relationships correlate fairly highly; hostility and love do not!

You may wonder about rage-reduction techniques, such as that of Dr. Robert Zaslow, where a therapist and a member of a therapeutic group deliberately tickle a person, hold him down, and throw taunts and invectives designed to enrage that person—until he feels relaxed and assertive rather than enraged. Almost any therapeutic technique will work—sometimes. Fight therapists, such as George Bach, sometimes endorse it, and are sure that Zaslow's claims are valid. Says Zaslow: "I'm doing for rage what Freud did for sex. Today, rage is socially unacceptable, just as sex used to be. But rage is really esthetic. When the tiger goes for his food in the jungle, it's an esthetic expression. That's the only way he can survive, and he's beautiful at it. As Dante said, hell is a place waiting for heaven to shine through. Rage is hell, and rage reduction propels you into heaven."

Brave words! But the actual results don't always seem to bear them out. Several clients of therapists using rage-reduction methods have reported feeling harmed. Although some individuals have probably received help by these rigorous methods, I would doubt whether they more than temporarily overcame their feelings of deep-seated hostility and would guess that most of them ended up more hostile. Other unfortunate results of this kind of treatment seem common and sometimes fairly severe. Dr. Hyman Spotnitz has commented, "The new development of encouraging physical contact with patients, I am sorry to say, leads to violent outbursts, as my own experience of many years ago showed. Therefore, I do not encourage such actions. A study of the literature and case reports will show that where therapists unnecessarily touch their patients or struggle with them physically, the therapy is unsuccessful."

Fritz Perls claimed that we have to give in to our aggression and express it directly toward others or toward the world because otherwise we will reflect it and take it out on ourselves. I disagree. We can, of course, refuse to display our anger toward others and then condemn ourselves for failing to do so. In this case this anger may be reflected back onto ourselves. But we can also, and probably more likely, directly take out our anger on others—and then *also* condemn ourselves for doing this. The main point that many fail to realize in their anger therapies is that no hydraulic force exists that makes us angry here (that is, against others). Our attitude *toward* our nonexpression may well make us feel depressed and self-downing. But the strain of not expressing our feelings remains like the strain of other kinds of nonexpression: a moderate strain that we can easily master. As a diabetic I strain myself to forgo eating sugar, which I really like to eat, but I merely tell myself, "Tough! Sugar does me much more harm than good; so I will force myself to give it up." I feel only moderate strain, and no anger against the world, from my decision to forbear.

As a human, I may strain myself to forgo expressing my feelings of anger toward my boss or my partner when I'd feel good—temporarily!—about letting them out. I then may foolishly tell myself, "I *shouldn't* have to control my anger. In fact, I wouldn't feel angry at all if that louse didn't act the way he does. Why can't he change, and not make me angry or, at least, let me express my anger? And why can't I 'strongly' express it and take the consequences, thereby proving how noble I am?" Because of these irrational ideas, I may make a federal case out of not expressing my anger—and I *therefore* choose to turn it inward and take it out on myself. But I can *stop* this crazy kind of thinking and acting if I choose.

12

More Ways of Overcoming Anger

The rational approach to anger involves a hardheaded, persistent, relentless effort to admit that you feel enraged rather than merely annoyed; that you largely brought on these feelings yourself; that you are responsible for continuing to feel them and can distinctly control and reduce them, although probably never to absolute zero; that they mainly bring you considerably more harm than good; and that it would seem advisable, though hardly necessary, for you to ameliorate and often eliminate your angry feelings.

You may accomplish this through:

Review of pragmatic results

Albert Bandura's investigations of hostility and the operant conditioning theories of B. F. Skinner call to our attention three major facts. (1) Anger and violence rarely arise from "good" social interactions but generally follow from experiences that include—or that *appear* to include—serious frustrations and unfairnesses. (2) Once we react in certain hostile ways to frustrations and annoyances, we are reinforced and penalized by our actions. Hostility either reinforces us by helping us to remove the stimuli that we find obnoxious or it brings us other satisfactions (such as the pleasure of feeling superior to the people we fight). Or else hostility penalizes us (helps us bring on counterattacks from those we hate and attack, for instance). (3) After getting reinforced or penalized for our aggressive feelings and moves, we finally can weigh the short-term and long-term advantages and disadvantages of the results we achieve and can, on a pragmatic basis, reduce frustrating conditions in the future and at least semirationally decide how we will react to remaining frustrations.

For example, I have promised to share an apartment with you and, after persuading you to go to great expense to fix it up, have refused to move in with you. I have thus set up a set of frustrating conditions for you to deal with. If you then choose to feel and act angrily toward me, you will get reinforcements and penalties. On the reinforcing side, you may remove yourself from my frustrating presence, influence me to make some restitution, and feel vastly superior to me since you act "good" and I act "bad." On the penalizing side, you may encourage me to treat you still worse in the future, be disapproved of by some of our mutual friends, and consume valuable time and energy futilely trying to get restitution from me. These reinforcements and penalties will tend, consciously or unconsciously, to make you feel more or less hostile when similar unfairness occurs in your life.

Finally, after feeling angry at me for quite a while and perhaps instituting vindictive feuding with me, you (as a human) can constructively review the entire situation with me and put it in the context of your general life. You can decide, for example, that your anger has some advantages—but that it also helps you get an ulcer or high blood pressure and therefore brings you more harm than good. You can decide that your hostility makes you feel superior to me—but that this kind of an ego game really isn't very rewarding. You can decide that you can live successfully with your pleasure at your anger—but that you could live more happily if you arranged to stay away from people like me in the future and thus could stop the frustrations that we would probably foist upon you.

If, in other words, you make yourself fully aware, in Bandura's terms, of how frustrations contribute to your anger, of what kinds of reinforcements and penalties immediately tend to accompany your angry feelings, and of what long-term consequences may result even from your "rewarding" angry "victories," you make a full-scale analysis of the complex roots of your hostility. A wide range of solutions then become available including changing the frustrating stimuli or Activating Events that contribute to your angry feelings, arranging for different kinds of reinforcers and penalties that will tend to make you feel less angry when still faced with obnoxious stimuli, taking a long-range instead of a short-range hedonistic view of the advantages and disadvantages of hostility, and changing your philosophic outlook toward frustrating people and events, so that again you make them seem less rage provoking.

Bandura, Skinner, and other advocates of social-reinforcement theories of anger seem to repeat the ancient Greek adage: Knowledge equals power. The more you understand the biological, social, cognitive, and other sources of your angry feelings and actions, the greater your chance of changing and controlling influences on you and of looking for more practical solutions to frustrations.

Frustration reduction

Although frustration does not seem to directly or invariably cause anger, it certainly significantly contributes! Most humans who suffer severe deprivation for considerable periods of time have a strong tendency to upset themselves about this—and to lash out angrily at frustrating people or conditions. Although, therefore, you had better work to raise your frustration tolerance and to reduce your whining about the unniceties of the universe, you can also wisely work to reduce these frustrations themselves.

You *don't* have to work at a boring job, stay with annoying friends, or let your mate or children keep taking advantage of you. Temporarily you may do yourself a lot of good by deliberately remaining in these unpleasant kinds of circumstances to work on your own low frustration tolerance and show yourself that you can stand what you don't like. Temporarily! But in the long run you almost always have better alternatives. Look for them. Work at instituting them. On the other hand, don't try to live with *zero* frustration (for you won't succeed!) or even at times with *minimal* frustration (for you may thereby lose out on real pleasures). But needless and enormous thwarting you really don't want. Do something to reduce some of it. If not immediately, at least ultimately. And often—soon!

High frustration tolerance

Anger and violence rarely stem from mere frustration but from low frustration tolerance. When you feel furious, your basic view consists of the idea that whatever frustrates you *should not* and *ought not* exist; that not only is it unfair, but this unfairness, again, *must not* prevail; that you *can't stand* frustration; and that those who unduly balk and block you are vermin who, once again, *should not* act the way they indubitably do.

Obviously, you can find an antidote to this kind of thinking by teaching yourself higher frustration tolerance. How? By seeing that frustration *should* exist (because it does), as likewise should unfairness and injustice. In this respect, you can heed the words of Erich Fromm:

> First of all, we might consider a basic fact of life: that nothing important is achieved without accepting frustration. The idea that one can learn without effort, i.e., without frustration, may be good as an advertising slogan, but is certainly not true in the acquisition of major skills. Without the capacity to accept frustration man would hardly have developed at all. And does not everyday observation show that many times people suffer frustration without having an aggressive response? What can, and often does, produce aggression is what the frustration *means* to the person, and the psychological meaning of frustration differs according to the total constellation in which the frustration occurs.

Fromm does not so indicate but "the total constellation in which the frustration occurs" also includes:

- Your basic tendency to demand that frustration must not exist.
- Your full acknowledgment that you *have* such a demand or command.

And then, it is hoped:

- Your realization that you will almost inevitably defeat yourself unless you ameliorate or surrender your demandingness.
- Your firm decision to give that up and replace it with a desire but not an absolutistic insistence that you receive little frustration.
- Your determinedly working—cognitively, emotively, and behaviorally—to live up to that decision.

Your philosophy *about* frustration, then, seems the real issue, and even when you have little control over being frustrated, you have several ways of modifying that philosophy.

Counterattacking narcissism and grandiosity

As Gregory Rochlin points out, narcissism or childish grandiosity has profound roots in human nature and tends to underlie much of our behavior. We don't merely want others to love and care for us; we utterly insist that they do, and we frequently feel completely shattered when they don't. Such shattering is self-induced since *we*, rather than they, down ourselves by our dire need for others' acceptance. We often foolishly claim that *they* destroy us by rejecting our "needs." This frequently leads to our feeling exceptionally angry and acting violently against those who presumably have "failed" us. Rochlin emphasizes how often hostility springs from wounded self-esteem and neglects its other important sources. But he does make a good point: Much of our fury against others originally arises from the "hurt" they give us—the "hurt" to our narcissistic demands for approval.

Moral: You can give up your infantile narcissism if this is one of the main sources of your anger. You don't *have* to run the universe. You don't *need* to feel good about yourself mainly because others acknowledge your outstandingness. No reason exists why you *must* take the center of the stage or why you *should* even receive minimum respect from others.

No, the world *doesn't* care too much for you and most likely never will. The more famous you get, moreover, the more enemies you may tend to make. The better you behave toward many people, the more they will take advantage of you. That's the way it often is. The universe most probably has no *special* interest in you. Nor ever will. Now, how can you fully face and accept that "cruel," "cold" fact and live happily in spite of it? If you can, one of the main sources of your hostility to others will end.

As both Freud and Adler noted many years ago and as I have stated in my early writings on Rational Emotive Behavior Therapy, much anger stems from childish grandiosity. As humans we believe that because the possibility exists that others *can* treat us very well—in fact, specially—and because we'd greatly benefit from this worshipful kind of treatment, they *should* bestow it on us. As H. Peters has noted:

> There have been philosophers, such as Bertrand Russell, who have held that jealousy is always inappropriate as an emotion, basically because it presupposes unjustifiable claims to a special relationship with another person. If psychologists could show that human beings were unable to avoid appraising situations in this way, that would be an important assertion to make. For there is a sense in which "ought" implies "can."

Peters somewhat overstates the case here. Humans *tend to* appraise situations in this way, but they *can* avoid, at least to some extent, doing so. Whenever you feel extremely angry at someone, you can fully face the fact that you inwardly state or imply a godlike command that this person *ought to* give you special treatment. You can then firmly rip up that *ought* many times and replace it with "I would find it very *preferable* if this person treated me specially, but the chances remain that he or she often won't," and thereby minimize your anger.

Childish grandiosity and ego aggrandizement create anger, including extreme violence, on two sides of the intellectual–dullness continuum. On the dullness side, Hans Toch found that a great many of the criminals whom he investigated, who in education and brightness clearly were on the dull half of the scale, could be classified as "self-image promoters" or "reputation defenders." They committed violent crimes largely because their social position, physical size, or group status seemed low and "obligated" them to compensate in a physically violent way—"a matter of 'noblesse oblige,' so to speak," as Toch notes.

At the other end of the continuum, highly educated and intellectual people also overreact to "oppression" and "ego insult" by behaving very angrily and violently. Theodore Gold, a twenty-three-year-old Weatherman who was killed in a dynamited town house in New York while assembling a bomb to fight for "liberty," told an old college friend before his death, "I've been doing a lot of exciting underground things, and I know I'm not afraid to die." One of his Weatherman friends defended his actions by stating, "We don't think in terms of being happy. We think in terms of being strong people."

Watch your own grandiosity and overrebelliousness. Certainly, the side you oppose may be wrong and unjust in some ways. Surely, your own cause may seem much more humane than "theirs." But you never know indisputably that your way will lead to much more good than harm and theirs to all kinds of holocausts. By all means, defend your own views—and fight, verbally and even actively, to see if you can get them to prevail. But watch your grandiosity! Watch your dogmatism! The stronger you feel about a cause, the more you will likely ignore its limitations and disadvantages. Try to bring these incisively to mind, too. And see if you can determinedly go after what you want—without enraging yourself and insisting that because you find it right and proper, it *must* prevail.

Liberalization of attitudes

Attitudes toward others and how you "should" react to them when they treat you unfairly correlate significantly with your general attitudes toward humans and the rules they "ought" to follow. Stuart Taylor and Jan Smith found that males with traditional beliefs reacted more hostilely to their opponents than did males with more liberal beliefs. If, therefore, you want to curb your tendencies toward making yourself angry at others, you might consider taking a distinctly more liberal general view of the world than the conservative, traditional, or reactionary view that you now may have.

Knowledge of history

History, as Daniel J. Boorstin points out, provides us with many striking illustrations of the consequences of hostility, ranging from the prolonged wars in ancient Israel and Greece, to Hitler's and Stalin's holocausts, and right up to the terrorism that still very much exists. Moreover, Boorstin reminds us, history also helps us scotch our utopianism and respect our possibilities for progress:

> "The voice of the intellect," observed Sigmund Freud (who did not underestimate the role of the irrational) in 1928, "is a soft one, but it does not rest until it has gained a hearing. Ultimately, after endlessly repeated rebuffs, it succeeds. This is one of the viewpoints in which one may be optimistic about the future of mankind." Beneath the strident voice of the present we must try to hear the insistent whisper of reason. It does not sound strongly. It speaks only to the attentive listener. It speaks a language always unfamiliar and often archaic. It speaks the language of all past times and places, which is the language of history.

Awareness of the harm of anger and violence

You might think that anger and violence have obviously wreaked so much harm on individuals and communities that virtually everyone, including yourself, has full awareness of the harm caused and uses this awareness to keep from reacting irately to others. What a wrong conclusion! You may indeed have a general awareness of some of the enormous disadvantages of rage, but how often do you bring this general awareness into specific focus and make yourself see exactly what harm you will most likely do yourself and others by making yourself enraged? Seldom, I would wager!

Let me briefly review some of the distinct disadvantages of resentment and anger that authorities on the subject have pointed out for many centuries:

Focusing on reprisal

Although you ostensibly make yourself angry at others in order to protect yourself from their wrong thinking and behaving, once you enrage yourself at these "wrongdoers" you tend to lose sight of the real issues involved and to obsess yourself with futile and harm-inciting revenge. Milton Schwebel indicates that even firebrands with legitimate grievances and good motivation to remove these grievances often will "use any excuse to stimulate confrontations, not in order to right wrongs or correct injustice but to provoke reprisal and repression in order to trap the great, uncommitted center to the side of revolution and anarchy."

Abuse of weaker individuals

As I point out elsewhere in this book, anger and even righteous indignation spur you to abuse some of your subordinates who act badly, including powerless children over whom you may, unfortunately, have control. In recent years an enormous amount of evidence has accumulated in regard to child abuse—up to and including maiming and killing of children by thousands of irate parents. Most of our statistics in this regard come from highly "civilized" countries like the United States—as shown by such authorities as Vincent Fontana and his associates, Ray E. Helfer and C. Henry Kempe, Naomi F. Chase, and David G. Gil and by a large bibliography of "Selected References on the Abused and Battered Child" published by the National Institute of Mental Health Communication Center. But other countries do just as poorly in this respect, as indicated by the statement of a British psychiatrist, Dr. John Howells, who told a Royal Society of Health conference that more children get beaten to death at home by parents than ever died in the workhouses of Victorian England. Said Dr. Howells: "Two children die each day in the United Kingdom killed by their parents . . . Many more are maimed in mind and body."

Political violence

Although the nations of the United Nations have so far managed to ward off another major holocaust like World War I and World War II, almost innumerable international and intranational conflicts continue to exist. Guerrilla warfare, hijackings, political murders, kidnappings, open warfare between political factions, and all kinds of terrorism remain rife in virtually every part of the civilized and less civilized world today.

Religious warfare

Just as political warfare stems from hatred of and bigotry against other groups, so does religious warfare. Religious warfare reigns all over the world today, including various overt and covert wars between Catholics and Protestants, Jews and Christians, Jews and Muslims, Muslims and Christians, Hindus and Muslims . . . each group, as usual, tends to believe that its views are sacred and that its opponent's views are utterly wrong—and that therefore, the opposing group has to be denounced, downed, and preferably eradicated. Even members of peace-loving groups, such as Jews and Christians, turn to bloodshed and murder when they make themselves grandiosely angry against members of other religious groups.

Belief in the power of aversive harm

Anger frequently includes the unwarranted belief that if you deal with others aversively and painfully when they disagree with you, they will learn by this aversive experience and will change their ways. How seldom they will! Usually, as Adah Maurer and her associates point out, people who suffer aversive responses to their aversive behavior learn that hurting others serves as an acceptable method of gaining power. They therefore often retaliate in kind rather than stop their vindictive behavior. Love begets love, and hate frequently begets hate. Punishing others encourages them to punish back in return. A vicious circle of violence leading to more violence ensues.

Prejudice against self and others

Hatred of others often leads you to view them as devils incarnate, and to magnify their possession of "evil" traits. Curiously enough, by attributing to them these traits and using them as an excuse for your own hatred, you frequently act bad yourself, and may end up with a doubly negative view of humans. Then, hating yourself for your angry feelings, you may drive yourself to hating others even more. As Marie Jahoda notes, "Despising others becomes a way of trying to bolster one's own shaky self-esteem by making others seem more inferior or contemptible. In fact, the only way some people can salvage their own self-respect is to feel 'lucky' they are not a Negro, Catholic, an Italian—or whoever is set up as the scapegoat for their own secret misery."

Taking on characteristics of those you hate

Ironically, you tend to hate others for their poor characteristics—bullying, prejudice, violence, arrogance—and through hating them and justifying almost any action you can perpetrate to stop them, you frequently take on the very features that you may loathe. As I have pointed out for many years, if you thoroughly hate Hitler, you tend to turn into a Hitler—one who condemns others in their entirety because he dislikes some of their traits. William Irwin Thompson points out that "we become what we hate" and notes that "in watching the conflict of the Irish Troubles, the Dublin yogi, George William Russell, developed the maxim into a principle of political science: 'By intensity of hatred nations create in themselves the characteristics they imagine in their enemies. Hence it is that passionate conflicts result in the interchange of characteristics.' "

Anger as a "pain in the gut"

Because we often feel highly pleased and self-righteous when we experience anger, we forget that we also experience it as a "pain in the gut"—and as a distracting, obsessive feeling that prevents us from doing many joyful things and that frequently leads to self-destruction.

Paul Hauck, in *Overcoming Frustration and Anger*, rightly notes that letting yourself get angry when someone tries to "get your goat" only does you double injury. He states:

> There are two statements I usually make to myself which help me keep my cool. The first is that I am not God and am neurotic to insist I have to have my way. This usually cools me off nicely. However, if that doesn't do the trick, I always throw in this next thought. "Hauck, be smart, someone is trying to shaft you. That's bad enough, old boy. Surely you're not going to be dumb now and do to yourself what that fellow is trying to do. No, sir! Maybe he doesn't give a hoot about my feelings, but I sure do. Therefore, I'm going to forcibly talk myself out of the angry mood which is beginning to come over me." Having trouble is one thing, and it's often unavoidable. But making *double trouble* for myself is another matter entirely.

Interference with individuality within groups

Alfred McClung Lee points out that group solidarity or group egotism may have certain advantages but has distinct disadvantages as well; that groups do *not* consist of individuals who act exactly like each other, who have the same tastes and preferences. One disadvantage of group solidarity is the enormous intragroup prejudice and hostility that it breeds. Says Lee: "Apologists for group-egotism praise its contribution to the participant individual's sense of identity with one specific part of a pluralistic society. But what of its cost in intergroup hostility, exploration, and bloodshed. Think of the untold millions . . . who have died or lived in deprivation because of their group identity!"

Dr. Lee could well have added sex warfare to his list of group ego centeredness. Certainly women have for many centuries been kept at a certain level in our society and males have acted chauvinistically to keep them there—because of group egotism and neglect of societal individuality. Now some feminist women tend to go to the same extreme and are overwhelmingly hostile to males, globally rating almost all men as bastards and carrying on what amounts to sex warfare. This prevents these women from seeing males as humans and in the long run probably makes for *greater* sex antagonism. Males, of course, who violently fight against feminism are in the same defensive, hating boat. Both sets of extremists nicely "identify" with ideal masculinity and feminity—none of whom ever seem to exist—and gain "strength," or what I call false integrity, by feeling and acting hostilely toward the other half of the human race.

Interference with activism

Revolutionists usually insist that only through making ourselves exceptionally incensed at injustices and inequities can we work to change poor social conditions. Partly true—and largely wrong! As Hannah Arendt has indicated, violent riots and rebellions give their participants a false sense of action, frequently include wrong moves on the part of the rebels, and tend to impede the careful planning, constructive action, and long-term follow-up procedures that would result in effective social change. Dramatic outbursts may serve as a prelude to constructive reorganization, but they frequently do not. Outbursts of verbal anger, moreover, can continue for years or decades and, if anything, prevent people from *doing* something about the execrable conditions against which they keep violently protesting.

Determined (rather than hysterical) *rebellion* against society or its conditions, on the other hand, has its distinct advantages. First, it lets you take a stand for what you really care for: a different set of conditions that you personally approve, rather than the given or traditional set under which you live. Second, instead of letting yourself stew about the "horrors" of what exists, determined rebellion gives you something constructive to do: permits you to let off some legitimate steam through expressing your real feelings and gives you something to work for in a busy, concerted way, thereby distracting you from musturbation and insensate anger. Third, constructive rebellion may well help change or ameliorate various kinds of frustrating conditions and thus remove some of the obnoxious Activating Experiences that would commonly encourage your fury.

So don't think that lack of anger means merely turning the other cheek or tolerating needless hassles. If you build, instead of rage, a powerful determination to do what you can do to modify unfortunate situations, you will head off most of your needless frustrations rather than childishly whining about their existence.

Interference with the rights of others

As Janet L. Wolfe points out, assertiveness differs notably from aggressiveness in that the former consists of "the ability to express feelings or legitimate rights straightforwardly, without attacking others or violating their rights. Aggressive behavior, to the contrary, violates the rights of others, or puts them down." Anger, too, has an intrinsically fascistic or elitist philosophy behind it, for it denies the rights of others in favor of one's own "special" rights.

Deification of all aggressiveness

When angry, you tend to deify all forms of aggressiveness and rationalize them as "good" or "healthy." Actually, we may call aggression "healthy" when it largely helps or abets some basic human goals, especially the goals of remaining alive, feeling relatively happy, living successfully in a social group, relating intimately to some selected members of that group, having a productive and enjoyable vocational life, and engaging in chosen and satisfying recreational pursuits. But intense feelings of anger help us to seek unhealthy as well as healthy goals. If we unangrily looked at these unhealthy goals, we would tend to see them as having dubious value.

Overgeneralized and unfair discrimination

When we anger ourselves against a group of individuals, we tend to overgeneralize and discriminate against even those who act much differently from the others whose behavior we might otherwise tend to favor.

Ignoring long-range values

Anger helps you look only at short-range rather than at long-range values and gains. As Marshall Gilula and David N. Daniels have shown, one of the major obstacles to our minimizing violence is our slowness to recognize that a violent style of coping with problems will often soothe current feelings and lead to immediate satisfactions—but that in the long run it will help destroy us and ultimately, perhaps—in some final nuclear holocaust—the entire human race.

The perpetuation of disturbance

Anger often involves some kind of temporary—or permanent—emotional disturbance. But when you indulge yourself in anger, you deny that you feel disturbed and thus block your ability to deal with and possibly eliminate your disturbance. In extreme cases you rage quite neurotically. You and your raging opponents may distract yourselves from acknowledging your severe disturbances and from doing anything to ameliorate them. In fact, your anger serves as a justification for your upsetness and provides you with a neurotic gain, and tends to keep you both angry and violent.

Interference with helping others to change

The angrier you make yourself at others who hold opposing views and the more you express that anger, the less you tend to help them change their views and come around to yours. On the contrary, they usually feel more justified in opposing you and claiming that your rage *proves* you wrong.

Encouraging feelings of depression

Anger may sometimes help you cover up or avoid feelings of depression, and, if so, it seems an advantageous reaction. But it can also lead to depressed feelings. For if you merely feel frustrated about something, you rarely make yourself depressed. But if you feel frustrated and dogmatically insist, to yourself and others, that this frustration *should* not, *must* not exist and that you find it *awful* that it does, you will not only anger yourself but often depress yourself as well. For if bad things *must not* exist, and they indubitably do, you can easily conclude that you have no power whatever over such things, that they will always exist, and that you can't stand them. If, instead of ranting and raving about frustrations, you focus on doing something to cope with them and think about how your angry behavior may augment them, you may help yourself feel neither angry nor depressed.

Psychosomatic reactions

Anger, both suppressed and overt, can easily result in psychosomatic reactions, including high blood pressure, heart problems, ulcers, and various other physical conditions. Although we often dramatize the effect of unexpressed anger, evidence shows that expressed rage also encourages physical pain and dysfunction.

Genocide

As noted above, anger-inspired wars have existed since time immemorial and still do! A most vicious aspect of war includes genocide, the deliberate conquering of an enemy group and the complete extirpation, if possible, of that group. Naturally, we think of Hitler in this respect and of his plans to exterminate the entire Jewish and Gypsy population of Germany—and, eventually, of the world. Examples of attempted extirpation of an entire group of people exist in ancient and modern times. And almost invariably these genocidal attempts stem from intense anger against a whole group when, at worst, only some of its members have acted badly in the eyes of the exterminators. This is *real* overgeneralization and consequent bigotry!

These, then, represent some of the distinct disadvantages of resentment and anger that our awareness will help to eliminate. Here are some more ways of working against your angry feelings and actions.

Understanding attribution theory

When someone treats us in a certain way, particularly a frustrating or unfair way, we tend to attribute various motives to this person, and we make ourselves more or less angry depending on the motives that we choose to attribute to him. In recent years a number of social psychologists have pointed out the importance of attribution theory in understanding human feelings and actions. Russell Geen and David Stonner, for example, set up an experiment whereby male college students—after having seen a violent movie—could presumably punish someone who had verbally attacked them. Under one set of experimental conditions the other subjects learned that the fighting stemmed from professional or altruistic motives and under another set of conditions that it stemmed from revenge motives. The results showed that those led by the experimenters to attribute the fighting to revenge motives acted significantly more angrily and punitively toward the people whom they subsequently punished than did those who believed that the fighting stemmed from altruistic motives.

If you have a tendency—as you probably do—to attribute highly negative, vindictive motives to people who frustrate or attack you, *force yourself to stop and question your attributions* and try to see *other* possible reasons for the frustration or the attack. In our usual illustration, I renege on my promise to share an apartment with you, and you assume that:

1. I truly want to do you in.
2. I knew all along that I would never share the apartment with you and deliberately misled you.
3. I now have no good reasons for pulling out of our deal, but I still viciously insist on pulling out of it.
4. I have no intention of compensating you in any way for the trouble I have caused you.

Stop and review the probability that I really do have such vindictive motives. Consider my possible other reasons for backing out on our deal, such as:

1. I had an honest change of heart after first thinking about the advantages of my living with you.
2. I cannot afford to go through with our deal, though I would really like to do so.
3. I think that you have somehow treated me unfairly, and therefore, I don't want to share an apartment with you.
4. The conditions of my life have radically changed, so that I really would find it quite handicapping if I went through with my original plans for you.

Look for and check your attributions! Others frequently frustrate, annoy, and treat you unfairly. But only rarely do they do so because they thoroughly and personally hate you; only rarely do they *intend* to act vindictively toward you; only rarely do they have no good reasons for treating you the way they do, or do they fully admit the iniquity of their ways and still persist in pursuing them. In many instances they have such severe disturbances that they cannot easily help treating you badly; or they have very little awareness of their injustices to you; or they believe that they cannot possibly solve some of their own basic problems unless they deal with you unfairly.

Seek, if you possibly can, their true motives and attitudes. And watch your exaggerated or invented attributions!

Combating romanticism and unrealism

Romanticism and utopian fantasizing have their assets: They give you something to look forward to in life, and while you feel romantically obsessed with a person or thing, you have some wonderfully exhilarating experiences. Your problem, as usual, consists of escalating romantic wishes and preferences into rigorous demands and commands. If you want Ms. Jones or Mr. Smith to love you devotedly and to have a continuing romantic involvement with you, fine! But if you absolutely, dogmatically believe that she or he must have that kind of attachment, and have it practically forever, beware!

Ingrid Bengis, author of *Combat in the Erogenous Zone* and a self-confessed man-hater, sagely notes: "When I was sixteen I commented to an adult that in my opinion all cynics were disappointed idealists. What I would add today is that most man-haters are probably disappointed romantics. Or at the very least, I would say, that is what I am."

So foster your own romanticism if you will. Look for high-level, imaginative, long-lasting involvements. But don't command, don't insist! You do not *need* the romantic attachments that you want. And if you believe this, really believe this, you will stop hating those who don't want to get into a rip-roaring romantic relationship with you.

Overcoming feelings of inadequacy

Many authorities correctly point out that feelings of hostility can compensate for feelings of inferiority, since hating others seems hugely better than downing oneself. Writers on crime and violence, such as Marvin Wolfgang and Franco Ferracuti and Hans Toch, show how certain subcultures in our society encourage their members to think that hostility and the use of force has fine, "manly" qualities, and consequently certain immature personalities in this subculture tend to employ violence as a compensatory tool, to cover up their basic feelings of inadequacy. If this thesis has a good deal to it—and it would seem that it probably has—then one solution to the problem of anger and violence would consist of helping basically immature individuals to act more maturely. This, of course, brings us right back to REBT and to some of the points on anger we made in the first few chapters.

If you want to minimize anger that stems from feelings of insecurity and inadequacy, read over this early material and learn to stop downing yourself. Your traits, deeds, and performances may indeed fall far below your desired level. For personal reasons or because you come from a certain "lower" socioeconomic class, you may have many cards stacked against you and may do decidedly worse than many other people. Too bad! Most unfortunate! Abysmally unfair! But if you really do have inferior characteristics or are looked down upon for what your social group wrongly defines as "inferiorities," *you* still do not have to see yourself as a bad person and deem yourself unworthy of joy.

The more you accept yourself unconditionally—because you *choose* to remain alive and to strive for happiness, and for no other reasons—the less you will have to cover up your "inadequacy" with compensatory anger. This does not mean that you cannot rightly fight against social injustice or act as a rebel *with* a cause. You can! But try to do so because you want to right wrongs and better your own life—and not to prove your "strength" or "manliness" or "nobility." Who needs that kind of self-justification? Answer: people who first foolishly put themselves down.

Familiarity and ritualistic behavior

Peter Marler, in studying the behavior of animals and humans, observed that "perhaps the most subtle and difficult to understand, and yet perhaps ultimately the most important, factor in reducing the probability of aggression is familiarity." He notes that strangeness seems to stimulate conflict and fighting, while living together leads to more peaceful coexistence. He feels that some animals have the involved ritual of prancing and preening before one another in order to gain familiarity.

Konrad Lorenz notes that the promotion of personal friendships between members of different groups and nations often goes a long way toward reducing hostility. Yehuda Amir, in reviewing the literature on contact in ethnic relations, observes that "there is increasing evidence . . . to support the view that contact between members of ethnic groups tends to produce change in attitude between these two groups" and that prejudice is minimized as this kind of social contact and mutual acceptance increases. Morton Deutsch indicates that cooperative and friendly contact will likely lead to conflict resolution because it encourages the recognition of the legitimacy of each person's interests and of the desirability of searching for a solution responsive to the wishes of both sides. It also leads to a trusting attitude that increases sensitivity to common interests, while minimizing the importance of differences that may lead to hostility.

You can sometimes reduce anger between yourself and others by making yourself more thoroughly familiar with them, and they with you. The more acquainted you become with strangers, the less danger you will tend to feel from them—and the less they will tend to feel from you. This does not necessarily relate to close ties, since when you have a close friend, mate, or relative, you sometimes make yourself more angry and violent at him than you would feel toward others, because you irrationally *demand* considerate treatment from this person while you merely *prefer* it from others. As Marvin Wolfgang and several other students of crime have reported, homicides and serious assaults generally occur among people who have a fairly close relationship with each other. But if you will teach yourself to expect your close associates to act humanly and fallibly, your intimacy with them may decrease your angry demandingness.

Fair fighting

In *Creative Aggression* Bach and Goldberg present a nine-step program by which you may engage in a "fair fight" with one of your intimates. As they note, "Fair fighting is not a verbal free-for-all but a controlled technique for assertive communication." It largely consists of formally requesting your opponent for a fight; arranging an open huddle and rehearsal; stating your beef and explaining how it affects you; getting your opponent to state your beefs back to him and making sure that you accurately report back his gripes; asking your partner to change; hearing his view after you carefully repeat it; agreeing on change or on no changes; and discussing, at a future meeting, the success or failure of your and your partner's agreement.

The distinguishing features of fair fighting include: agreeing on a limited kind of fight, listening carefully to your opponent, restating this opponent's views before trying to answer them, agreeing on whether or not you both desire a change, and restating this agreement. Essentially, then, in fair fighting you agree *not* to fight in the usual bellyaching, disruptive manner, but to do so in a civilized way, largely using the listening and restating methods developed by Thomas Gordon and by me and Ted Crawford in our book *Making Intimate Connections*.

This does not mean that fair fighting will solve everything. With some people, it will merely bring out into the open their differences, and they will agree that they will continue or agree to part. But it does, at least implicitly, eliminate the *musts* that lead to anger. For when you agree on fair fights, you agree that you do not *have* to get your way, that you *can* listen carefully to your partner, that you *may* legitimately compromise, and that you *do* feel able to stop your demandingness and to give your partner the right to control his own beliefs and feelings.

In analyzing a fair fight, according to the Bach and Goldberg method, you also look at your and your partner's style of blaming and damning, get some understanding of how each of you resorts to self-defeating rage, and manage to get some insight into your anger-creating philosophies. So even though the technique seems mainly behavioral, it includes antimusturbational elements, and may help you and your partner halt your anger. As Bach and Goldberg note, "Fair fighting is designed to avoid a win-lose approach and provide a procedure that results in a mutually comfortable resolution and learning experience."

Avoidance of drugs and alcohol

Abusers of drugs and alcohol frequently turn up as very angry people, even after they have stopped their use for a number of years. In all probability, part of their drinking and drug abuse stems from their upsettability. Alcoholics, for example, may either drink heavily to control and mask their anger, or only feel able to express their anger when under the influence of liquor. So their hostility tends to drive them to drink.

At the same time, both drugs and alcohol also increase anger in many instances. Sedative drugs, such as marijuana or phenobarbital, may tend to make some people less enraged than they would normally feel. Amphetamines tend to increase irritability and nastiness, and some people act angrily whenever they get high on these kinds of substances. Alcohol also often helps increase low frustration tolerance. Even the *belief* that you have consumed alcohol may result in more aggressive behavior, regardless of the actual alcoholic content of the drinks you may have had—as an experiment by Alan R. Lang, Daniel J. Goeckness, Vincent J. Adesso, and G. Alan Marlatt showed.

If you have any serious problems with hostility, watch what drugs and drinks you take. This doesn't mean that you necessarily have to remain a teetotaler, but monitor your own drug-taking and alcohol-imbibing behavior.

Lack of reinforcement

Aleksandr I. Solzhenitsyn has pointed out that if we keep reinforcing outbursts of violence, letting their perpetrators get away with assaultive behavior, we encourage their perpetuation.

This also tends to hold true for self-angering. If you let yourself get away with outbursts of assaultive behavior, especially if you reinforce yourself by falsely letting yourself "know" how strong and noble you are for letting yourself act violently, you will tend to increase your anger-inciting tendencies. But if you very firmly insist that you'd better stop this kind of nonsense, and definitely penalize yourself every time you indulge in an outburst, you will tend to condition yourself to be less assaultive.

A philosophy of fallibility

I can hardly overemphasize the point that all humans remain incredibly fallible and that this seems our basic nature. Naturally, we can change and do better. But only within limits! We have just about no choice of acting completely fair, just, ethical, right, or proper.

People also sometimes have the ability to accept the fallibility of others and to forgive them for their enormous crimes. An excellent case in point consists of the incident that John M. Gullo and I included in our book *Murder and Assassination*. When a young man in the city of Philadelphia sexually attacked and killed a three-and-a-half-year-old girl some years ago, her father, Professor Anatol Hold of the University of Pennsylvania, wrote a remarkable letter to the *Philadelphia Bulletin*, in which he said he hoped that the murderer would be brought to justice, psychologically treated, but *not* made to suffer the death penalty. For as much as he missed and grieved over his dead child, this father wrote, he acknowledged that the slayer was an exceptionally disturbed individual, driven to his deed by enormous feelings of inadequacy and worthlessness, and he could not, in all conscience, desire the death of such a disordered person. Wrote Professor Hold: "My final word has to do with the operation of the machinery of justice. Had I caught the boy in the act, I would have wished to kill him. Now that there is no undoing of what has been done, I only wish to help him. Let no feelings of caveman vengeance influence us. Let us rather help him who did so human a thing."

In a remarkably similar case, Joseph Sturek, a mental health therapy aide at Central Islip State Hospital in New York, felt exceptionally sad when his sixteen-year-old son and several of his friends found Sturek's twelve-year-old daughter, Jennifer, who had been brutally murdered a few days before. But when evidence clearly seemed to show that a fifteen-year-old boy, a neighbor of the Stureks, had committed the murder, Sturek said, "We must forgive the boy. He is very sick. Jennifer would have wanted us to forgive him. . . . The fifteen-year-old's father should have known that there was something wrong, and should have done something about it, perhaps through psychiatry." Sturek added, "I feel so sorry for the boy's parents, because whether they are good or bad, they're going through their own hell now."

Sturek's hinting that the boy's parents might *be* good or bad—rateable as whole persons for some of their traits—is not the REBT view. People may well have good and bad traits—meaning characteristics that help and that harm themselves and others—but we'd better not designate them, holistically, as good or bad people. Obviously, however, Sturek accepted the possibility of forgiving the murderer of his daughter, even though he did not condone his wrong acts.

Can you do anything to aid this kind of compassion in yourself and others? Yes—if you acknowledge your philosophy of revenge and substitute for it that of accepting human fallibility. Also, if you see what harm revenge frequently does to you and others and realize that it mainly confirms your tendencies to carry on rather than to drop unfortunate altercations. Dr. Harry Harlow pointed out that although humans and primates have the innate tendency both to love and to hate, they will tend to feel and behave less angrily in their later life if they have had early experiences that bring out their love and friendliness.

Even though human aggressive tendencies have a strong biological underpinning, that does not mean that they *have* to flower. So try to see that your children or pupils interact more socially with their peers, and you can give them a head start on their unangry behavior. Don't expect miracles in these respects, since strong innate predispositions toward combativeness don't easily disappear. But if we can train "naturally" antagonistic animals, such as dogs and cats, to live together peacefully—which we definitely can—we can also encourage "naturally" antagonistic humans to behave much less assaultively. Why not try?

Michael Efran and J. Allan Cheyne, in commenting on an experiment, note that "the mundane encounters which we all experience each day constitute unpleasant, even stressful, events. The ubiquity of these events may make them more potent contributors to the 'stress of modern life' than has previously been assumed." You could try to reduce the number of ordinary social encounters of a "stressful" nature that you experience on a day-to-day basis. This solution, however, has its distinct limitations since it involves social withdrawal. You reduce stress but possibly also reduce many socially satisfying experiences.

A better solution involves changing your attitude *toward* social stress. If you work on yourself so that you do not *have to* do well in social encounters and do not find social frustrations *too hard*, you can make yourself more accepting (though not necessarily approving) of the unpleasantness of everyday living. You may thereby react less angrily when common social stresses occur.

Countering abuse of children and subordinates

We have given increasing attention in recent years to the abuse of children, to parents and other caretakers who strictly discipline their offspring and physically abuse them and even beat them to death. Studies made of such parents, including one of the cases that John M. Gullo and I presented in *Murder and Assassination*, show that they frequently have great frustrations and feelings of inadequacy in their own lives and that they sometimes take these out on their young victims. As Linda Charlton has noted, "Above all, there is the abuse that is the product of stress, of parents striking at children because of unbearable pressure."

While we rightfully dramatize incidents of child abuse, we fail to observe the frequent ill treatment of adults. Professors, for example, can unfairly treat college and graduate students. Bosses, union officials, supervisors, and police and military officers can abuse their subordinates. Public inspectors and other officials can tyrannize those over whom they have some power. Mates who know that their partners neurotically need them can act as little Hitlers over such partners. Physically or intellectually strong adolescents often savagely abuse those they find weaker or less capable.

The main causes of this almost ubiquitous phenomenon of the "strong" victimizing their less powerful subordinates? Again, feelings of great inferiority on the part of the former, which they avoid facing or compensate for by hopping on the backs of those they can command. Again, continual stresses and frustrations experienced by the victimizers may make them more than willing to seek out enjoyable combative or abusive pursuits.

Dealing with counteraggression

When someone deals with you angrily or seems angrily to make unreasonable demands of you, counteraggression commonly arises. The history of humanity shows that it leads to innumerable arguments, feuds, and even national and international wars. *Let us list some rules that you can use to put a stop to your own counteraggression:*

Assume that the aggressors have something to their point of view. Yours may have more "rightness" than theirs; but it seems unlikely that they have no good points whatever. Try to look for and give some value to their point of view.

Even if you conclude—rightly or wrongly—that your opponents have no good arguments, assume that they definitely *think* they do. They rarely fight for what they call "right" when they don't believe in it. However deluded, they just about always believe in their point of view. Acknowledge to yourself that they do believe in it. Often use a creative listening attitude, such as Ted Crawford's technique, Resolving Discussion Sequence (RDS). You may *think* you really know the other's outlook, but to make sure that you do and to show her that you really *want* to see the other side of the argument, repeat back to an aggressor your own interpretation of that person's presentation, and then check with him whether you have heard it correctly. Keep checking and repeating the other's view until it seems almost certain that you have understood it. You can use this procedure with your friends, with your coworkers, with your family members, and even with your pronounced enemies. At least *know* what their opposing views consist of, show them that you do know, and don't try to argue them out of a conviction that they really don't hold.

More details of Ted Crawford's technique of combating anger can be found in his and my book, *Making Intimate Connections: Seven Guidelines for Great Relationships and Better Communication.*

Sometimes use REBT methods with your opponents. If a male friend, for example, severely castigates you for your lateness when you are sure you came to an appointment on time, you can say something like: "Well, naturally, I don't see it just the way that you do. But let's assume you acted rightly and I behaved wrongly. I knew, let us say, that we made the appointment for nine, and I deliberately or carelessly came at ten, really inconveniencing you. Okay. In that case, I behaved badly. But even so, why do you have to upset yourself about my poor behavior and make yourself incensed at me? If I do wrong, I do wrong, and I certainly have a problem. But don't keep telling yourself, 'He *shouldn't* come late! He has *no right* to make a mistake! He is a *total worm* for acting that wormy way!' If so, don't you *also* have a problem? Wouldn't it be good for you to think about your problem of anger and to do a little work on that?" Watch it, for with many angry people this kind of REBT argument may well backfire! But at times it may be useful.

Remember that when someone is angry at you, even most unfairly in your eyes, you don't *have to* show this person the error of his ways and you don't *have to* make a "strong" rebuttal. Usually, you will *want to* present your own view and present your argument. But don't think you have to. Real strength often consists of your letting your opponent "win" the argument, in spite of the unfairness of this outcome, and then going on to more constructive things. Your goal had better not be showing your opponent, and the world at large, your correctness. Let it, instead, be your trying to get more of what you want and less of what you don't want out of life. Letting others, at least temporarily, "win" arguments with you may lead to the fulfillment of *this* kind of goal.

Beware of vindictiveness! When you have lost an argument or

been assaulted, don't focus on getting even with your opponents at all costs. Revenge keeps you emotionally involved with your opponents practically forever, consumes enormous amounts of time and energy, distracts you from more constructive goals, gives you a needless pain in your own gut, encourages counterrevenge and prolonged feuds, rarely convinces your opponents that they are wrong, makes them feel that you are weak, and harms innocent bystanders. Revenge and vindictiveness may help you have a less boring life. But at what a cost!

You do not have to incense yourself when your opponents seem to have overweening demands. If you *look* carefully at these demands, you will usually see their more reasonable aspects. For one thing, your opponents may have deliberately overstated their demands, knowing that you would not accede, but hoping for a more reasonable compromise. For another, they may have little knowledge of your attitudes and your wishes. Or they may not see the impracticality of what they keep asking. Just because they have an emotional stake in their requests and frequently feel that they simply *have to* achieve them, they may not easily see the consequences of what they demand and may even defeat themselves by some of the things they put in their ultimatums.

In dealing with the "demands" and the "unnegotiable" requests of some of the student protest groups at the University of Illinois, David D. Henry, president of the university, discovered that their terms often did not carry the harshness of their surface meaning. "While the word 'demand' normally offends me," Henry said to reporters, "I translate it to mean 'proposal.'" He then felt much better able to cope with these "demands" and to negotiate "unnegotiable" requests of the students.

If, similarly, you really try to see your opponent's point of view, the negotiability of his "demands" on you, and the possibility of your reaching out to him without hostility, you will tend to act much less angrily toward the demander—and probably encourage him to be less aggressive toward you. Remember that just as almost all of us seem to have probably innate tendencies to fight vehemently against people's "demands," so do we have natural tendencies to fight less and to compromise more when we see that other people give our "demands" due consideration. While, on the one hand, we natively tend to fight, we also natively tend to compromise. So give your opponents' compromising proclivities a more-than-even chance to assert themselves!

Nonviolence as a philosophy

Violence as a philosophy has tended to rule the human race. Only in a few notable cases has nonviolence risen as a planned, practical method of getting your way without open warfare between you and your opponents. Gandhi's prolonged fight to get the British to abdicate as the political ruler of India represents one such case; and although the nonviolent approach might well *not* work with certain other kinds of opponents than Gandhi had—with, for example, the Nazis—recognize that it has great advantages.

As Christopher Lasch points out, the Indian doctrine of nonviolence, or *Satyagraha*, assumes decency is latent in all people: "To decide in advance that certain adversaries are incapable of decency is therefore to accuse them of inhumanity and to fall into precisely that arrogant moralizing from which Satyagraha proposes to deliver us in the first place."

Erik Erikson has nicely portrayed Gandhi's nonviolent approach. He points out that Gandhi's truth consists of the acceptance of the idea that violence against your adversary really amounts to the same thing as violence against yourself. Martin Luther King subscribed to this same truth: "For practical as well as moral reasons, nonviolence offers the only road to freedom for my people. In violent warfare, one must be prepared to face ruthlessly the fact that there will be casualties by the thousands."

Barbara Deming also indicates the practical, hardheaded results of the difficult path of nonviolence:

> [When noncooperation] is nonviolent, I believe it is immensely more powerful in the long run, because one has, as it

> were, two hands on the adversary; with one hand, one shakes up his life drastically—makes it impossible for him simply to continue as he *has been;* with the other hand we calm him, we control his response to us, because we respect his rights as well as ours, his real, his human rights, because we assure him that it is not his destruction we want, merely justice.

In your own life, you do not have to practice passive resistance or complete nonviolence against any opponents. But you can, if you wish, show your subordinates, your peers, and your supervisors that you firmly believe in nonviolence and that although you may sometimes or often resist doing what they want you to do, you will do so in a physically unassaultive manner.

Personally, I don't advocate taking this view to extremes. If a thug attacks me and I feel convinced that he would most probably harm me physically, I think that I would choose either (1) to run like hell or (2) to unangrily return his assault to protect myself.

Joan Baez notes in her nonviolent way: "If all recourse to violence is taken away, you're forced to really use your mind to search for alternatives. And you're forced to acknowledge—and this is what *I* mean by revolution—that no man has the right to do injury to another person or to be an accomplice in the doing of injury. This means you have to recognize that everybody is equal and there's no such thing as an enemy."

When questioned by Nat Hentoff, "Wouldn't you have considered Adolf Hitler an enemy?" she replied:

> No, he was a human being, too. But recognizing his humanity didn't mean that you had to like him and it certainly didn't mean you had to carry out his orders. In a civilized society, people wouldn't have followed him. They would have seen that he was a wreck, a very sick man; and seeing that, they would have gotten him some help. The term *enemy* just gets in the way of understanding that we are all human beings. Admittedly, it takes an awful lot of unbrainwashing to come to that point. To be this kind of revolutionary requires the right-

winger to throw away his flag and the left-winger to forget all those posters about power coming out of the barrel of a gun.

I agree with Joan Baez. To live without designating those who seriously disagree with you as "enemies" means to take an unusually revolutionary point of view. But if you can work on yourself to adopt this view, you will make yourself much less hostile—yet, as she indicates, by no means a nonactivist.

Some empirical confirmation of this point of view comes from the experiments of Harry Kaufmann and Seymour Feshbach. They found that disruptive behaviors were substantially reduced by prior exposure to constructive but not to punitive communication.

This would tend to show that if you deal with the Hitlers of the world in a nondamning, constructive manner, you may actually help them modify their behavior more than if you view them in a castigating, hostile way.

You can, if you wish, adopt a philosophy of nonviolence. You can sanely do so not only to decrease your own feelings of hostility, but also to set a fine human example for others to follow.

Recognizing the irony of hatred

Hatred can consume you more than almost any other feeling and, like jealousy and a few other passions, can literally obsess you and run your life. It usually goes far beyond your feelings of frustration and brings with it an illusion of self-interest. On the surface, you seem absorbed in getting what you want and removing what you don't want. But what an illusion!

Your feelings of anxiety—spurred by the Irrational Belief that "I must do well and win others' approval and would find it *horrible* if I didn't!"—make you other-directed rather than self-directed. But your feelings of hatred produce a similar result. You can make yourself so horrified about people who treat you unfairly that you thereby make *them* the center of your attention and normally lose yourself in the process. You *seem* to want greater satisfaction for your own life, but you really obsess about changing *them*, doing *them* in, gloating over injuring *them*.

If you will make yourself realize how other-directed this kind of behavior is, you can see how you defeat yourself by hating, while deluding yourself that your hatred helps. You can then go back to your main interest: "What, in view of the disadvantages of their treatment of me, can *I* do to make *my* life happier?" As Ken Olsen notes, "Hate is a means by which we punish and destroy ourselves for the actions of others." How ironic! See that you sink this irony into your brain many times—until you replace most of your hostility with self-interest and with unconditional other-acceptance (UOA).

Let us go back to still more ways of overcoming your feeling and acting angrily.

Humanistic values

If you see yourself as an integral part of the human race, if you see that all humans have a right to live and achieve happiness merely because they exist, and if you see that your own right to live and enjoy will most likely be enhanced if you act humanely to others, you will tend to feel much less angry against others even when they treat you shabbily. That does not mean that you have to go far out of your way to help or to sacrifice yourself for others. But it does mean that the more humanistic you are, the less cruelly you will tend to treat others.

To acquire a more humanistic philosophy, try to remember that you and others abhor mistreatment; that concern for others tends to foster conditions you would like; and that just as you can, alas, enjoy hurting others, you can also enjoy helping them. Without being a Florence Nightingale or St. Francis, you can find real satisfaction in trying to make the world a better place in which to live.

Bernard J. Siegel points out that some tribal groups (such as the Taos American Indians) and international groups (such as the Jews) form "defensive groups," which make a conscious attempt to instill peaceful values "by requiring constant exercise of control over behavior potentially destructive to the group in relation to external threats." Such groups maintain inner peace in order to mobilize themselves more effectively to survive in a hostile world.

Focusing on the pain of the victim

When angry, we tend to enjoy our own emotional outburst and to assume that somehow the victim of our anger will ultimately benefit from our fury. Nothing of the sort may occur! Some individuals may take our rage badly, may feel acute emotional pain, and may internalize our criticism and feel affected by it forever. Don't delude yourself into thinking that your victims only benefit from your hostility. Vividly imagine the negative results of your anger, and use these to inhibit your further expressions.

Don't, of course, go to the other irrational extreme and down yourself for displaying anger. However mistaken and "rotten" your deed, you don't become a *rotten person* for performing it. But your anger does have consequences—and, often, very inhumane consequences to others who are really vulnerable. Keep their vulnerability in mind; try to see that even if their angry acts harm you, they do not really "deserve" to keep suffering because of your rage. Try to realize that their suffering will not necessarily eliminate their assaultive behavior.

Focusing on relating to others

An obvious advantage of your making yourself unangry at others includes your getting along better with them when they are not bothersome. Amazingly, however, you easily tend to forget this—and you concentrate on other goals, many of them mistaken. As a parent, for example, you focus on teaching your children to do the right thing and insist that they *have to do* this. Consequently, when they do the wrong thing, you incense yourself at them—and scream that they'd better change. Result: You have poor relations with them even when they are behaving "properly."

Haim Ginott notes the case of a boy of seven who broke a toy gun and, frightened by his own ineptness, hid the gun. In finding parts of the gun, the father tried to get him to say where he had put the rest of it, and the boy replied that he didn't know. The father said, "You broke the gun! If there's one thing I hate, it's a liar!" And he gave the boy a good spanking. But as Dr. Ginott notes:

Instead of playing detective and prosecutor, the father would have been more helpful to his son by saying:

"I see your new gun is broken.
"It didn't last long.
"It's a pity. It was expensive."

The child might have learned some valuable lesson:

"Father understands. I can tell him my troubles. I must take better care of my gifts."

So remind yourself: "If I make myself angry and express my anger to others, I will usually antagonize them and encourage them to keep acting badly. If I accept them with their poor behavior and do not demand that they stop behaving that way, I will get along better with them and also frequently be a more effective teacher of good conduct. The less angry I feel and act, the more effective a teacher of the 'right way' I shall probably be."

Discriminate the constructive aspects of anger

Anger, as many authorities have pointed out, has its constructive aspects. Without feeling some degree of irritation, frustration, and annoyance, we would hardly reduce others' obnoxious behavior and human progress might stop. H. H. Wolff has pointed out that we can act against others "constructively in many fields, including self-preservation, and defense of basic physical needs, sexual conquest and experience, as well as for other predominantly psychological purposes such as competition, the defense of one's rights as an individual or those of one's family or the group one belongs to, the struggle for the development of one's identity, the maintenance of value systems and ideals and especially for creative purposes of all kinds."

Paula Heimann and Arthur Valenstein also note that "normally every child has a thrust toward activity, toward asserting himself and toward mastery; it need not necessarily become an overweening urge toward destructiveness, which in itself suggests a possible neurotic quality."

Albert Rothenberg separates anger from hostility and notes that anger has strong communication aspects for humans and, therefore, great constructive potential despite its dangers and its frequent tie to feelings of anxiety. If we can rid ourselves of the anxiety, Rothenberg hypothesizes, we can constructively use our feelings of anger.

Albert E. Trieschman shows that children often use temper tantrums as a problem-solving device since they cannot easily devise better means of coping with a crisis. The wild threats and insults of these children "represent a primitive effort to feel some sense of competence."

Usually, when you feel angry, you very much want to get your own way, to remove unpleasant stimuli, to control others, and to preserve your own physical and emotional health. Good! Why shouldn't you want what you want and try to decrease what you don't like? At the same time, you would do well to recognize fully that most *other* humans want exactly what you do—their *own* way. They have just as much a right to their preferences as you have to yours. Obviously both you and they frequently cannot get what you want—especially when your and their desires are incompatible.

If you give yourself the full right to want and give others a similar right and if you don't demand that they *have to* acknowledge your right, you can better accept the constructive while minimizing the self-defeating aspects of your ardent wishes.

Cooperative outlook

REBT does not hold that competition is always evil and that you should at all costs avoid it. On the contrary, it assumes that as a human you will often try to get what you want, to acquire more than others acquire, and to obtain things at others' expense.

Although we usually think of competition in professional and business affairs, it also applies to gaining someone else's approval for love. You want to establish an intimate relationship with someone and another person wants to have an intimate relationship with him as well. The person you choose only is monogamously inclined, so either you or your competitor will lose out. Shall you withdraw from competition? Angrily fight for the single "prize"? Obsessively plot and scheme to win the competition? What?

The usual REBT answer: Try, as strongly as you can, to win the competition, but don't insist that you *must* win it or you will be a total loser. And don't see your competition as a complete villain. Feel fairly determined—but not absolutely insistent—on gaining what you want. At the same time, consider the advantage of a more cooperative outlook. Sometimes both you and your opponent can "win"— though neither of you completely. You may even find it enjoyable to help that opponent achieve partial satisfaction. The goal you seek—whether another's love, money, professional success, or what you will—need not constitute your *only* preference. Sharing with another; cooperatively planning so that both of you may partially gain what you want; feeling friendly toward your opponents—you may also choose these goals.

Competition, remember, may include both short-range and long-range disadvantages and losses. It takes time and effort. It encourages enmity from others. It overemphasizes winning. It has distinct social consequences for third parties. In a wider social context, extreme competition can lead to international conflict and war.

The more you train yourself to *want* but not to *need* monogamous bonding and the more you accept the virtues of cooperating with many individuals in your community rather than a small selected group of family members, the less competitive and hostile you may become.

You may not, of course, crave the satisfactions of cooperativeness over competitiveness and may therefore not work for them. But you do have at least two viable options here, and the mere fact that you naturally and as a result of your upbringing have tended to favor one of them—competition—doesn't mean that you have to favor it exclusively.

Diversionary methods of overcoming anger

REBT views hostility as mainly stemming from your thoughts, ideas, beliefs, and philosophies, and it therefore tries to help you *change* them. However, it also realizes that you can temporarily shunt aside or divert yourself from your own upsetting beliefs by a variety of methods, such as relaxation, meditation, games, attachments, physical exercises, and a host of other pleasure-seeking distractions. Even anger itself, as several writers have shown, can divert you from certain other forms of hostility, as when the people of one community incense themselves at the people of another group and thereby are less hostile toward members of their own group.

Some diversionary pastimes can also help you remove, and not merely sidetrack or palliate, your anger. If you feel unassertive, and hate yourself for your unassertiveness, you can play games like chess or football or sell others on your political ideas to overcome your unassertiveness. You thereby rid yourself of much of your "reason" for self-downing. This isn't an elegant cure since you can also choose to remain unassertive, continue to down yourself, and finally wind up feeling angry at others who "suppress" you. Not so good!

Hans Toch, who has particularly studied violent individuals who cover up their self-deprecation with angering themselves against others, notes that diversionary activity may sometimes help in cases like these:

> It might be possible to offer such an individual the alternative of joining extracurricularly an activity or club involving contemporaries who have shown themselves similarly troublesome. In this setting, group discussions of violence could occur, violence-related games could be played, skits or plays could be produced, and behavior patterns could be generated that could meet the boy's requirements for self-affirmation, without its destructive consequences.

If you feel prone to hostility and violence, you may consider the possibilities of diverting your angry urges in these more constructive ways. You can sometimes arrange for limited or playacting forms of competition that will give you some satisfaction and self-expression and thereby more easily refrain from more global forms of violence that will "satisfy" you at the expense of other values and lead to certain dangers. Again, diversions of this kind will probably not completely solve your problems of hostility. But in some respects they may help.

Antidepressive methods

The psychological literature may exaggerate the extent to which anger may cover up depression and depression may cover up anger. These kinds of cover-ups do at times occur, but not all anger consists of depression turned outward, nor does all depression consist of anger turned inward. Nonetheless, at times you may anger yourself for taking on a self-pitying (depressed) attitude, and you may then go on to lash out at others who presumably have "caused" the "horrible" events that you think you can't stand.

You can deal with the depressed feelings that underlie your feelings of anger by using Rational Emotive Behavior Therapy. First determine the Activating Event or Adversity that precedes your depressed mood. Generally, you will have failed at something or been rejected by someone whose approval you want to achieve. But feelings of failure and rejection do not in themselves lead to depression. In addition, you probably would be downing yourself for failing. Then you might angrily put others down for rejecting you.

In the REBT formulation you would have, at B, told yourself a set of sensible or Rational Beliefs (RBs), such as "I don't like failing. I wish that I had succeeded and been accepted by this person. How unfortunate for me to fail and get rejected!" These Rational Beliefs would lead you to feeling sorry, sad, and frustrated about what happened to you at point A.

At point IB, however, your set of Irrational Beliefs would tend to take over: "How awful for me to fail and get rejected. I'll never really get what I want! This shows that I am a *rotten* person! How hopeless! I'll go on forever, never really getting what I most desire!"

At this point, you will begin to feel the undesirable Emotional

Consequence (C)—your depression. Which you would then Dispute (D) with the usual Rational Emotive Behavioral questioning: "Why is it *awful* for me to fail and be rejected? What evidence exists that I'll never get what I want? Even if I continue failing and being rejected, how does that make me a *rotten person* who will hopelessly go on forever, never getting what I most desire?"

The cognitive Effect (E) of your Disputing would be along these lines: "Nothing makes it *awful* for me to fail and be rejected. Only inconvenience and annoyance result. Just because I fail *now* hardly means that I have to keep doing so *in the future*. In fact, the more I try, the more I'll most probably succeed. But even if I never get exactly what I want and keep getting many rejections, it will prove, at the worst, that my behavior is bad, not at all that I am a totally rotten human."

If you keep doing your ABCDEs in this manner, you will most likely wind up feeling sorry, concerned, frustrated, and displeased, but not depressed; you will have no particular incentive to rationalize away or otherwise cover up your depression with raging at others. Since you won't, in your own eyes, feel like a no-goodnik for failing and getting rejected, you may not anger yourself at people who reject you.

In order for you to decrease your disturbability, I cannot too strongly emphasize overcoming your feelings of self-downing, vulnerability, and inadequacy, since these arise so frequently and intensely. And they have pronounced relationships with anger. If you use your temper flare-ups as indicating that you probably have a general negative attitude toward yourself and others and if you acknowledge that you have *chosen* this way of life, you will increase your ability to reevaluate your choices and to change them.

In the REBT framework, feelings of inadequacy largely stem from convincing yourself, at point B, that you have some weakness, inferiority, or inadequacy at point A, and that this is *awful* and you have to down yourself as a person for having it. To reduce your self-downing you'd better convince yourself that you may well have some failing but that you cannot legitimately rate yourself as a rotten person for having it. Failing is unfortunate, but you have the ability to live reasonably happily in spite of this misfortune. Using REBT in this fashion, you can surmount your feelings of self-deprecation and undermine the angry emotions to which they may easily lead.

Training courses and workshops

You can learn how to deal with others, including your intimates, more effectively by taking suitable training courses and workshops. Many individuals and organizations now give fight training courses. These have their value, when presented by effective leaders, but they also have their limitations. They may help you feel and act more angrily, under the guise of having you assert yourself. Assertiveness training along rational and behavioral lines is more helpful, usually, than any course or workshop that includes the word *fight* in its title.

Human relations courses, such as those pioneered by Norman Kagan, can also help you considerably with your social skills and thereby decrease your tendency to interact combatively with others. Child management procedures, such as those outlined by W. Becker, Don Dinkmeyer, and Thomas Gordon, also show you how to relate more effectively to your children. They have, as well, abuse prevention potential. Some organizations, such as the Albert Ellis Institute in New York and other American and foreign cities, teach people how to relate more other-acceptingly and less angrily. Look for these kinds of seminars and workshops. But again: Watch out for "growth centers" that specialize in psychomotor, bioenergetic, primal, and Reichian methods of "creative expression"—they will sometimes teach you have to augment your "assertiveness" in a highly angry way.

If you find that courses and workshops, as well as the other techniques suggested in this book, don't help you prevent your self-defeating rages, you might well consider intensive individual or group therapy. Rational Emotive Behavior Therapy, Cognitive Behavior Therapy, Adlerian therapy—therapies such as these that include a highly cognitive element and that help you understand and significantly change your basic philosophic assumptions that create anger (and other disturbed feelings) may help considerably.

As you can see by the large number of cognitive, emotive, and behavioral methods that can be used to interrupt and reduce angry feelings and actions—as indicated in this chapter and other chapters of this book—you have a wide choice of techniques to reduce your own. *Choice* is the word for REBT and other cognitive-behavioral therapies, as shown in my book, *Overcoming Destructive Beliefs, Feelings, and Behaviors.*

A multimodal approach to your dealing with dysfunctional rage is espoused by practically all clinicians and researchers who have tackled anger problems in recent years. You can find details of their recommendations in the references at the end of this book, including publications by Jerry Deffenbacher, Raymond DiGiuseppe, Christopher Eckhardt, Howard Kassinove, His Holiness the Dalai Lama, Raymond Chip Tafrate, and Leonore Walker.

13

Accepting Yourself With Your Anger

Hopefully this book has so far clearly shown you how to reduce your anger and other unhealthy feelings. Because you remain a fallible human, however, you will in all probability find yourself slipping back, from time to time, into self-defeating attitudes. So we'd better look at how you can best deal with yourself and others when that happens.

Let us say that with some skill and success you have practiced the various techniques introduced in this book. Yet just the other day your boss acted so nasty and stupid toward you that you felt like really letting him have it. Fortunately he had to leave the office before you had a chance to blow up in his presence, but even after he had gone, you took more than an hour to cool down. Now let's see how you could have dealt with your anger better under those conditions.

First—importantly—you can acknowledge fully to yourself that you had enraged feelings against your boss rather than denying them or rationalizing them away; and you can fully acknowledge that *you* brought them on. You made yourself angry—your boss didn't. And you mistakenly did so. You rightly felt annoyed and irritated at your boss's presumably nasty behavior. Why should you like it when it went against your own desires and interests? But you then angered yourself about his nastiness. You could have chosen not to do so and only made yourself sorry and disappointed with your behavior.

Second, and perhaps even more important, you can accept yourself *with* your raging feelings. You can acknowledge the wrongness of your feelings, but not the badness of you. Humans not only act bad, but see that they do, and they frequently take their bad behavior and make it into a new Activating Experience and then belabor themselves mightily for acting that way. As a fallible human person you have a right to be wrong, to make yourself unhealthily angry. You aren't a louse or a worm for doing so. You only are a person who has acted stupidly—not a stupid *person*.

Say to yourself something like, "I really behaved self-defeatingly in incensing myself at my boss, but I can easily do so and have a right, as a human, to act that way. My behavior is wrong, but I can't legitimately see myself as a really rotten person." In other words, accept yourself while *not* accepting your behavior. Fully acknowledge its mistakenness: that it most likely brings you more harm than good. Review your anger and see why it does you harm. It gives you a "pain in the gut"; it doesn't help you solve your problem with your boss; it easily may communicate itself to him and make your relationship much worse; it may lead to poor physical reactions on your part (high blood pressure and more); it makes you preoccupied with your boss and his apparent irrationality, instead of focusing on how to do your job better and please him more; and it sabotages your efficiency in many ways. If you feel determined to accept you, your humanity, in spite of your anger, you can fully acknowledge it as self-sabotaging, whereas if you insist on downing you, your totality, for your anger, then you will tend to deny, repress, and excuse your anger. And you will find yourself dealing unsatisfactorily with it. Look at it as bad but correctable!

Review what you mistakenly told yourself to make yourself angry. Resolve to tell yourself something different in the future—and practice doing so in your head. Perhaps you'll see that you *demanded* that your boss act nicely and that when he didn't fulfill this demand, you told yourself, "How *awful!* He has no right to act that way! I *can't stand* his stupidity! I hope he drops dead!"

Now you ask yourself—at D for Disputing—why is it *awful* for your boss to act nasty? Why has he no right to act that way? Where is it written that you really *can't stand* his stupidity? Is he really a total villain who should drop dead to please you?

You might answer thus: "Nothing makes it *awful* for my boss to act nastily. It's only annoying and inconvenient! He does have the right to act any way that he acts. Even though he acts wrong and I don't like this behavior, I *can definitely stand* his stupidity. I certainly am not a villain when I displease him. So he isn't either!"

Note that by approaching the situation with the ABCDEs of REBT, you have not chosen to feel irresponsible about your fury at your boss, thereby encouraging future fury. You have honestly acknowledged your anger—but realized *its* wrongness. You have made an attempt to understand what you did to make yourself angry and what you can do in the future to reduce making yourself enraged again. That is the main point. You can live most successfully with your anger by *understanding* it; by realistically seeing that humans easily and naturally make themselves angry, just as they easily and naturally overeat and avoid going to the dentist; *by accepting* yourself for creating it; and *by showing yourself how to Dispute it.*

Israel Charny states, "The key to the psychotherapist's contributions, I believe, is that he teaches an awareness and acceptance of the universality of *angry feelings* and inner wishes to destroy another human being, but that *overt acts* of such violence at another's person are never to be condoned except in clear self-defense against physical attacks." I agree. Then Charny goes on: "However, to feel like hitting is not wrong. Even to feel like killing is human." I agree that to feel like hitting your boss or killing him when he acts bad is a human, natural emotion. But I still think it is wrong since your feeling goes with the overgeneralization that he has no right to act that way and deserves to be assaulted for acting that way. He does have the right. No matter how human your anger, you'd better acknowledge it as mistaken while still fully accepting you, yourself, with this destructive behavior!

You can follow certain practical procedures that will help let off steam relatively harmlessly and also, perhaps, help those at whom you feel angry to reconsider their own behavior and perhaps modify it. For example:

Try to assert yourself to the people at whom you feel angry in I-statements rather than in you-statements. If you hate your boss for making you work overtime and not compensating you, don't say to him, "You are unfair for making me work overtime! I don't understand how you can do that!" Such a statement distinctly accuses the other of rotten behavior and assumes that because he is responsible for that behavior he therefore *absolutely must not* perform it.

Instead, you can give the same message in this kind of I-statement: "I feel that you are asking me to work overtime without additional compensation, and I don't like that. I wonder whether this is fair. But assuming that from my point of view it is unfair, I wonder how you see it from your point of view." This kind of I-statement shows your feelings and shows that you think his action wrong, but it does so open-mindedly and diplomatically. It reveals your displeasure, but not your immense anger—even if you happen to feel angry while stating it.

When you are enraged at people whom you think have acted bad and don't admit it, try to speak authoritatively rather than authoritarianly. If, for example, you have an employee who keeps coming in late, you don't have to say, "How can you do that all the time? You know goddamned well that we don't tolerate any lateness here!" You can say, instead, "I don't know whether anyone pointed it out to you clearly when you joined this firm, but we have a very strict policy about lateness. Anyone who comes in even a few minutes late several times gets talked to by his supervisor and strictly penalized if he does not thereafter start coming in on time. The company has had this rule for a long time and finds it advisable to stick to it; I therefore have called you in to talk about the problem of your lateness."

Or if you notice that someone in your class keeps asking to borrow your homework in order to copy it and you feel angry about this, you can say something like: "Maybe you don't agree with this homework rule and think it silly. But I have personally found that I really don't understand what goes on in class unless I regularly do my homework. It seems to be that the only real way to learn this subject is to practice it on your own. So I feel that lending you my homework to copy won't really do you much good and that you'd do yourself a disservice by copying it. Therefore, I don't think I will lend it to you." This kind of response seems much better than your authoritarianly telling the attempted borrower, "Look, dear! One just does not borrow homework to copy in this class. That won't do at all!"

Usually you will get along much better in life if, when someone puts you down and you feel angry about it, you refrain from following suit and putting her down. A revengeful retort will often make you feel better—but not get better. It will tend to make you feel more angry, and you will win the other's enmity. So your best retort frequently consists of seeming to agree with the put-down; ignoring it; agreeing with it in part; or showing the other person that you do not take it too seriously, do not agree with it.

If an acquaintance of yours, for example, laughs at you for dressing in a certain manner, you can make these kinds of retorts: (1) "Yes, my jacket does seem on the loud side"; (2) "I see that you really don't like the way I dress"; (3) "I guess my jacket does seem on the loud side, but I find it exciting and attractive"; (4) "I can see what you mean and that others might agree with you, but I don't consider things like this that important"; (5) "Apparently we just don't agree on what constitutes loudness"; (6) "You may think it loud, but almost everyone seems to wear this kind of color these days, and you therefore may be in a minority."

With these kinds of retorts, you hold your ground but do not display hostility toward and put down others. Even when you feel angry as you respond in this way, your responses tend to calm down and make you feel less irate. You never lose integrity by acting this way, for even if your "put-downer" thinks that you act weakly, that remains his problem, and you need never feel put down.

As Herbert Fensterheim and Jean Baer rightly point out, this does not mean that you had better give an apologetic or self-downing retort when someone puts you down and you feel angry. If someone criticizes your taste in a jacket, you do not, in order to avoid a confrontation, have to reply, "Yes, I guess people do think less of me when I wear loud colors like this," or, "Oh, I thought everyone was wearing this color this year, and that led me to buy this jacket." Acting weakly frequently encourages the other person to keep trying to put you down further and sets a bad example for still others, who may similarly try to take advantage of you. As I have stated in *How to Live With a "Neurotic,"* I normally advocate an attitude of firm kindness. Not unfirm kindness; not firm unkindness. Simply firm kindness—and the maintaining of your own integrity no matter what others may think of you.

Occasionally you will find it best to retort to put-downs in a sarcastic, mean, or very critical manner, just as you will sometimes, though seldom, find it the better part of valor to fight physically with an opponent rather than to run away. For in certain groups—such as tough street-corner groups—if you don't combatively stand up for yourself and return unkindness in kind, the group members may view you as weak and may plague you practically forever.

Fensterheim and Baer give some good examples of how to respond in such circumstances, including (1) forcing yourself to answer instead of running away from the situation; (2) taking time to think of a good retort; (3) using I-statements instead of you-statements; (4) not asking the other to elaborate on what he finds wrong with you; (5) using some stock phrases, such as "What do you find so damned wrong with my behavior?" or "How come you seem so critical today?" However, I still would say: Make this the exception rather than the rule, even when others have clearly tried to down you and you feel angry about this.

Don't think perfectionistically about your dealing with your own anger and replying to people when you are angry at them. Inevitably, you will at times retort badly and weakly, or you will make yourself so incensed that you will reply to them in an extremely bottled-up or chokingly furious manner. So you will! It would be lovely if you always handled yourself beautifully when angry and did not act like a horse's ass. But you surely *will* act that way at times.

If so, learn to accept yourself with your weakness—as well as with your anger. Your stupidity merely shows your humanity. (Leonardo da Vinci, Isaac Newton, and Albert Einstein sometimes acted idiotically. And so will you.)

Acknowledge your ability to change and to act less angrily. You will never achieve perfect lack of hostility, but you can make yourself less frequently furious. Try, and don't give up too easily. Give yourself practice at talking yourself out of your rage, and try, at the same time, to talk some of your close friends and associates out of their rage. If you can show some of them how to feel much less hostile, you will then practice how to calm yourself down.

When you do feel angry, try to acknowledge this to both yourself and others. Not always, of course! If you feel very angry at your school principal or at one of your students, perhaps you'd better pretend that you don't. But with your friends and associates—with whom you can be fairly honest—by all means be honest. Admit to them how angry you feel—and also to yourself that *you* made yourself angry. By admitting this, you will avoid squelching your anger and keeping it under strong wraps.

If you want to live successfully with your anger, you'd better do some of the same things that you would do if you wanted to lessen it. Rational-emotive-behavioral techniques work in much the same way whether you want to minimize your emotional disturbance or live more happily while you still experience it. You can see this, for example, in Paul A. Hauck's book, *Overcoming Frustration and Anger*, one of the few treatises written on low frustration tolerance and rage. Dr. Hauck gives several good rules for avoiding hostile feelings and actions, but you can successfully use some of them if you want to survive happily while you are still anger-prone.

He points out, for example, that righteous indignation gives you no good excuse to remain angry, for all anger tends to include righteousness: "In fact, anger wouldn't arise in the first place if you didn't think you were completely right in your opinion and that the other person was completely wrong. That even applies to things and nature. When you give your flat tire an angry kick you really are trying to tell the world that that tire had no right to go flat on you, that it has done a mean and dirty trick, and that it deserves a kick for being such a lousy tire."

Recognizing your "righteous indignation" and fully facing its foolishness will help you stop kicking the tire—and also help you angrily kick it while humorously acknowledging your own anger and accepting it as part of your fallible all-too-human condition.

Dr. Hauck shows that when you feel angry, you frequently note real failings of a person and can legitimately make yourself problem-oriented (to remove those failings), instead of blame-oriented (condemning the person or object for having deficiencies). Here he brings out the REBT view that you'd better make yourself problem-centered rather than self-centered about unpleasant happenings, whether caused by you or anyone else. But he goes a little beyond this to point out that when you feel angry, you can make yourself fault-oriented. "If you don't know what's at fault, you can't very well change the trouble. So being fault-oriented is good and not at all the same as blame-oriented."

Your anger can help you see that something has serious faults and that you can try to remove or minimize these faults. In this sense you can constructively use and live with your anger—if you employ it to help you detect your own, and others' deficiencies, and to tackle the problem of doing something to correct these deficiencies.

Along the same lines, Dr. Hauck notes that "the trick is to *forgive everything*, and *forget nothing*." Nicely stated! By forgiving me for promising to share an apartment with you and then reneging on my promise, by accepting me as a human *with* my crummy behavior, you can deal with other incidents of this sort if and when they occur. Again, if you do this, you can live successfully with your feelings of anger by using them to assess my failings, to figure out what to do about them, and to feel less angry and more problem-solving.

Paul Hauck also recommends the diversion technique of counting to ten to help you deal with your anger: "As corny as this may sound, the method nevertheless has merit. It will not of course prevent you from thinking angrily (only challenging the idea that you must have your way can do that). But it will aid you in controlling your anger long enough to prevent you from putting your foot into your mouth and will give you time to collect your thoughts."

Quite so. And similarly, you can use many of the other diversion techniques mentioned in the chapter on behavioral methods to give yourself time to become less angry and also to live more successfully with your feelings of rage. As long as you see that these methods temporarily interrupt but do not really cure your anger, as long as you acknowledge that you still wrongly enrage yourself, and as long as you use diversions to calm yourself so that you can continue to reduce your anger, you can almost happily live with feelings of rage. So count to ten, take a walk, turn on the TV set, or otherwise give yourself a breathing period that interrupts your hostility and gives you time to work against it.

Let me say that just about all the anger-reducing methods outlined in this book can also help you live much better and suffer much less while you still feel enraged. In the course of your wrathful experiences you can recognize that you basically create your own feelings; that you can think and act your way into unangry channels; that you can divert yourself temporarily into less intense pathways; that you can focus on solving your problems with people and things rather than on upsetting yourself about them; and that although rage seems to control you, you have remarkable powers to control and change it. These recognitions will help you live much better, with far less penalizing results, with and without your severe hostile feelings.

You may find behaving in this manner sufficiently satisfying to stop right there. You don't *have to* make yourself unangry almost every time you create your anger. You can accept yourself with your resentful feelings and do yourself a lot of good by this very acceptance. I think you will often find, however, that when you consistently start to reach this stage, when you stubbornly refuse to down yourself when you feel angry, and when you look more at the problem-solving aspects of obnoxious situations and less at their "horrible" unfairness, you will probably want to go on to the next and more elegant step: reducing your anger for a more forgiving, less damning attitude toward the world and the people in it. Not that you have to. But why not try it and see?

14

Postscript: How to Deal With International Terrorism

The first edition of this book was written in 1976 and published in 1977, when international terrorism was rampant but not as serious as today. The events of September 11, 2001, and continuing incidents of world strife have multiplied international raging and the threats to peace. How can you deal with terrorism?

Not very easily! I gave an invited address, "Fanaticism That May Lead to a Holocaust: The Contributions of Scientific Counseling and Psychotherapy," to the American Counseling Association's annual convention in New York in 1985 (published in 1986 in the influential journal of the ACA). Although in 1985 our world was not in imminent danger from fanatical terrorists, my paper highlighted several important ways that it might well soon be at risk: (1) Political governments of the world are unlikely to start nuclear warfare because they are led by responsible leaders who fear reprisals in kind. (2) Small groups of dedicated fanatics may, if they can, start a nuclear conflagration because they are out to prove that they are 100 percent right and that their opponents—the rest of us—are 100 percent wrong. (3) Such groups of fanatics include kamikaze fighters who are certain that they will be rewarded in an afterlife if they kill themselves and others in terrorist attacks. (4) Modern technology, which keeps improving, makes it possible for a few bigots to decimate much greater numbers of the rest of us than was previously possible. (5) Eventually the day will come when a paltry few individuals can use nuclear (and other) weapons to wipe out billions of people and other living creatures. Billions? Yes, billions.

"Is there," I asked in 1985, "any feasible answer to this grave, impending problem?" Yes, I optimistically answered: the worldwide use of scientific counseling and psychotherapy to minimize bigotry, prejudice, grandiosity, and other elements of absolutistic thinking. But I faced the hard fact that effective psychotherapy takes too long and is too expensive to be used with billions of people. I said that "we had better adapt it to educational applications so that virtually all humans from kindergarten onward can be shown what they are doing to endlessly upset and infuriate themselves and are presented with cognitive, emotive, and behavioral techniques they can use to calm themselves to think and act more rationally. Large-scale education—in the schools, in community groups, in religious institutions, and in every mass media format—had better incorporate therapeutic technologies and bring them to the masses. Yes, all the masses." Brave words for 1985!

I had forgotten these specific antiterrorist words when I wrote on September 12, 2001, my monthly response to the Ask Albert Ellis question for our institute's Web site. The terrorist attacks on the World Trade Center and the Pentagon had just occurred. I briefly presented the REBT view on terrorism without consulting my 1985 paper. Here is my Web site response to a current question:

Ask Albert Ellis, September 2001

How would one go about using REBT in order to cope and to help others cope with the tragic events that took place on September 11? I am looking for a proactive way to deal with the brutality of this act, but find that my Irrational Beliefs and *shoulds* are getting in my way.

Dr. Ellis answers:
Your Irrational Beliefs and *shoulds* that get in your way probably include:
1. "I absolutely *must* be able to figure out a way to stop terrorists from acting so brutally and killing and maiming so many people, and there is something very weak and inadequate about me because I can't find a way to stop this kind of terrorism."
2. "The terrorists and their backers have perpetrated some of the worst deeds imaginable; this makes them *completely rotten people* who *should absolutely be exterminated*—quickly—since only killing all of them will stop this deed from happening again."
3. "Because the world is so full of cruel violence and terrorism, it is a totally despicable place and I cannot continue to live in it and be at all happy."

These ideas are irrational because, as Alfred Korzybski noted in *Science and Sanity* in 1933, they are unrealistic and illogical overgeneralizations that render people "unsane." My 1962 book, *Reason and Emotion in Psychotherapy*, showed that all three of these beliefs—and many similar absolutistic *shoulds* and *musts*—lead you (and innumerable other people) to make yourself not only very sad and displeased with the terrorists' abominable behavior, but also to dysfunctionally overwhelm yourself with panic, rage, and depression. Thus, the first of these Irrational Beliefs will cause you to loathe your entire self, or personhood, not to only deplore your weakness and inadequacy to halt terrorism. The second of these Irrational Beliefs will make you thoroughly despise the terrorists (and all other people who do cruel deeds) and consume yourself with rage. The third of these Irrational Beliefs will make you hopelessly depressed about the present and future state of the world and encourage you to obsessively contemplate—and perhaps actually commit—suicide.

Ironically, these three self-defeating *shoulds* and *musts* are probably very similar to those held by the terrorists, who un-sanely killed themselves and thousands of innocent people for what they considered a holy crusade. They first considered themselves powerless because they could not stop America from "cruelly" siding with their enemies; and they therefore felt that they *absolutely had to* punish America to prove that they themselves were powerful and worthwhile individuals. Second, they devoutly believed that Americans *absolutely must not* oppose their position and that *all Americans are complete devils* who deserve to be wiped out. Third, they dogmatically convinced themselves there is no use living in and trying to lead a happy life in such a totally evil world; and therefore, by killing the infidels, they would attain eternal, blissful life. So, with these unsane beliefs, they enthusiastically killed themselves along with countless innocent people.

If you and the rest of America and world citizens keep reinforcing your Irrational Beliefs, you will enrage yourself against the terrorists and their backers and in the process will likely encourage them to increase their fury against Americans and other people who oppose them, and will encourage more retaliation by them, by us again, until the cycle of retaliation precipitates a worldwide war and quite possibly the end of our planet. As ancient lore and modern history have amply shown, love begets love and hatred and violence beget increased hatred and violence—with no end in sight!

You ask how REBT would help you cope with and help others cope with the tragic events of September 11. That requires a long answer, which I can only briefly summarize here.

First, you can use REBT to teach yourself—and all others—*unconditional self-acceptance*. That is, you fully accept yourself with all of your warts and flaws, while heartily disliking and doing your best to change some of your self-defeating behaviors and bad behavior toward others.

Second, you can use REBT to *unconditionally accept all other people* as persons, no matter how bad they act. You can, of course, firmly try to induce them, in a variety of ways, to change their self-sabotaging and immoral thoughts, feelings, and actions.

In Christian terms, you unconditionally accept all *sinners* but not their *sins*. Ultimately some behaviors may require sanctions or imprisonment for individuals.

Third, you *unconditionally accept life*, with its immense problems and difficulties, and teach yourself to have high frustration tolerance. As Reinhold Niebuhr said, you strive to change the unfortunate things that you can change, to accept (but not to like) those that you cannot change, and to have the wisdom to know the difference.

If you achieve a good measure of these three REBT philosophies—that is, unconditional self-acceptance, unconditional other-acceptance, and unconditional life–acceptance—will you therefore be able to convince terrorists to change their absolutistic bigoted ways? Not exactly. But you will cope much better with terrorism, help others to cope with it, and model behavior that can, if you strongly encourage it to be followed around the world, eventually reduce it to a minimum. This will take many years to effect, and will require immense and persistent educational efforts by you and others to promote peaceful and cooperative solutions instead of hateful and destructive "solutions" to serious national and international difficulties. If we fail to work on our own belief systems to produce this long-term purpose, we will only ensure renewed terrorism for decades, and perhaps centuries, to come.

Are you willing to keep relentlessly working for REBT's recommendations for self-peace, peace to other humans, and peace to the world? If so, you may help people of goodwill to think, plan, and execute eventual answers to terrorism and many other serious world problems.

As you can see and as you might expect, my REBT philosophy of how we can react to terrorism, and how you can use it to possibly save the world from its assaults, is still the same. I promise no perfect or short-range solutions to this problem. None.

Using the REBT thinking, feeling, and behaving methods described in this book, you can do what I have recently shown many of my individual and group therapy clients as well as my workshop participants—that is, how to react to terrorism. *Minimize your anxiety about terrorism.* Terroristic incidents will reoccur. For the time being, there's no stopping them. So be very concerned about dealing with terrorism and helping others, especially your children, to cope with it. And do as much as you can to promote a psychological educational attitude in yourself and others that will help to minimize terrorism.

Be concerned—but not overconcerned and panicked. Incidents will occur, but not often to you and your loved ones. Fortunately, only a few fanatics will find it feasible at present to plot, scheme, plan, and carry out terroristic attacks. These few may disrupt and kill thousands, but not millions. You and your loved ones will most probably be affected but still spared. You and they will survive. But if you don't, you will merely die before your time. So live and try to enjoy your life while you may!

Minimize your depression about terrorism. Terrorism is expectantly bad—one of the worst things that can happen to you and to others. But it is not *totally* bad, as bad as it could possibly be. It always could be worse—like a shooting star that destroys the entire earth. It is never *awful,* meaning badder than it *absolutely should* be. You can *stand it*—find some happiness in a terroristic, war-filled world. It is *just* very, very bad. Period. If you accept the REBT antiawfulizing philosophy, you will be quite sad about present and future terrorism—but not make yourself feel depressed and hopeless.

Minimize your rage about terrorism. Terroristic violence is, by normal social standards, extremely unfair—to its murdered and maimed victims, to you and your loved ones, and to humanity as a whole. It may possibly have some advantages—such as the removal of present and future unpleasantness—but it wreaks so much harm and encourages so much continuing hatred and reprisals that its gains are most questionable. Its cost-benefit ratio is, in both the short and long run, distinctly minus. So also with your rage about terrorism. Your strong distaste and dislike about it, if unaccompanied by rage and vindictiveness, may well help you to survive, to prepare, and in some practical ways to reduce or prevent it. But your raging about it, and your damning its practitioners as *evil people*, will most likely encourage more terrorism.

Your raging against terrorism, moreover, has many personal disadvantages. It encourages you to be obsessed with people you hate. It consumes much time and energy. It brings you more frustration than the actual problem it creates. It may easily lead to several psychosomatic ailments, such as cardiac and intestinal problems. It augments your overgeneralizing and your musturbatory thinking. It makes you as bigoted and damning as the terrorists themselves. It helps make you act impulsively and foolishly. And so forth and so on!

Instead of raging against terrorism, you can achieve most of the advantages of making yourself incensed by powerfully disliking it, steadily denouncing it, intensely thinking about it, and determinedly doing everything you can do to plan and scheme to teach others to act against it strongly, but not frantically!

This brings me to consider in more detail spiritual and religious techniques of dealing with your terror of terrorism, which I have only briefly mentioned so far. Spiritual methods largely go together with a humanistic–existentialist approach, which REBT heavily supports. You could, of course, believe in spirits, such as angels and tooth fairies, whom you could endow with peace-loving qualities and thereby help calm your fears and enable you to cope with and predict the end of terrorism. Few of you probably do these days, and certainly I personally don't. If it serves you well, use it.

"Spiritual Goals and Spirited Values in Psychotherapy" one of my papers (recently published in the main Adlerlian journal) shows how therapists have increasingly used spirituality. But they largely give it an existential–humanistic meaning, and have encouraged their clients to create a vital, absorbing meaning and purpose to their lives and to devote themselves to helping others, their community, and the world instead of only to individual "selfish" interests." This kind of spiritual approach is one of the main teachings of REBT. As shown throughout this book, it espouses unconditional other-acceptance (UOA) together with unconditional self-acceptance (USA) and unconditional life-acceptance (ULA). As I indicate in

Overcoming Destructive Beliefs, Feelings, and Behaviors, it also favors the developmental therapy of Allen Ivey and Sandra Rigazio-DiGilio, which encourages therapists to use cognitive, emotive, and behavioral methods to cope with their clients' stressful social conditions but also to try to better these conditions.

This, then, is a kind of spirituality you can embrace when faced with terrorism. Try as best you may to develop a long-lasting and meaningful purpose for your own life; aid as much as you can the benevolent purposes of others; and persistently strive to help the present terroristic world change for the better. Try, aid, and strive!

Allen Ivey and his associates, along with many other psychologists such as Derald Wing Sue, have pioneered in promoting multicultural aspects of therapy. As I indicate in my newly revised edition of *Overcoming Resistance*, anger, rage, terrorism, and other serious disturbances are accompanied by rigid, absolutistic thinking—which to some extent afflicts all humans, including human therapists. Consequently, therapists from one culture tend to be prejudiced against and in important ways oppress clients of another culture. As Drs. Ivey, Sue, and other multicultural therapists emphasize, we had better make enormous efforts to counterattack this bigotry.

You, too, may tend to be strongly biased against multiversity, and to view people of a different sex, ethnic group, political and economic status, or religious persuasion with prejudiced attitudes. Almost inevitably! Your narrow-minded, one-sided views may create and maintain the many aspects of anger and rage we have been discussing in this book. Strong multiverse thoughts, feelings, and actions are required to counteract all-too-human bigotry and help alleviate rage and terrorism. Are you ready to think, feel, and act to do so?

Terrorism has many severe psychological and physical disadvantages. Like emotional disturbance itself, it has important secondary symptoms that often exacerbate its primary symptoms. As explained earlier, when you make yourself enraged at people who treat you badly, you suffer the primary feeling of anger. But then you may enrage yourself at your raging, and thereby suffer the secondary symptoms of guilt, self-downing, and depression. These secondary symptoms are sometimes worse than the primary rage because they may lead to all kinds of emotional pain as well as serious external disadvantages. Thus, if you damn and depress yourself about your raging, you may turn off other people, work inefficiently, enjoy practically nothing, and even commit suicide. You feel hopeless and you act hopelessly.

Secondary symptoms are acknowledged and can be treated with REBT and many other forms of therapy. They are so devastating that they can hardly be ignored. But are the secondary and also the tertiary symptoms of terrorism equally clear? Probably not—let us look at some of them.

Some primary results of urban terrorism are fairly obvious. Citizens are killed or maimed. Buildings and other structures are destroyed. Transportation is disrupted for months. Jobs are lost, some never to be replaced. People are hospitalized and may require long-term medical treatment. Residents may become temporarily homeless and some may never find good living quarters again. Billions of dollars can be lost by individual businesses, governmental agencies, charitable and other institutions. People who found themselves in the center of the terrorism and others who were far from there but who witnessed it on television or who read about it can be emotionally terrorized with intense anxiety, rage, and depression during or after their experiences. On and on! Too many grim results to count. But what about the secondary results? Again, too many to count.

Let us first consider the normal concern, vigilance, and caution that people follow when terroristic incidents occur. These feelings were and still are being experienced by thousands of American and other people and will lead to improved cautions at airports and other dangerous places now and in the future. This will result in all kinds of difficulties, time expended, and expense for tens of thousands of people. I personally travel a great deal—about forty flights a year—to American and foreign cities to give workshops and lectures. Though I haven't cut down on these trips, because I rationally think that the chance of my getting hurt or killed is still very slight (less than one chance in a million for the year 2002), I still am quite inconvenienced on my trips. I have to leave earlier for the airports, take extra time to check in and clear my baggage, cut to a bare minimum the items I take with me (no little pair of scissors), make sure that I pack everything myself, and so on. But I can't avoid these extra troubles, so I unupsettedly put up with them. However, I and many other people are inconvenienced by them, and that is our penalty for the authorities' exerting normal caution. Yes, even healthy caution—like paying for fire insurance—exacts penalties.

Serious anxiety or panic about terrorism (or anything else) also brings on many difficulties and penalties. Thus, if I were panicked about the slight possibility that terrorism would kill or harm me, especially if I take plane flights, I would probably cancel all my trips and thereby limit myself and lose money for the Albert Ellis Institute, which gets all the income from these trips. But since I am only *concerned* and *not* panicked, I put up with the inconvenience that follows from the authorities' natural caution and take my trips as usual. Concern and anxiety (overconcern) lead to many difficult inconveniences!

Concern, however, usually does not create secondary symptoms—concern about concern. This is because concern is helpful and I (and the authorities) favor it. But anxiety (overconcern) is often very uncomfortable and leads to anxiety about anxiety. People tell themselves, "Since anxiety is uncomfortable and brings about such bad results, I *must not* feel anxious, *must not* feel anxious!" Then they feel anxious *about* their feelings of anxiety—they produce a *secondary* symptom. They also then get *worse* results!

Anxiety itself and anxiety about anxiety often lead to irrational and self-defeating phobias. The view that "Elevators must always be perfectly safe!" creates phobias about riding in elevators—which are fantastically safe and result in perhaps a few accidents every year out of billions of elevator rides. "I must not be anxious about riding in elevators!" creates anxiety about elevator anxiety—and produces worse phobias. People unnecessarily walk up and down stairs, refuse to work in skyscrapers or live in apartments in tall buildings, and panic about living on higher floors when they do reside in them. None of these phobics have been hurt or have even heard of people who were seriously hurt in elevator crashes. Still they panic and still they panic about their panic. This is what is happening, and will continue to happen, as the result of September 11 terrorism. Millions of Americans and other people who were nowhere near the World Trade Center and their friends and relatives did not directly suffer from the attacks are now terrified about tall buildings, loud noises, taking airplane flights, walking in the streets, using bridges, tunnels, and subways, living in New York, visiting New York, and scores of other things that before the terrorist attacks they unthinkingly, unfearfully enjoyed. Yes, millions!

The dismal results of this kind of panic have multiple levels. *First: panic.* "I *should be* perfectly safe and obviously I'm not and that's *terrible!* My friends and relatives and other people *absolutely should not* be in danger and obviously they are, and that's awful!"

"I absolutely should be able to do something to stop this kind of terrorism and I can't do anything to stop it. I'm an inadequate weakling!" "Stopping terrorism is hopeless, so I can't be happy in any way while it continues."

Second: panic about panic. "I must not panic! I'm a weakling for panicking! Not everybody panics as badly as I do and I should have much more control over myself than I have!" "My panic makes me feel very uncomfortable and I can't stand such discomfort! I can't be happy *at all* with it!"

Third: panic about restrictions and personal and other losses caused by terrorism. "I *can't stand* the restrictions and losses caused by the terrorism and the precautions we must now take!" "The discomforts and sorrows stemming from the terrorism absolutely *should not* exist. They're *too* hard to bear, *too* depriving and *awful*!"

Fourth: panic about responding so badly to the results of the terrorism. "I *absolutely shouldn't* take the restrictions and the losses caused by the terrorism so badly! I must not be such a ninny and make myself completely desolate when I am *merely* deprived by those losses and restrictions!"

On several levels, then, you can panic yourself about the existence of terroristic dangers. You can panic about your panic, about your panic about your restrictions and losses connected with terrorism, and about your weakness and low frustration tolerance in not bearing up under these restrictions as well as you supposedly *should* tolerate them. The ways in which you can upset yourself and upset yourself about upsetness are almost endless!

On a personal level, disturbing yourself about terrorism (primary disturbance) and disturbing yourself about disturbing yourself (secondary disturbance) have many emotional and practical consequences. But, fortunately, you are a constructionist who has been born and raised with the ability to reduce your disturbances. Yes, even your disturbablity. That's what I keep showing how to do in this book. However, you have little ability to quickly help reduce other people's primary and secondary disturbances or to reduce the economic, political, and social results of their upsetablilty. What about *that?* Can you alleviate these grim results of what we can call tertiary consequences of disturbance? I think you can.

The terrorism of September 11, 2001, together with people's panic (and panic about their panic), has led to many socioeconomic problems, such as job losses, boycotts of tall buildings, reduced air travel, tourism losses, and more. Can you personally do anything to curtail these considerable problems? Yes. Although you cannot create miracles in this respect, here are some of the specific things you can do if you apply the theory and practice of REBT as described in this book to your and other people's panic about terroristic attacks.

1. *Be realistically concerned.* For many reasons that I have given in this chapter, terrorism like that of September 11, 2001, had better be one of your prime concerns. Especially given the developments of deadlier and more easily applied technology, it could—and already has—wreaked great havoc and could one of these days possibly wipe out the human race. Nuclear and medical "advances" march on. Do everything you can, politically and socially, to let your legislators know of your concern and your determination to act on it.

2. *Watch your unrealistic and illogical panicking.* Terrorism probably won't kill you and your loved ones, nor the entire human race, at least not today or tomorrow. Most likely, it can be cut down and perhaps ultimately abolished. But panic, raging, and damning of all terrorists may augment rather than reduce it. Terrorists commit evil

deeds but are not evil people. Accept the sinner but not the sin. Dispute your overgeneralizing about terrorism, terrorists, and everything else. As Alfred Korzybski said in 1933, you *are* not and can't *be* what you *do*. For you do tens of thousands of things in your lifetime—and will keep doing them until you die. You and the terrorists cannot be totally and finally evaluated. You and they are an ongoing *process*.

3. *Watch your panicking about your panicking.* It is bad, but you are never a *bad person* for experiencing it. Intensely telling yourself, "I must not panic! I must not panic!" will usually *increase* your panicking, and its dismal results. Hate your panic, but never hate *yourself* for panicking.

4. *Don't horrify yourself about the restrictions and personal and social losses caused by terrorism.* They are bad enough without your demanding that they *absolutely must not* exist and that you *can't stand* them and be happy *at all* if they do. As Reinhold Niebuhr noted at the beginning of the twentieth century, stoically *accept*—not *like*—what right now you cannot change.

5. *Don't panic about taking the losses and the restrictions of terrorism so seriously.* And don't panic about panicking about them, either. It would be lovely if you were stronger and less upsettable in this respect—but you don't *have* to be. Accept the grim results of terrorism when you cannot, for the present, change them; and accept your panicking reactions to these facts while you work at making your reactions healthy negative feelings, like strong sorrow and regret, instead of unhealthy negative feelings like panic and rage.

6. *Work at achieving less upsettability.* You will inevitably die anyway, so focus on living as happily as you can while you're alive and on finding some degree of happiness in spite of some of the worst things—such as terrorism—that may happen to you. When exceptionally bad things like terrorism occur, choose to feel strong but nondestructive emotions like constructively savoring your possible last moments. Practice this in advance, and be prepared for the worst that could happen.

7. *Try to teach others how to follow some of the foregoing principles and practices.* Try to teach your children, relatives, friends and acquain-

tances how to make themselves less disturbed about terrorism and less disturbed about their disturbances. This kind of teaching REBT to others may well help you use it more thoroughly on yourself!

8. *Do your best to aid community and social interests.* Try to see that antidamning, accept-the-sinner-but-not-the-sin philosophies are routinely taught to all children in the public, private, and parochial school system so that terroristic urges become minimized. If you choose, acquire a vital absorbing philosophy of social interest that will add to your healthy self-interest and thereby benefit you and other people.

Once again, I realistically emphasize that terrorism will not immediately go away, and that only in the long run will we minimize it. Education, not bickering and arguing, can presumably work. Meanwhile, here are some practical steps that you personally can take, even while terrorism and its exceptually harmful results continue. Take the above self-changing steps and consider acting constructively against some of the destructive consequences of terroristic activities.

- Stay with most of your usual personal and interpersonal pursuits even though there is *some* greater danger of your being harmed.
- Take the normal risks of traveling, and especially of flying, that you took before September 11, 2001, and don't contribute to airline disruption and economic losses.
- Take vacations and tours that you would normally take in "good" times.
- Have normal fears of living or working in extremely tall buildings—such as the Empire State Building—but not of *all* high-rises.
- Spend your income as you regularly would. Don't contribute to economic problems in your community by underspending on "dangerous" trips and vacations that are statistically only slightly riskier than they were before the terroristic events of September 11, 2001. Don't convince yourself that they are "terrible" risks for you just because the terroristic attack of September 11, 2001, made them fatal to others.

As you consider doing—or not doing—these "risky" things, don't go to ridiculous extremes. On the one hand, don't escalate your possible dangers and radically avoid them. Don't, for example, avoid *all* flying, *all* trips, or frequenting all tall buildings on the false assumption that these activities are *exceptionally* "dangerous" and that your phobias about them will *absolutely* save you and your loved ones from harm. These are dubious assumptions, will be overly restrictive, and will, if you and many others follow them, lead to severe economic and social consequences. They will—perhaps!—protect you, but create much communal, including ultimate *personal*, harm.

On the other hand, don't throw all caution to the winds and insist on flying carelessly checked planes, in very bad weather, with a group of strangely acting people, and without any flight insurance. Even under these conditions, your plane will most probably not be hijacked and you will be safe. But I wouldn't risk it, if I were you.

To review: In the short run, terrorism has been with us for many centuries and is, because of technological advances, getting worse. Stopping it will probably take many years of individual and group education. While doing your best to aid its demise, you can use REBT and other aspects of Cognitive Behavior Therapy to surrender your primary anxiety stemming from your insistences that terrorism *absolutely must not* exist. You can change them to strong preferences and thus minimize your ego anxiety ("I and my loved ones *must* have a guarantee that we will succeed in stopping it and *must not* be harmed!") and your discomfort anxiety ("The great inconvenience and dangers caused by terrorism *absolutely must not* plague me and my loved ones!"). You can also minimize your secondary anxiety ("I *absolutely must not* be self-destructively panicked or depressed about my disturbing myself about terrorism!").

You could also stop yourself from agonizing about the dismal consequences of terrorism and from agonizing about your agonizing. You can then take several steps to live with real concern about terrorism and its prevention while taking practical steps to stop yourself and encourage others from unconsciously contributing to the social, political, and economic consequences that tend to follow terroristic acts and to distinctively exacerbate these consequences. By stopping to think before you act out of panic, you may contribute to cutting down the tertiary costs of terrorism, which often accompany the costs of primary panic and secondary panic *about* panic.

References

Note: I have made every effort to include in these references the authors mentioned in the text. But many of them were famous writers whose classic works can easily be found and others were, for one reason or another, unavailable. Consequently, the majority of the important authors, but not all of them, are listed in these references.

Alberti, R., and Emmons, R. (2001). *Your Perfect Right.* 8th ed. Atascadero, Calif.: Impact.

Bach, G., and Goldberg, H. (1975). *Creative Aggression*. New York: Avon.

Baez, J. (July 1970). "Playboy Interview." *Playboy*, 53–64, 136, 152–57.

Bandura, A. (1997). *Self-Efficacy: The Exercise of Control.* New York: Freeman.

Bandura, A., and Wittenberg, C. (1971). "The Impact of Visual Media on Personality." In Segal, J., ed., *Mental Health of the Child*, (pp. 247–66). Washington, D.C.: National Institute for Mental Health.

Barton, R. A, and Bell, P. A. (1971). "Effects of Heightened Sexual Arousal on Physical Aggression." *Proceedings 81st Annual Convention of the American Psychological Association.*

Beck, A. T. (1988). *Love Is Not enough.* New York: Harper & Row.

Berkowitz, L. (1964). "The Effects of Observing Violence." *Scientific American* 210 (2), 2–8.

Berkowitz, L. (1990). "On the Formation and Regulation of Anger and Aggression." *American Psychologist*, 45, 494–503.

Berkowitz, L., Green, J. A., and Macaulay, J. R. (1962). "Hostility Catharsis as the Reduction of Emotional Tension." *Psychiatry* 25, 221–31.

Bernard, M.E., and Wolfe, J. L. eds. (2000). *The REBT Resource Book for Practitioners.* New York: Albert Ellis Institute.

Boelkins, R. C., and Heiser, J. F. (1970). "Biological Basis of Aggression." In Daniels, D., ed., *Violence and the Struggle for Existence* (pp. 15–52). Boston: Little, Brown.

Bond, F. W., and Dryden, W. (2001). *Handbook of Brief Cognitive Therapy*. Chichester, England: Wiley.

Boorstin, D. J. (July 6, 1970). "A Case of Hypochondria." *Newsweek*, 27–29.

Buss, A. H. (1961). *The Psychology of Aggression.* New York: Wiley.

Charney, I. W. (1968). "The Psychotherapist as Teacher of an Ethic of Nonviolence." *Voices* 3(4), 57–66.

Cline-Naffziger, C. (1974). "Women's Lives and Frustration, Oppression and Anger." *Journal of Counseling Psychology* 21, 51–56.

Crawford, T. (1982). *Some Difficulties to Sharing Differences.* Santa Barbara, Cal.: Author.

Danysh, J. (1974). *Stop without Quitting.* San Francisco: International Society for General Semantics.

Deffenbacher, J. L. (1999). "Cognitive-behavioral Conceptions of Anger." *Journal of Clinical Psychology/In Session: Psychotherapy in Practice* 55, 295–309.

Deming, B. (1968). "Nonviolent Battle." *Direct Action* no. 90, 8.

Denenberg, V. H. and Zarrow, M. J. (1970). "Rat pax." *Psychology Today* 3 (12), 45–47, 66–67.

Deutsch, M. (1969). "Conflicts: Productive and Destructive." *Journal of Social Issues* 25, 7–14.

DiGiuseppe, R. (2000). "The Top 10 Reasons to Give Up Your Disturbed Anger." In M. E. Berner and J. L. Wolfe, eds., *REBT Source Book for Professionals*, pp. III, 62. New York: Albert Ellis Institute.

———, and Tafrate, R. (In press). "Anger Treatment for Adults." *Clinical Psychology: Science and Practice.*

———, Tafrate, R., and Eckhard, C. (1994). "Critical Issues in the Treatment of Anger." *Cognitive and Behavioral Practice, 1,* 111–32.

Donnerstein, E. (1975). "Erotic Stimuli and Aggression." *Journal of Personality and Social Psychology* 32, 237–44.

Dryden, W. (1990). *Dealing with Anger Problems: Rational-Emotive Therapeutic Interventions.* Sarasota, Fla.: Professional Resource Exchange.

———. (2001). *Reason to Change: A Rational Emotive Behavior Therapy (REBT) workbook.* Hove, East Sussex, England: Brunner-Routledge.

Ellis, A. (1957/1975). *How to Live with a "Neurotic": At Home and at Work.* Hollywood, Cal.: Wilshire Books.

———. (1977). "Fun as Psychotherapy." *Rational Living* 12 (1), 2–6. Also: Cassette recording. New York: Albert Ellis Institute.

———. (Speaker). (1977b). *A Garland of Rational Humorous Songs* (Cassette recording and songbook). New York: Albert Ellis Institute.

———. (1986). "Fanaticism That May Lead to Nuclear Holocaust." *Journal of Counseling and Development* 65, 146–51

———. (1988). *How to Stubbornly Refuse to Make Yourself Miserable About Anything—Yes, Anything!* New York: Kensington Publishers.

———. (2000). *How to Maintain and Enhance Your Rational Emotive Behavior Therapy Gains.* New York: Albert Ellis Institute.

———. (2000). "Spiritual Goals and Spirited Values in Psychotherapy." *Journal of Individual Psychology* 36, 279–84.

———. (2001a). *Feeling Better, Getting Better, Staying Better.* Atascadero, Calif.: Impact.

———. (2001b). *Overcoming Destructive Beliefs, Feelings and Behaviors.* Amherst, N.Y.: Prometheus Books.

———. (2002). *Overcoming Resistance: A Rational Emotive Behavior Therapy Integrated Approach.* New York: Springer.

———, and Crawford, T. (2000). *Making Intimate Connections.* Atascadero, Calif.: Impact.

———, and Gullo, J. (1972). *Murder and Assassination.* New York: Lyle Stuart.

———, and Harper, R. A. (1997). *A Guide to Rational living.* North Hollywood, Calif.: Melvin Powers.

———, and Harper, R. A. (2001). *How to Stop Destroying Your Relationsips.* New York: Citadel.

———, and Tafrate, R. C. (1997). *How to Control Your Anger Before It Controls You*. New York: Citadel.

Erikson, E. (1969). *Gandhi's Truth, or the Origins of Militant Nonviolence*. New York: Norton.

Fensterheim, H., and Baer, J. (1975). *Don't Say Yes When You Want to Say No*. New York: Dell.

Feshbach, S. (1971). "Dynamics and Morality of Violence and Aggression." *American Psychologist* 26, 281–92.

Freud, S. (1949). *Civilization and Its Discontents*. London: Hogarth.

———. (1963). *Collected Papers*. New York: Collier Books.

Fromm, E. (1955). *The Sane Society*. New York: Rinehart.

Geen, R., and Stonner, D. (1974). "The Meaning of Observed Violence." *Journal of Research in Personality* 8, 55–63.

Gilula, M. F., and Daniels, D. N. (1969). "Violence and Man's Struggle to Adapt." *Science* 164, 396–405.

Ginott, H. (1965). *Between Parent and Child*. New York: Macmillan.

Gordon, T. (1971). *Parent Effectiveness Training*. New York, Peter Wyden.

Hague, P. (1975). "Accepting Anger." *Radical Therapist* 3 (4), 11.

Harlow, H. F. (December 1975). "Harlow's Lecture on Love in Relation Aggression." *APA Monitor*, 3.

Harris, M. B., and Samerott, G. (1975). "The Effects of Aggressive and Altruistic Modeling on Subsequent Behavior." *Journal of Social Psychology* 95, 173–82.

Hauck, P. A. (1974). *Overcoming Frustration and Anger*. Philadelphia: Westminster.

His Holiness the Dalai Lama, and Cutler, H. C. (1998). *The Art of Happiness*. New York: Riverhead.

Ilfeld, F. W., Jr. (1969). "Overview of the Causes and Prevention of Violence." *Archives of General Psychiatry* 20, 675–89.

Ivey, A. E., Ivey, M., and Simek-Morgan, L. (1997). *Counseling and Psychotherapy: A Multicultural Perspective*. Boston: Allyn & Bacon.

Jaffe, Y., Malamuth, N., Feingold, J., and Feshbach, S. (1974). "Sexual Arousal and Behavioral Aggression." *Journal of Personality and Social Psychology* 30, 759–64.

Jahoda, M. (1961). "What is Prejudice?" *World Mental Health* 13, 38–45.

James, W. (1922). *Essays in Radical Empiricism*. New York: Longmans Green.

Joseph, E. D. (1973). "Aggression Redefined—Its Adaptational Aspects." *Psychoanalytic Quarterly* 42, 197–213.

Kassinove, H., and Tafrate, R. C. (2002). *Anger Management*. Atascadero, Calif.: Impact.

Kaufmann, H., and Feshbach, S. (1963). "The Influence of Antiaggressive Communications upon Responses to Provocation." *American Psychologist* 18, 387–88.

Kermani, E. J. (1969). "Aggression, Biophysiological Aspects." *Diseases of the Nervous System* 30, 407–14.

King, M. L. (October 1966). "Nonviolence: The Only Road to Freedom." *Ebony*, 27–34.

Korzybski, A. (1933/1990). *Science and Sanity*. Corcord, Calif.: International Society of General Semantics.

Lang, A. R., Goeckner, D. J., Adesso, V. J., and Marlatt, G. A. (1975). "Effects of Alcohol on Aggression in Male Social Drinkers." *Journal of Abnormal Psychology* 84, 5080, 508–18.

Lange, A., and Jakubowski, P. (1976). *Responsible Assertive Behavior*. Champaign, Ill: Research Press.

Lasch, C. (1978). *The Culture of Narcissism*. New York: Norton.

Lazarus, A. A., and Fay, A. (1975). *I Can if I Want to*. New York: William Morrow.

Lee, A. M. (1972). *Toward Humanist Sociology*. Englewood Cliffs, N.J.: Prentice-Hall.

Liebert, R. M., and Baron, R. A. (1972). "Some Immediate Effects of Televised Violence on Children's Behavior." *Developmental Psychology* 6, 100–21.

Lorenz, K. (1968). *On Aggression*. New York: Harcourt, Brace and World; Bantam.

Lowen, A. (1966). *The Betrayal of the Body* New York: Macmillan.

Lunde, D. T., and Hamburg, D. A. (1972). "Techniques for Assessing the Effects of Sex Hormones on Affect, Arousal, and Aggression in Humans." *Recent Progress in Hormone Research* 28, 627.

Mace, D. (1976). "Marital Intimacy and the Deadly Love-Anger Cycle." *Journal of Marriage and Family Counseling* 2, 131–37.

Marler, P. (1976). "On Animal Aggression." *American Psychologist* 31, 239–46.

Maslow, A. (1968). *Toward a Psychology of Being*. New York: Van Nostrand Reinhold.

Maultsby, M. C., Jr. (1971). "Rational Emotive Imagery." *Rational Living* 6 (1), 24–27.

Maurer, A. (1972). "The Real Roots of Violence." *Proceedings 80th Annual Convention American Psychological Association*, 923.

Meadows, C. M. (1971). "Constructive View of Anger, Aggression, and Violence." *Pastoral Psychology* 21, 9–20.

Meehl, P. E. (1962). "Schizotaxis, Schizotypy, Schizophrenia." *American Psychologist* 17, 827–38.

Meichenbaum, D. (1997). "The Evolution of a Cognitive Behavior Therapist." In J. K. Zeig, ed., *The Evolution of Psychotherapy: The Third Conference* (pp. 95–106). New York: Brunner/Mazel.

Meissner, W. W. (1972). "Toward a Theology of Human Aggression." *Journal of Religion and Health* 3, 324–32.

Montagu, A. (January–February 1967). "Original Sin Revised: A Reply to Recent Popular Theories on Aggression." *Vista* 2 (9), 47–48.

Moyer, K. E. (July 1975). The Physiology of Violence: Allergy and Aggression." *Psychology Today*, 77–79.

Murdoch, B. D. (1972). "Electroencephalograms, Aggression and Emotional Maturity in Psychopathic and Non-psychopathic Prisoners." *Psychologia Africana* 14, 216–31.

Novaco, R. (1974). *A Treatment Program for the Management of Anger through Cognitive and Relaxation Controls*. Ph.D. thesis, Indiana University. Also published as *Anger Control*. Lexington, Mass.: Lexington Books, 1975.

Papanek, H. (1962). "Expression of Hostility: Its Value in the Psychotherapy Group." *Journal of Individual Psychology* 18, 62–67.

Parker, R. S. (1972). *The Emotional Stress of War, Violence and Peace*. New York: Stanwix House.

Perls, F. (1969). *Gestalt Therapy Verbatim*. New York: Delta.

Peters, H. (1970). "The Education of the Emotions." In Magda Arnold, ed., *Feelings and Emotions* (pp.187–203). New York: Academic Press.

Phadke, K. M. (1982). "Some Innovations in RET Theory and Practice. *Rational Living* 17 (2), 25–30.

Reich, W. (1960). *Selected Writings*. New York: Farrar, Straus and Cudahy.

Rochlin, G. (1973). *Man's Aggression: The Defense of the Self.* Boston: Houghton Mifflin.

Roth, M. (1972). "Human Violence as Viewed from the Psychiatric Clinic." *American Journal of Psychiatry* 128, 1043–56.

Rothenberg, A. (1971). "On Anger." *American Journal of Psychiatry* 128, 454–60.

Rubin, T. I. (1969). *The Angry Book*. New York: Macmillan.

Ryterband, E. C. (1968). "The Naked Ape." *Psychology Today* 2 (3), 10.

Sanford, N. (1976). Quoted in "Violence and Psychological Sources of Aggression," *Wright Institute Report*, p. 4. Washington, D.C.: Wright Institute.

Schwebel, M. (1970). "Confrontation." *American Journal of Orthopsychiatry* 40, 183–87.

Siegel, B. J. (1969). "Defensive Cultural Adaptation." In H. D. Graham and T. R. Gurr, eds., *Violence in America*. New York: New American Library.

Skinner, B. F. (1971). *Beyond Freedom and Dignity*. New York: Knopf.

Solnit, A. J. (1972). "Aggression: A View of Theory Building in Psychoanalysis." *Journal of the American Psychoanalytic Association* 20, 435–40.

Spock, B. (1970). *Decent and Indecent*. New York: McCall's.

Spotnitz, H. (1971). Quoted in "Handling Violent Feelings in Group Psychotherapy." *Frontiers of Psychiatry* 1(18), 2.

Storr, A. (1968). *Human Aggression*. New York: Atheneum.

Sue, D. W., Arrendo, P., and McDavis, R. J. (1993). "Multicultural Counseling and Impotencies and Standards: A Call to the Profession." *Journal of Counseling and Development* 70, 477–86.

Sue, D. W., and Sue, D. (2003). *Counseling with the Culturally Diverse: Theory and Practice*. New York: Wiley.

Tafrate, R., and Kassinove, H. (1999). "Anger Control in Men." *Journal of Cognitive Psychotherapy*, *12*, 187–211.

Taylor, S. P. and Smith, I. (1974). "Aggression as a Function of Sex of Victim and Male Subject's Attitude Toward Women." *Psychological Reports* 35, 1095–98.

Toch, H. H. (1969). *Violent Men: An Inquiry into the Psychology of Violence*. Chicago: Aldine.

Vandenberg, S. G. (August 24, 1968). Quoted in "Research on Twins Suggests Hostility May Be Inherited." *New York Times*, 22.

Van den Berghe, P. L. (1974). "Bringing Beasts Back in: Toward a Biosocial Theory of Aggression." *American Sociological Review* 39, 777–88.

Wachtel, A. S. and Davis, M. P. (1969). "Riots: Psychologic Techniques of Prevention and Control." *Journal of the Tennessee Medical Association* 62, 1129–31.

Walen, S., DiGiuseppe, R., and Dryden, W. (1992). *A Practitioner's Guide to Rational-Emotive Therapy*. New York: Oxford University Press.

Walters, R. H. (1966). "Implications of Laboratory Studies of Aggression for the Control and Regulation of Violence." *The Annals* 364, 60–72.

Wolff, H. H. (1969). "The Role of Aggression in the Psychopathology of Illness." *Journal of Psychosomatic Research* 13, 315–20.

Wolfe, J. L. (1992). *What to Do When He Has a Headache*. New York: Hyperion.

Wolfgang, M., and Ferracuti, F. (1967). *The Subculture of Violence*. London: Tavistock.

Zaslow, R. (1969–1970). "Rage Reduction." *Explorations*, No. 17, 17–20.

Index

THE SUSPECT IN POETRY

by

JAMES DICKEY

1964

THE SIXTIES PRESS

For permission to reprint, the author is grateful to *Poetry, The Sewanee Review, The Hudson Review, The New York Times Book Review,* and *The Virginia Quarterly Review,* in which some of these essays and reviews have appeared.

Library of Congress Catalogue Card Number
62 — 21968

Printed in the Republic of Ireland

CONTENTS

THE SUSPECT IN POETRY

THE SUSPECT IN POETRY

AT one time or another, and perhaps at most times, the long-term reader of poetry must marvel at the hundreds and hundreds of lines, stanzas, themes, and whole poems which seem to be sheer effrontery to his sense of what the truth of their subjects must be or could possibly be: that seem to have been invented to satisfy the rules of some complicated but learnable (for many have learned) game which keeps changing from generation to generation, but which always, whether it means to or not, brings into being a truly remarkable amount of utter humbug, absolutely and uselessly far-fetched and complex manipulation of language. The touch upon words of a humanly perceived beauty, terror, or mystery is rare indeed, for a fundamental kind of unliterary innocence is necessary in a writer before he can undergo these feelings. They cannot be expressed out of nothing but good will and the current fashions of an art. For all readers, then, almost all poetry contains elements that are suspect, having no relation to what the readers believe in as "reality," and even in a sense degrading it by offering experience as a series of unbelievable contrivances, none of which has the power of bringing forth a genuine response. Oddly enough, it is only in poems wherein we forget that our feelings have been deliberately evoked that poetry as an art justifies itself. One thing is certain; if the reader does not, through the writing, gain a new, intimate, and vital perspective on his own life as a human being, there is no poem at all, or only a poem written by a collective entity called "Modern Poetry, Period 1945-1960." What makes the whole thing difficult, of course, is that what may be suspect to me may well be genuine to you, and consequently we enter into a thorough critical chaos.

This is, I suspect, where we should be, anyway. What matters is that there be some real response to poems, some passionate and private feeling about them: that for certain people there be certain poems that speak directly to them as they believe God would. And it is hard to regard most of the poems we read in this light. Most of our contemporary poets are writing out into a Climate of poetic officialdom, or pre-tested Approval, based largely on the principles which the New Criticism has espoused, and on the opinions of those who Count in modern letters. We have lost all sense of personal intimacy between the poet and his reader, and even between the poet and his non-poetical self, the self that eats, walks down the street, fills out forms, pays taxes, not as a poet, but in the same ways everybody else does. A very real invasion of privacy has taken place and turned the poet into a kind of monster whose very efforts to appear human, forgiving, compassionate, and lovable must be looked upon with suspicion, as just so many devices, comparable to the brochures used by salesmen or the broadcasts of the Voice of America. Because he knows with Eliot that art is autotelic, he also knows a great deal of what there is to know about evoking, by means of the craft of verse, selected emotions in his readers. For this reason, everything he does comes to seem a manipulation, much in the same way that advertising or any other propaganda is. This air of falseness, of the Suspect in poetry, is one cause of the fatal and much-deplored rift between poet and audience in our time. Very subtly, the feeling of basic honesty, of emotional honesty (but what, exactly, is that?) has evaporated from our poetry; there is no longer a sense of communion involved: that communion upon which all meaningful communication in the arts depends. " The poets lie too much " has grown from a still small voice into a thundering accusation, though it has been with us at least since Plato. When we sit down to a book of poems, to a poem, we need to get back to something as simple as Norman Douglas's "What has this fellow got to say to *me*?" I don't wish to blink the question of form and content, with which I have no ability to contend, anyway: only to point out some of the reasons we don't really experience poetry any more, but only judge it. And therefore care little about it except as the fodder necessary to nourish our literary opinions. And that is too bad. Too bad for poetry, certainly, but worst of all for us.

THE WINTERS APPROACH

I—DONALD DRUMMOND

Donald F. Drummond is a writer whom I have watched for several years with some admiration, but with more dismay and regret. That he is one of the best of a generation of the pupils of Yvor Winters I have no doubt at all. His poems, thoughtful, cleanly conceived and executed, and displaying almost a control-beyond-control of their material, have a great deal of compression, intelligence, and wit. Yet he seems to me a completely unsatisfactory poet. In common with almost all other Winters-trained writers, Drummond appears to have assimilated entirely, and to have put to extremely effective use, the well-known principles and techniques upon which Winters insists with his characteristic air of finality. This enables Drummond to operate with a certain measure of success within disastrously narrow bounds, and cuts him off entirely from writing poems of permanent value. Worse; one often has the feeling that Mr. Drummond is not a poet at all, in the Platonic sense, but is by choice a kind of minor artisan in words, who has learned all he can from his guild-master, and is unwilling or unable to contribute anything of his own beyond. Many of the pieces in *The Battlement* are quite obviously (to use a phrase of F. R. Leavis) no more than " occasions for the exercise of the verse craft." Drummond writes

> Excess of light, prohibited
> By the double-rayed diffusive terms
> At source and sorcerer, becomes
> The mystery which is scarletness

Seen in its whole, the violent red
Of quick, aerated blood, arterial
And central near the body's heart.

When one determines from the rest of the poem that this elaborate passage, involving human eyes seen as burning-glasses, a "mystery," and the color of the blood as it leaves the heart, is simply an overingenious trope meant to define the color of a woman's dress, it is hard to suppress an unbelieving smile at the wasted seriousness and effort which concocted it; it is even more difficult to avoid a certain amount of impatience regarding a system of values that would reduce the rich, multiple excess of the imagination to the bare, starved, and creatureless bones strewn through this book and some of the others like it which Alan Swallow makes available to us.

In spite of their admirable concision, all of Drummond's poems are denatured, dry, and in their lack of physical concreteness strike me as being no refutation at all to William James' belief that "the deeper features of reality are found only in perceptual experience." Rather than a refining and "understanding" of experience, a kind of calculated bleaching-process has taken place, wherein life is reduced to a colorless abstraction of itself. The body does not, for example, hurt, but "suffers indignity." Something "portends" something else, so that a third thing may "misinterpret where it apprehends." And so on. The result of Drummond's practise: his carefully-staged conceits, his logical-as-a-time-table metaphors, his merciless regularity of accent, is not the massive sense and depth of inevitability and rightness of the great practitioners of the strict forms (Dryden, Yeats, Valéry), but neatness merely: tidiness: the wrapping up of a small ordinary parcel with habitual skill and dispatch.

I cannot, however, for the life of me get rid of the notion that Drummond is a larger poet than he has yet appeared to be. The release of this poet (if he exists) from the stone, will, of course, have to be effected by Drummond himself. I should like to see him lose himself for a year or so in the huge variety of Shakespeare, read modern continental verse, even wade shamelessly about in sentimentality. A glacial and sanctioned " purity " of the sort displayed in *The Battlement* has but little chance of contributing anything of value to either the language or the human beings who use it. In a few shocking, rebellious fragments in his book, Drummond appears to possess more individuality and insight than any of the other poets of his persuasion I have read; I would, if I could, enlist him on the side of humanity, rather than that of the Angels, whatever desperate remedies were required.

The Battlement, by Donald Drummond, Alan Swallow, 1956. $2.50

II—ELLEN KAY

Ellen Kay is a tractable student of the Wintersian virtues, and seems to take as axiomatic that learning to concoct acceptable little quasi-philosophical proposition-making verses that scan constitutes all that one can hope to achieve in the way of human expression. One sees immediately that nature is never itself in Miss Kay's poems; nor does it belong to Miss Kay in any intimate and revealing connection. It belongs to the Proposition which it may be made to yield, if the poet rigs a satisfactory set of syllogisms. For this kind of writing, the myths do as well as (or perhaps better than) things seen and known; consequently there are poems on Pluto and Ceres, Eve, the unicorn, Tiresias, The Living Narcissus, and, no less wonderful in the pantheon of West-coast neo-classicism, One Intent upon the Doctorate. Perhaps this is all just as well, for Miss Kay's powers of observation are decidedly slight. But when one sees, also, that her ability to make decisive generalizations is not much above that of the average graduate student, one becomes restive. She says that a stone found in the sea is "licked small and smooth by rough/Tongues of wave, in beauty/ Its own cosmography . . ." Isn't this a kind of predictable dressing-up of a poetic commonplace? What more haggard cliché could the poet have come upon than waves seen as tongues, albeit rough ? I find this going-a-platitude-one-better occurring so frequently throughout Miss Kay's book that it has all the appearance of being systematized, and I can't, despite my best efforts, escape the conclusion that Miss Kay is an almost frightening example of all the worst faults, quickly acquired, and middling virtues, come by somewhat more slowly (but I should think not much) of the average Winters-trained poet, primly preaching a set of academic homilies (" the mind is . . . " " lust is . . ." " love is not . . ." etc.), wherein painfully-contrived arguments in rhyme substitute for genuine insight, and the whole is delivered in diction like nothing ever spoken in truth or understandable error : " Comfort cannot insure./Life is no sinecure . . ." or (my personal favourite), " April holds their last breath;/ Catabolic law, guiled/By the mind's strategy,/Moves to finality/Without return." In the end one reads this kind of writing only as another more serious-minded and semi-codified form of jargon verse; in any meaningful sense it is subjectless, all " strategy " and no passion, all will-power and no luck.

A Local Habitation, by Ellen Kay, Alan Swallow, 1958, $2.00.

ALLEN GINSBERG

I—*Howl*

I admit, as anyone must, that my own sensibility may exhibit terrible failures of eye, ear, mind, and nerve. Such an admission has grave consequences, and a good many of the terrors of responsibility. Because of my own defects of taste, I fear, for example, that I may diminish some perfectly respectable reader's pleasure in the work of Allen Ginsberg, who has written the following lines.

> What sphinx of cement and aluminum bashed open their skulls and ate up their brains and imagination?
> Moloch! Solitude! Filth! Ugliness! Ashcans and unobtainable dollars! Children screaming under the stairways! Boys sobbing in armies! Old men weeping in the parks!

It is at least theoretically possible that I may do a certain amount of harm, also, to the celebrated "Bay Area Renaissance" if I say, with a tone of condescension I don't like but find myself using anyway, that Ginsberg's writings are of the familiar our-love-against-their-machines-and-money variety, strongly akin to those of Henry Miller, Kenneth Patchen, and Kenneth Rexroth, but lacking entirely the memorable and individual qualities of these: Miller's surrealist sexual humor, Patchen's occasional beauties of imagery, and Rexroth's serious and moving contemplation of Time. There are some chances one must take, however; among contemporary poets, Ginsberg is the perfect inhabitant, if not the very founder of Babel, where conditions do not so much make tongues incomprehensible, but render their utterances, as poetry, meaningless. *Howl* is the skin of Rimbaud's *Une Saison en Enfer* thrown over the conventional maunderings of one type of American adolescent, who has discovered that machine civilization has no interest in his having read Blake. The pattern of introduction of works of this type is familiar: they are offered as "confession," with the warning (here by William Carlos Williams) that their authors have indeed "descended into Hell" and come back with a marvellous and terrible Truth to tell us, all about ourselves and the world we have made. The principal state of mind is thus hallucination; everyone in Ginsberg's book is hopped-up on benzedrine, reefers, or whiskey, and is doing something as violently and loudly as he can, in "protest" or "fulfillment." What emerges from all this is an Attitude, since most of the writing itself is in no sense distinctive. The Attitude, however, is really not worth examining either, since Ginsberg's idea of "revolt" seems essentially to consist in making of oneself "cocksman and Adonis of Denver."

If I pay Ginsberg more attention than he perhaps merits, I do so because I have long harbored what now seems to be a rather frightening assumption: that among the unschooled, self-educated, brash, and relatively mannerless poets whose books are issued by small publishers like "The City Lights Bookshop," there might one day appear a writer to supply the in-touch-with-living authenticity which current American poetry so badly needs, grown as it has genteel and almost suffocatingly proper. *Howl* is certainly not the work I have been awaiting. And yet, and yet . . . Having established Ginsberg in (or as) Babel, is one, then, utterly sure that in this estimate some important things have not been left out? Isn't it true of his work, for instance, that somewhere amongst its exhibitionist welter of unrelated associations, wish-fulfillment fantasies, and self-righteous maudlinness, a confused but believable passion for values is struggling? Are there not a few indiscriminately scattered passages which indeed do have upon them a good deal of the constricted, screaming fury Ginsberg feels against his world? And is it quite fair to say that he lacks *entirely* the better qualities of his literary kin: Patchen, Miller, and Rexroth? Is not, say, his description of the baggage racks in "In the Baggage Room at Greyhound" one of the funniest and most horrifying catalogues (and typical baggage racks) in contemporary writing?

> It was the racks, I realized, sitting myself on top of them now as is my wont at lunchtime to rest my tired foot,
> it was the racks, great wooden shelves and stanchions posts and beams assembled floor to roof jumbled with baggage,
> —the Japanese white metal postwar trunk gaudily flowered and headed for Fort Bragg,
> one Mexican green paper package in purple rope adorned with names for Nogales,
> hundreds of radiators all at once for Eureka,
> crates of Hawaiian underwear,
> rolls of posters scattered over the Peninsula, nuts to Sacramento,
> one human eye for Napa,
> an aluminum box of human blood for Stockton
> and a little red package of human teeth for Calistoga—

No; I must admit that the comic talent that noted and collected these items seems to me considerable. And if a measure of craft were to be exercised? What then? It is hardly fair to hope that Ginsberg will ever come to agree with himself that this is necessary, but I for one will buy and read what he writes, should he do so.

Howl, by Allen Ginsberg, City Lights Books, 1956, $.75.

II—*Kaddish*

It is fun to imagine the exhilaration that must seize people who " always thought they might be poets " when they try the Allen Ginsberg method and find out that, after all, they *are* poets. In each case the needed equipment is very simple : a life, with its memories, frustrations, secret wishes (very important, these !), an ability to write elementary prose and to supply it with rather more exclamation points than might normally be called for; these show transport, awe, horror and other important emotions.

Later, refinements may be introduced, such as Zen Buddhism and the frequent use of words like " strange," " mad," " tragic," " visionary," " angelic," " apocalyptic " —and lo ! the neophyte is revealed as a full-blown Ginsbergian or beatnik poet, qualified to read in coffee houses, wear a beard and serve as a " living symbol " of protest and freedom.

Mr. Ginsberg's new poems in *Kaddish*, like his old poems, seem not so much themselves as a convenient prototype of all such writing : a strewn, mishmash prose consisting mainly of assertions that its author is possessed, is often if not always in " holy ecstasy," and so on. But the writing belies all such claims quite heartlessly; there is nothing holy about it in any sense that I can understand, and its obsession is evidenced only by its efforts to be so. Confession is not enough, and neither is the assumption that the truth of one's experience will emerge if only one can keep talking long enough in a whipped-up state of excitement. It takes more than this to make poetry. It just does.

Kaddish, **by Allen Ginsberg, City Lights Books, 1961, $1.50.**

THOM GUNN

As far as I am concerned, chiefest among all current suspects is Thom Gunn. He has already taken quite a beating from some very good American reviewers, notably John Thompson in the November, 1959 issue of *Poetry*. On the other hand, he is very highly regarded in England, wins all sorts of prizes there, and has things like this said about him by critics as acute, learned, and perceptive as Alfred Alvarez: "Gunn's *Fighting Terms* is the most impressive first book of poems since Robert Lowell's." I see him somewhat differently: as a fashionable, rote versifier of some skill and intelligence, the very perfect model of the young, Americanized British poet, writing solemnly about the sect of eagle-jacketed motorcycle riders and about Elvis Presley, who turns out (naturally!) to be a Symbol of impending war. All his work is smoothly executed. It can exercise your logical powers by putting before you a number of problems and resolving them neatly, but it has not the slightest power to touch you (or to touch me, perhaps I should say), or to make you feel that the situation with which it is dealing has any importance whatever, except as material for the kind of poems Gunn writes. Here are the motorcyclists:

> A minute holds them, who have come to go:
> The self-defined, astride the created will
> They burst away; the towns they travel through
> Are home for neither bird nor holiness,
> For birds and saints complete their purposes.
> At worst, one is in motion; and at best,
> Reaching no absolute, in which to rest,
> One is always nearer by not keeping still.

This sort of writing invites you to go on and on, line

after line, stanza after stanza, murmuring, " Yes, I think I see . . . Yes . . . Yes . . . Yes . . ." without actually assenting, or doing so only because the poet seems to have such utter confidence that what he is saying is true, and because some of the problems involved look pretty knotty, and would probably take some work to unravel. Eventually, though, you get a little tired of this diet of half-ideas, and begin to read the book all over again. And you ask questions like these, about the above quotation: Isn't it a little silly to characterize a group of sideburned toughs on Harley-Davidsons as " the self-defined, astride the created will " ? How about the reference to " the towns they travel through " ? Doesn't dragging in the supposed fact that birds and saints are *not* in the towns introduce a whole train of possibilities that, when examined, turns out to be completely irrelevant? For example, what if birds and saints *were* in the towns? Even though they " complete their purposes " (whatever that may mean), would this make any appreciable difference to the cyclists? Is it even true that there are no birds in the towns? I had thought previously that some birds can make a home anywhere. Perhaps I am being over-literal, but over-literalness comes to seem the only defense against Gunn's pedantic, pontifical manner, and his irritating pose as a universal Wise Man. From these poems you go back to the things and beings Gunn has written about, to the cities, the women, the magicians, the airedales of Yvor Winters, even to the motorcyclists, with relief, realizing that, after all, they're not, they *can't* be like these poems at all. And you feel, too, what a very sad thing it is that the poet in our time is an intellectual, and that his thinking sets him increasingly far from his subjects. If the poet's search is for " truth " and " reality," and for means by which to communicate these, one must drearily conclude that he is now farther from being able to do it than he has ever been. He has taken on a knowing, wise-seeming no-voice, a limbo voice like Gunn's, completely unconvincing, mannered, unmattering. He performs endless labours to make simple ideas complex and important-sounding. I have seldom read a duller book than *The Sense of Movement*, and I have nightmares thinking of the energy and the good intentions that went into it. Before the concrete of his approach and his " style " hardens around him, Gunn would do well to remember that his two favorite words, " will " and " define," are, in poetry, uneasy bed-fellows. It is not the will but the imagination that defines, or better still, holds, embodies, presents, and finally gives.

Gunn's book brings up the whole question of the recent influence of American on British poetry. In my opinion, it has not been good. The chief culprit, I am afraid, is Wallace Stevens, whose mannered artificiality and poetry-about-writing-poetry-about-poetry have driven large numbers of writers delightedly back into their shimmering, wordy sensibilities and buried them there. Gunn resembles Stevens no more than he does, say, Yvor Winters, but he has picked up the attitude that Stevens' work has fostered in the now influential next-to-youngest generation of American poets. According to this view, writing a poem is simply inventing a complex proposition about life or one of its manifestations, and illustrating it with whatever material appears to fit in. It seems to me that this leads to a particularly debilitated kind of puzzle-making sterility, where to over-complicate and then resolve is considered the criterion of artistic excellence. The great simplicities, the illuminations that should come like the sun from behind the cloud of ordinary perceptions and everyday judgments are not given a chance to come through, even if they could.

These moments are hard to have, hard to discover and embody. Why bother, when it is so easy to be a " career poet " and to make one's way in a society of opinion which gives good marks to poems like Gunn's? Reading book after book of these poets, one is reminded of nothing so much as of Edmund Wilson's wonderful remark about the poems of Stephen Vincent Benêt, which are " just about the same kind of poetry that the ordinary man would produce if he'd gone in for writing poetry instead of for investment banking or selling real estate." No; we must look to writing in other languages than English for the creative *joie de vivre* that poetry must above all embody: to the poems of a thousand young Frenchmen full of sentimentalities at which Brooks and Warren might laugh, but which come out of an unself-consciousness that enables these writers to use their imagination at full stretch, resulting in poems that are as far as anything could possibly be from the constipated verses we are accustomed to reading, with their carefully market-tested and approved kind of significance. Or we would profit by going to the South Americans, especially to Neruda, whose magnificent abandon includes whole schools of wonderfully good and atrociously bad poets with the strength and delight of a demiurge. We have had enough of calculated effects in poetry, or at least of effects calculated as we have calculated them. Even the beatniks, though none has much imagination, can teach us things about opening up, for what we need most is the simple belief that a human being has said something because it matters.

The Sense of Movement, by Thom Gunn, University of Chicago Press, 1960, $2.75.

NED O'GORMAN

For a long time after I first read him, I didn't know what to make of Ned O'Gorman, and I am still not sure I do. In the beginning I felt I should admire what appeared to be his desperate lunges to get hold of something important, but having since gone back through *The Night of the Hammer* several times, grasping with only a shade less fervor than the poet himself, and continually coming up empty-handed, I no longer wish to pursue the assumption that the thing was ever there in the first place. Many of Mr. O'Gorman's titled pieces make intense, semi-articulate sounds and talk about God, but they do not seem to me to be poems, if organization and intelligence have anything to do with the definition of poetry. It is true enough that Mr. O'Gorman is not in the current mode of university-cultivated garden-poets, but in his case this fact doesn't seem to be in his favor. The structure of his work, when it is discernible at all, is so poor that most of his writings appear to be no more than arbitrary assemblages of half-observed people and objects, half-understood ideas and notions, thrown together in a slapdash, breathless, quasi-mystical and maddeningly assured manner, as if genius were at work, did we but have the sense to recognize it. I have never been brought so near to real agony by the remarks of a dust-jacket as I have by this one, with its talk of "delightful, sometimes wild gaiety," "gusty humor," and of Mr. O'Gorman's having "the poet's essential gift of making all things new." This last may very well be so, but if it is, one resolves, grimly and not without a certain amount of selfless dedication, to set about making them old again. The fact is that Mr. O'Gorman's work is absurdly farfetched, without being in the least imaginative. For example, who in his right mind, or in his wrong mind, would want to begin a poem on Yeats with " He played too long on passion's calliope " ? Who could think there might be any conceivable kind of good, even comic good, in addressing his father in terms such as " O thou sweet dumb-bell " ? In addition to a great many other such failures of taste, Mr. O'Gorman must also own up to having written most of his book in prose: prose to make the prosiness of William Carlos Williams and Kenneth Rexroth sound like the singing of Elizabethan nightingales in comparison. Mr. O'Gorman's writing nearly all depends for its seeming energy on the primitive device of chopping up quite ordinary prose sentences, seeing to it that a fair number of the " lines " end in conjunctions or prepositions, and delivering the whole as verse:

> In the gamble for sacrifice Cain lost and
> Abel won; but winning in that family was a curse
> And Abel's head got broke apart for that.

What good moments there are in *The Night of the Hammer*—bees " with hammers in their wings " and a snake seen as " the twist of choking in the grass "—are hidden among such a deal of inconsequential, confident, earless chatter that one must hunt them down like protectively-colored animals. I suppose it may be construed as of some importance that they are there at all, but what we wish of a poet is poems, and there is none here, unless perhaps the title itself.

The Night of the Hammer, by Ned O'Gorman, Harcourt, Brace, 1958, $3.75.

ROBERT MEZEY

Robert Mezey is right in there with the rest of the poets of his generation, having studied " with John Crowe Ransom at Kenyon College and Paul Engle at the University of Iowa," and with this book has won the Lamont Poetry Prize, surely the most infallible badge of accepted-and-forgotten mediocrity our culture can bestow. Between the Yale Series of Younger Poets (if you feel in the mood for a sad, unbelieving laugh, look at Yale's list all the way back to the beginning, and *read* a few of the books) and the Lamont Prize, given to the likes of Ned O'Gorman and Donald Justice, I don't believe we could choose, and I'm glad we don't have to; both show the dismal state of our verse, and both go on awarding and publishing as though it mattered. This, of course, isn't Mr. Mezey's fault. And it isn't as though he can't write, either. He can; he writes very well, and he's not entirely school-gelded. The trouble is that the quality of his thought isn't much. His ideas are not interesting—at least not to me—and his commitment to experience is not deep and passionate enough, however much he may talk about passion and all its works, and is only connected to language at all because it is so easy, once you have learned, to connect " life " and words at a superficial level. I quote out of context because I haven't room for a whole poem, but one should be able to judge something of a poet's larger movements by his smaller ones:

> I am in love with you —
>   And the moon, so lately spent,
> Will kiss your immaculate stillness
>   In the dark pond of my consent.

Anyone could have fastened on such commonplaces and made them rhyme. But why should anyone want to? It is the *compulsion* to write one way rather than another, to say what one has to say in one way rather than another, the personal necessity for it, that makes good poets. And this Mezey seems to me to lack. He must struggle for the painful ground where his personality and the English language can inflict wounds on each other, and not lie down together like the lion and the lamb, not even suspicious at the beginning.

The Lovemaker, by Robert Mezey, The Cummington Press, 1961, (no price listed).

CHARLES OLSON

Charles Olson is one of the elder statesmen of the Grove Press poets, and his "Maximus" poems have been appearing in the very small and very rebellious magazines over the past several years. They have apparently gained a fairly enthusiastic reputation among the readers of these periodicals, and their collection has been anticipated with a good deal of excitement in some quarters, for at such a time the master plan was to be revealed, the relation of the parts to the whole shown; there was even speculation that the completed work would bring about a radically new kind of American poetry. Olson helped this supposition along by generously furnishing his followers with his theory of "projective" verse or "open" verse, which notion I should imagine he picked up from the French critic René Nelli, author of *Poésie Ouverte Poésie Fermée.* The kind of poetry which he describes is written, evidently, by means of a method entitled "composition by field." The poem, according to this, is "energy transferred from where the poet got it . . . to the reader." It must therefore be "a high energy-construct, and . . . an energy-discharge." Stripped of the language of physics, which in his use turns quickly to jargon, Olson's theory comes down to the simple and ancient one of organic form: "right form, in any given poem, is the only and exclusively possible extension of content under hand." As to the process by which this laudable goal may be reached, Olson tells us that "ONE PERCEPTION MUST IMMEDIATELY AND DIRECTLY LEAD TO A FURTHER PERCEPTION." These dicta, when taken in conjunction with a less easily understood set of ideas concerned with the relation of breathing to "the line," make up most of what Olson has to say about poetry. For the reference of those who might wish to put it into action, I reproduce Mr. Olson's key formula. "Put baldly," he says, "the two halves are:

the HEAD, by way of the EAR, to the SYLLABLE
the HEART, by way of the BREATH, to the LINE."

If rightly applied to syllable and line, this process is supposed to give "the play of the mind" which shows "whether a mind is there at all." In the poem—or the "field," as Olson calls it—the syllables, lines, images, sounds, and meanings "must be taken up as participants in the kinetic of the poem just as solidly as we are accustomed to take what we call the objects of reality." These elements "are to be seen as creating the tensions of the poem just as totally as those other objects create what we know as the world." Well, fine. But this is all nothing very new. And when you come, finally, to see that Olson's trump card, very nearly, is "the advantage of the typewriter," which ostensibly gives the poet "for the first time" the "stave and the bar a musician has had" it is pretty evident that Olson's contribution to the aesthetics of poetry is likely to be something less than epoch-making. All the things he says are in various ways true enough, but "projective verse" has no claim on them; most of them are true of any poetry, or at least of any that is worth reading. Certainly organic form—the poem growing naturally from its own materials and creating its own best internal relations and overall shape—is the form that all good poems must have: do have. What Olson's notion of "open" verse does is simply to provide creative irresponsibility with the semblance of a rationale which may be defended in heated and cloudy terms by its supposed practitioners. All "schools" theorize endlessly, it may be noted.

The Maximus Poems themselves, issued in a handsome format by Jonathan Williams' small and splendid Jargon/

Corinth Press, are reasonably interesting, though by no means as original as one might have been led to expect. I kept looking in them for the HEAD by way of the EAR to the SYLLABLE, but found only a great number of syllables which go back to Ezra Pound's head via the kind of jigsaw organizational techniques of William Carlos Williams' *Paterson*. Instead of "Mr. Paterson" we have Maximus, and instead of Paterson itself we have Gloucester, Mass. There is much of the history of Gloucester; there are lists of the crews of ships, what they carried, descriptions of their figureheads, and so on, evidently selected around one of Mr. Olson's principles, though I'm not sure which one. There are also a great many small, terse, prosy snapshots of Gloucester life both past and present, with Maximus now participating, now reading, now remembering, now dreaming. Some of these episodes are effective, especially a short prose section on cod-fishing, but I have difficulty in taking the whole seriously as a poem, as I do with *Paterson* also. Yet I have a weakness for long poems of this kind, for the *Cantos*, for *Paterson*, for *Maximus*, and particularly for the most obscure and ambitious of them all, David Jones' *The Anathémata*, which perhaps provides in its brilliant, thorny introduction the best justification for this kind of writing, for this kind of organization (or anti-organization), that could be made. Jones says, quoting Nennius (or whoever composed the introductory matter to the *Historia Brittonum*): coacervavi omne quod inveni: "I have made a heap of all that I could find." Jones then goes on to explain that he has allowed himself "to be directed by motifs gathered together from such sources as have by accident been available to me and to make a work of this mixed data." This, essentially, is what Olson has done also, and there is always some amount of fascination in seeing what things have been made available to another's mind "by accident" and have emerged in print as the details of a poem. In presenting his material, Olson is both observant of the way his world, including its history, looks and feels, and determinedly bookish, with the cantankerous and pedantic bluster of his self-educated colleagues Rexroth and Edward Dahlberg. But with or without the help of his theories, he has managed to write a few moderately interesting sections of a long, unsuccessful poem which must have been the labor of years, and these are worth reading. The structure of the poem is only the structure of fortuitous association plus the more obvious devices and literary mannerisms of Pound and Williams, but his mind seems to me quite a capable one, and at all points is working hard to say what has been given it. That is enough, because it has to be.

The Maximus Poems, by Charles Olson, Jargon-Corinth Book, Citadel Press, 1960, $1.95.

HAROLD WITT

Harold Witt says that " close observation of what is most familiar—the regional and known—is the way to universals." This is probably true or at least it ought to be, but it is hard for me to believe that things like " the in absentia bees " constitute much of value in the way of " close observation." *The Death of Venus* displays a good deal of verbal busyness, an air of brilliant slap-dash improvisation, and very little real feeling or consequence. The poems only infrequently engage their subjects: instead, they take off from them, circle them, skirt them, and, in essence, play with them. Despite Witt's avowal of " close observation," his clever figures are maddeningly vague; to say of a " strayed opossum " that it is " disturbing as *stars* " (italics mine) is to say little more or less than that it is disturbing as diamonds, raspberries, head-colds, birds, airplanes, atomic bombs, or almost anything else you might want to pick, for all things, seen in some perspectives, are " disturbing " in some sense; in point of fact, stars are usually counted (unless you are Pascal) as relatively reassuring.

Most of his work shows Witt to be a decorative poet, the decorative being defined as the writer who, because he cannot say exactly the right thing, hopes to say the interesting thing. If, as Malcolm de Chazal maintains, poetry is the art of transmitting life, or the sense of life, at its most meaningful, then the presence of a living human being must somehow make itself felt behind the language. This does not happen in *The Death of Venus* any more than it does in the sardonic and contrived poems of Weldon Kees, which Witt's somewhat resemble. As must be apparent, I don't much like Witt's kind of writing. Nevertheless, he has an enviable store of energy, and obviously he loves the language. He may yet go through a thousand changes, and one of them may be the right one.

The Death of Venus, by Harold Witt, The Golden Quill Press, 1958, $2.50.

ANNE SEXTON

I—*To Bedlam And Part Way Back*

Anne Sexton's poems so obviously come out of deep, painful sections of the author's life that one's literary opinions scarcely seem to matter; one feels tempted to drop them furtively into the nearest ashcan, rather than be caught with them in the presence of so much naked suffering. The experiences she recounts are among the most harrowing that human beings can undergo: those of madness and near-madness, of the pathetic, well-meaning, necessarily tentative and perilous attempts at cure, and of the patient's slow coming back into the human associations and responsibilities which the old, previous self still demands. In addition to being an extremely painful subject, this is perhaps a major one for poetry, with a sickeningly frightening appropriateness to our time. But I am afraid that in my opinion the poems fail to do their subject the kind of justice which I should like to see done. Perhaps no poems could. Yet I am sure that Mrs. Sexton herself could come closer than she does here, did she not make entirely unnecessary concessions to the conventions of her literary generation and the one just before it. One can gather much of her tone and procedure from quotations like " You, Doctor Martin, walk/from breakfast to madness," and " All day we watched the gulls/striking the top of the sky/and riding the blown roller coaster." " Riding the blown roller coaster " is a kind of writing I dislike to such an extent that I feel, perhaps irrationally, that everyone else including Mrs. Sexton ought to dislike it, too, for its easy, A-student, superficially-exact " differentness " and its straining to make contrivance and artificiality appear natural.

One would hope that a writer of Mrs. Sexton's seriousness, and with her terrible story to tell, would avoid this kind of thing at any price. Yet a large part of her book is composed of such figures. In the end, one comes to the conclusion that if there were some way to relieve these poems of the obvious effort of trying to be poems, something very good would emerge. I think they would make far better short stories, and probably in Mrs. Sexton's hands, too, than they do poems. As they are, they lack concentration, and above all the profound, individual linguistic suggestibility and accuracy that poems must have to be good. As D. H. Lawrence once remarked in another connection, they don't " say the real say." But Mrs. Sexton's candor, her courage, and her story are worth anyone's three dollars.

To Bedlam and Part Way Back, **by Anne Sexton, Houghton Mifflin, 1960, $3.00.**

II—*All My Pretty Ones*

In Anne Sexton's work the main sense is that of indignity—of being outraged by the world and its henchmen, like surgeons and alcoholic lovers and dying parents. It would be hard to find a writer who dwells more insistently on the pathetic and disgusting aspects of bodily experience, as though this made the writing more real, and it would also be difficult to find a more hopelessly mechanical approach to reporting these matters than the one she employs.

Her attitude, widely cited as " compassionate," is actually a curious compound of self-deprecatory cynicism and sentimentality-congratulating-itself-on-not-being-caught, as when Mrs. Sexton sees her stomach, after surgery, as being "laced up like a football/for the game" (as though footballs were laced up for games) or when she says to " K. Owyne ": " I washed lobster and stale gin/off your shirt. We lived in sin/in too many rooms." Most of Mrs. Sexton's book is like this; her recourse to the studiedly off-hand diction favored by Randall Jarrell and Elizabeth Bishop and her habitual gravitation to the domestic and the " anti-poetic " seem to me as contrived and mannered as any romantic poet's harking after galleons and sunsets and forbidden pleasures.

The confessional quality in much recent verse, of which the works of Robert Lowell and W. D. Snodgrass are also cases in point, is giving rise to a new kind of orthodoxy as tedious as the garden-and-picture-gallery school of the forties and fifties. Though it is eminently orthodox in this respect, Mrs. Sexton's work seems to me very little more than a kind of terribly serious and determinedly outspoken soap-opera, and as such will undoubtedly have an appeal in some quarters.

All My Pretty Ones, by Anne Sexton, Houghton Mifflin, 1962, $3.00.

PHILIP BOOTH

When one writes of individual collections, one comes under the important obligation to submit as much as possible to each poet's viewpoint and his methods, and to understand the poems as " parts of a world " in a sense in which those of anthologies are not. I read Philip Booth's *Letter From a Distant Land* with this in mind, trying as best I could to see the poems as coming from and illuminating a crucial center. There is none, however. Booth's is an American Georgian poetry, thinly descriptive, replete with easy answers, vacant, amiably bucolic. There are many attempts to feel, or at least to talk about feelings, but precision is lacking, and therefore consequence. Booth tries hard to particularize, but, though he lists many objects, none comes through with the immediate and fierce *haecceitas* that good poems demand and exact. Instead of being concrete, as some reviewers have claimed, Booth's verse is actually quite diffuse and vague.

> We floated on hope at flood,
>   and over, over, the tide-
> sunk bar; there where the run
>   of current, the waving sun,
> showed clear on the waterglass
>   sand, on the seawind grass,
> how the islands were one.

Well, how *were* they one? Why is it " hope " on which the poet floats? Further, why " hope at flood," which implies some tremendous inner expectancy? True, Booth has previously stated that he and another had rowed ashore to swim " for love, a summer whim/When our limbs were all July," but that hardly seems adequate to justify the melting, grandiose assertion of the close. No; Booth's writing is undiscriminating in detail and thus mechanical, and so his feelings come to seem mechanical, too, and do not even seem possible without the full support of the Mode. Someone has remarked of this book that " there is not a really bad poem in it." This says exactly the reverse of what the statement intends. The fact that the poems are all no better than acceptably good, means, *sub specie aeternitatis*, that they are no better than unobtrusively or damnably bad; both good and bad, in these senses, will be equally lost. It reveals also, and devastatingly, one of the most pernicious results of the influence of the New Critics: the approval of poems on principle, as it were, if they sound like the thousands of others brought out by the same poetic weather. Booth sounds enough like the other poets his age and of his time to be all of them in one; in addition, he has a strain of complacent sentimentality which I find very much not to my liking. It may be that he will turn out well; I hope so. As far as I am concerned, however, his beginning does not indicate this as a strong possibility.

***Letter From a Distant Land*, by Philip Booth, Viking, 1957, $3.00.**

In The Presence Of Anthologies

NEW POETS OF ENGLAND AND AMERICA I (1957)

In a sense, every poem of every new book is presided over and judged by an imminent Anthology. Anthologies are perhaps the most important harbingers of lastingness that a writer's work may know during his lifetime; thus they have come to seem a kind of trial immortality for all good poems. In them, poets look for their names and their best or most typical poems, or their atypical, one-shot successes with fear, pride, satisfaction, and awe: in the presence of anthologies the mighty tremble; the lesser know fantastic hope, and the plainly unworthy are exalted. Doubts are many, on the part of the anthologist no less than on that of the poets, for what type of book is more open to attack? Anyone who reviews or even reads it is almost certain to use it merely to throw out in favour of the one *he* would edit, if he could ever get round to it, or if he were ever asked. Into the presence of this celestial and awesome Book all others come at their own risk, and are withered in the impossible light of Heaven. Reading earthly collections does, however, lead one to certain conclusions about the function of the genre, which is not at all what we sometimes suppose it to be. The *raison d'être* of the anthology is only secondarily to indicate trends, groups, schools, and periods, or to show what the young are writing, or what the old have written at different times, under different cultural conditions, or to demonstrate what Louis Untermeyer considers to be *A Treasury of Great Poems*. It is not to present a reflection of " the sensibility of an era " as seen in the eyes of its editors, or, more fragmentarily, in those of its poets. It is to lead readers to the poets on their home ground, their own books, where they present their worlds as fully and deeply as they are able. Such, especially, is the value of a book like *The New*

Poets of England and America (I), since only a few of these writers are at all well-known. Reading through *New Poets*, I found myself, after a first, free-wheeling and very enjoyable game of " Put-in, Take-out," objecting less and less to the selections, for the book is superbly edited, and, though its inclusions and exclusions are questionable in many cases, most of these poets have every right to admission, being as well as any others representative of a generation that has as yet exhibited very little passion, urgency, or imagination. I am still disturbed at not seeing John Logan, Wilfred Watson, Claire McAllister, and Ernest Sandeen, from this side of the Atlantic. From among the English poets, I miss Burns Singer, Christopher Logue, the brilliant Hilary Corke, and, most of all, Robert Conquest, editor of the important *New Lines* collection, and certainly superior to seven-tenths of these writers. The editors promise subsequent editions, however, and it may be that one day we shall have them all, and shall then be able to construct our ideal Anthology merely by exclusion.

Aside from Robert Lowell, represented only by his first and best work, *New Poets* shows only a few American writers who could not be exchanged one for the other without appreciable loss. Two of the editors, Hall and Simpson, are good; Hall is tasteful and delicate, with a generous sense of humor and a nice understanding of structural balance; Simpson is agreeable and sharp, using history lightly and imaginatively in "The Green Shepherd," and building an enveloping and moving dreamwork in " I Dreamed That in a City Dark as Paris." I also liked poems by Howard Nemerov, William Jay Smith, Howard Moss, William Meredith, and Reed Whittemore. The rest all seem to be each other.

The fault of most of this poetry—and perhaps of most poetry—is that one simply doesn't believe it. One longs in vain for some standard by which to measure the capacity of works of art to reach us " where we live " : to be able to say something definitive about the mysterious enlightening conjunction between the good poem and the inner life of the beholder, without which poetry is an exercise differing from any other linguistic usage only in format. It is easy enough to like the poems in *New Poets*; they fulfill many of our notions of what poems should be; they are by turns clever (Amis), elegant (Hecht and Wilbur), ploddingly " sincere " (Wright), learned (Davie and Gunn), humbly aspiring (Pack and Justice), funny (Causley and Whittemore), ingenious (Coulette), and sardonic (Finkel), but never any of these things in a way that matters very much. It is easy to like them, but difficult to care about them. Most of these are occasional poets; most have been schooled or have learned to pick up pretty nearly any scene or object from memory and make acceptable poetic currency of it. Yet this wider field of choice actually reduces the chances for an absolute and personal fatality of viewpoint to occur: the Inevitable tends to get blurred, obscured, and finally swallowed up by the imploring crowd of pretty and quite serviceable Possibles. Facility is not alone at fault; we have given a charming and deliberate smallness far more than its due. There are many poets here who may eventually emerge as significant, but at present, as this excellent selection makes clear, most of them are exemplars of the thing they must overthrow in order to do so.

The main English bloc here is formed of the so-called " Movement " poets, and the American, less well-defined but still quite identifiable, of the university-taught, New-Criticism-oriented writers whom I am tempted to label collectively the " School of Charm." Though assuredly not of great moment, the " Movement " poets are considerably more interesting than ours. In their work, an uneasy alliance has been joined between Auden and Empson, and fitted with a special Outlook best exemplified in the poems of John Wain (not represented here) and Kingsley Amis. There are the familiar " lists " from Auden (" The . . . the . . .the . . . /The . . . the . . . the . . the . . ") and many waggish instances of zeugma (" . . tickled up with ghosts/That brandish warnings or an abstract noun "). There are the terse, laconic statements learned from Empson (" For one month afterwards the eye stays true . . ."). But these devices are only background for the Outlook, which may be defined as a mutually-understood helplessness, in the face of which, much as Hemingway's hero displays " grace," the poet must show wit. I am reminded by the Outlook of nothing so much as of T. E. Hulme's statement that " philosophical syntheses and ethical systems are possible only in arm-chair movements. They are seen to be meaningless as soon as we get into a bus with a dirty baby and a crowd." Amis, particularly, is so strongly in sympathy with the man happy to forget his " philosophical syntheses " under such circumstances that he appears continually to be half-apologizing for writing at all. Reading Amis' own book, *A Case of Samples,* one sees that his real theme is this embarrassment about writing : his assumption, which he expects us to share, that it is amusingly futile at best: he not only believes, but must *confess* he believes his poems bear not the slightest real relation to the tiresome, routine, scrubby existences that people live. Yet Amis is not empty; only thin, bright, and somewhat brittle. He is amusing, and should make his contribution to light verse, wherein he is perfectly assured, quite funny, and certainly in fashion.

Of the other " Movement " writers included in *New Poets*, only Philip Larkin is worth considering. He is said to exemplify the best of the group's work, and I am inclined to agree with the judgment. He is assuredly a great deal more interesting than Thom Gunn, John Holloway, or Donald Davie, all of whom seem to me derivative, cautious, and nearly profitless. Unlike these, Larkin is in a continuously right and meaningful relation to his material. Without straining in the least, he gets a little more out of each subject than one would have thought likely; one understands at last that this small, characteristic difference between his poems and the quite ordinary ones he might have written stems simply from his warm, penetrating way of seeing his subjects, and of thinking clearly about them. He has an easy, conversational voice that strikes me as being very nearly flawless in pitch, and a tender gravity I find most attractive.

In keeping with my earlier pronouncement about the "true function" of anthologies, I want to mention two young English writers whom I had not previously known, in hopes that the reader will be led to seek out their other publications, as I intend to do. Geoffrey Hill and Jon Silkin are both under thirty, and promise much. Hill's "Genesis" is one of the few very fine poems in *New Poets*. I can think of no better compliment to pay Hill than to say I was all but persuaded that, were God a very talented young poet, the six days of the Creation might very well have been as the poem says they were.

Silkin is a strange, breathless, visionary yet energetic poet who deals with the world largely in terms of the deaths of birds, insects, and animals, viewing these not only as portents of human death and perhaps of universal dissolution, but as happenings in themselves unfathomable: terrible, unforgivable. His work brings home to us again the fact that the poet must, inevitably, be obsessed: that it is his obsession that gives urgency and point to his use of the craft, being the thing that the words must at all costs embody. Beside Silkin's pathetic and passionate writing one is eager to forget the *New Poets'* pages and pages of neatly worked-up situations, such as " Or let me think I pause beside a door/And see you in a bodice of Vermeer . . . " and the countless other wearisome rehearsals of known, usable qualities that seem mostly the property of the American contingent, here.

The New Poets of England and America, **edited by Donald Hall, Robert Pack, and Louis Simpson, Meridian Books, 1957, $1.45.**

THE GROVE PRESS NEW AMERICAN POETS (1960)

There are four or five main ways of reacting to poems, and they all matter. In ascending order of importance they are (a) "This probably isn't so, and even if it *were* I couldn't care less," (b) "This may be true enough as far as it goes, but, well . . . so what?" (c) "This is true, or at least convincing, and therefore I respond to it differently than I do to poems in the first two categories," and (d) "This is true with a kind of truth at which I could never have arrived by myself, but its truth is better than the one I had believed." The first two classifications are useful because they are what we feel about bad poems, very bad ones in (a) and half-bad or unsuccessfully realized ones in (b). In (c) are most of the poems we like well enough to call "good" in reviews and to which we may want to return occasionally, and in (d) are those we continue to call great when conversing only with ourselves, and which we would hope to die hearing or remembering. Almost all writers of verse aspire simply to reside in (c), and many a solid reputation—such as that of Robert Graves—has been founded on just such a semi-permanent residence, which is by no means as easy of attainment as I may make it seem. Even those whom we call "major" poets catch only a few glimpses of the world I have designated (d), or at most stand for a handful of moments in that bewildering light, in the certainty that they are bringing about an entirely new kind of human communication compounded of about equal parts of the commonality of all mankind and the unique particularity of the poet's vision and his language. The achievement of even a small but steadily authentic flame is immensely difficult, as we all know, and requires, as well as a great deal of luck, a lifelong attention to those means by which we might best hope to feed it. With each poem, the difficulties come at us from all sides anew. How far, the poet thinks, should I entrust my poem to the flux of images and memories that are its only hope? The stream of consciousness (and unconsciousness) is the source of all good things, but it is also the source of all bad things. If I inhibit it with too many rules, it is likely to give me nothing, and I will end up writing a poetry of the pure will, like Lee Anderson's (true, Paul Valéry insisted that he wrote this kind, but if so his will was a better imagination than my imagination). The opposite thing to do is to let everything out, and for a brief dazzling moment which some poets never outlive, this looks like the answer, the philosopher's stone, the Comstock Lode of poetry. Abandoned to that stream, and with all kinds of subterranean creatures thrusting words into your mouth by the bucketful, it is hard not to ride thus forever, singing and shouting whatever comes to mind. If someone were to tell you that your "song" was only a kind of monstrousness that has to be understood and ordered according to some principle to be meaningful, you might be likely to bring up in refutation what the French refer to as the Surrealist Breakthrough, and the marvelous poems of Éluard and Desnos, which (these poets assure us at great length) could not have come forth in any other way. And if you are young, and if you get the proper kind of encouragement from your elders, men like Kenneth Rexroth and Charles Olson, you can coast down-stream forever, perfectly mindless and jubilant. This is, I think, a fair description of the writers in Mr. Donald Allen's anthology. And to an era weary of over-refined, university-pale subtleties they look interesting; at least they look *different*. Nothing on God's earth can shut them up, and the fact that a good many of their own kind and a few curio-seekers from other walks of life listen to them bellow in coffee-houses convinces those who wish to be convinced that they are " bringing poetry back to the public," restoring it to its true role, making it prophetic, and so on. Meanwhile their mentors keep telling the genteel, mildly-interested middle-brow public that this is a " real movement ": that, as Mr. Rexroth said recently in the *New York Times* Book Review section, these writers are aware of their " unchanging responsibility to poetry's most ancient utterances," that this one is " unquestionably the best " of the lot and that that one is a " rough, startlingly honest poet," and so on, as if these estimates were indeed of some value, much as if I were to say that a grade-school sprinter displays " startling leg drive " or is " explosive off the blocks " and said nothing at all of what would happen to him if he were to line up on the same track with Dave Sime or Armin Hary. The fact is that few of those who fill up the 454 pages of *The New American Poetry* can write a lick. These few are occasionally good in some of the ways in which it matters to be good, but put against a really intelligent and resourceful poet like Howard Nemerov even they show up pretty drably. The fact that a reasonably large segment of the reading public might now be persuaded that the " New Poets " are " real " and that poets like Nemerov are only " mandarin " writers (as Rexroth, using Cyril Connolly's term, says) indicates as nothing else has done for a long time how little we really care about poetry, how little we love it for what it is to us (and not for what we have been told it is), and above all how little we have learned about it.

Perhaps poetry is by nature a realm where only extremes and things of more than life size, more than life intensity are valid. But there is a vast difference between the extremes of Rimbaud, a genius who screamed, and Allen Ginsberg, an ordinary and somewhat pretentious man who screams. It may be, too, that the answer deserved by the sober constipation of the Yvor Winters school and the chatty, knowledgeable aesthetic elegance of the likes of Anthony Hecht and George Starbuck is the aggressive gabble of the "Beats" and the other and similar poets whom Mr. Allen puts before us. And perhaps, again, what we really want (or perhaps I had better say what *I* really want) has very little to do with either.

When I stop to examine them, as I frequently do these days, I find that my tastes in poetry are actually quite simple. I wish merely to be able to feel and see and respond to what the poet is saying, and with as much strength and depth as possible. The difficulty is that much contemporary (and other) poetry is made up of a number of totally unconvincing postures, and induces a kind of disbelief in the reader completely different from that cited by Coleridge. It is a disbelief which refuses to be suspended either willingly or unwillingly, for it is occasioned by a growing certainty that the writer has wilfully betrayed his own experience. The most unconvincing of these postures—all so remarkably alike that they posit a new poetic conformity-in-anarchy which may well presage the death of all authentic expression in this generation—are to be found in Mr. Allen's collection. If the first blow is dealt the reader's belief in the poem by any hint of insincerity, this belief is simply annihilated by such yowling for attention (not in order to communicate anything, but merely to be noticed, to be discovered saying something ostensibly poetic and/or philosophical) as this "line" from Michael McClure: OH BEAUTY BEAUTY BEAUTY BEAUTY BEAUTY BEAUTY IS HIDEOUS. I think this is not an unfair sample of Mr. McClure's approach, if such it may be called. Mr. Ginsberg's is similar, though even less interesting, despite the fact that some of it has to do with narcotics and homosexuality. Ginsberg's comic abilities, which I still enjoy, are not much in evidence here, which is a shame. But then Mr. Ginsberg's poems are not the best in this anthology, either, though certainly the most publicized, and so my regret over the omission of his poem about the luggage room at the Greyhound bus station is balanced by some work by other writers in which there are certain glimmers of talent which may eventually lead to better poetry than these poets are able to come up with at present. Of these, Gary Snyder comes closest to valid expression. The example of Pound has helped him, and that probably explains his superiority to the others. I think, too, that Robert Duncan is quite imaginative, though somewhat pretentious, and that there are some good passages in the selections from Charles Olson, Paul Blackburn, Paul Carroll, Larry Eigner, Jonathan Williams, and Denise Levertov. The rest, as far as I am concerned, are a complete and dead loss, and must bore even their authors.

Both the public and " critical " (or Rexrothian) success and the actual failure of these people (or the majority of them, at any rate) can be traced to the absence in each of them of what W. H. Auden calls " the censor " : the faculty or indwelling being which determines what shall and what shall not come into a poem, and which has the final say as to how the admitted material shall be used. It is basically the same as Coleridge's " architectonic " faculty: that which builds the good details into coherent wholes. But if everything we come out with is called " good," what basis is there for the selection of the real good? Much less the ordering of authentic materials into significant communicative structures? If I feel a little guilty about using this kind of academic language I do so with some defiance, for I recognize that even academism, much as I have inveighed against it in the past, is (as Dr. Winters tells us) a defense of the mind, and so of the only way in which permanently valuable poetry may be written. It is quite true—and has been amply demonstrated over the last twenty years—that the censor can censor you to death, and can cut off the life-stream of the unconscious entirely, or poison it in subtle and sterilizing ways. To make matters even more complicated, the censor can even write poems out of virtually nothing, much as if a man were to build a house only of nails, or as if a poem were to fancy itself the subject of Roy Campbell's justly celebrated quatrain about the South African novelists, using " the snaffle and the curb " on a non-existent horse. And this is not good, either. But when the stream of images is rich and full and the censor is at his best: when he (or it) knows what to look for and seize on and what to do with it when it appears, poetry has its only legitimate chance to come into being. It is precisely this chance that the " Beats " are systematically denying themselves, with the help of (again) Mr. Rexroth, William Carlos Williams, Charles Olson, and editors like Donald Allen, who has the temerity to label his book *The New American Poetry*. What he has given us, instead, is an enormous amount of fairly low-grade whale-fat, at least part of which might, with the help of the censor, render down into usable oil. But this is something we are unlikely ever to see happen. There is too much encouragement given it to remain what it is: " natural."

The New American Poetry: 1945-60, edited by Donald A. Allen, Grove Press, 1960, $1.95.

The Second Birth

THE SECOND BIRTH

Most people interested in poetry (which means those who write it, those who aspire to write it, and those who criticize it) must notice at one time or another how few " born poets " there are, and how many poets: how few, like Orpheus and Rimbaud and Dylan Thomas, who find themselves early in life with the complete instrument in their hands, and have only to accord its strings to make the rocks dance and posterity rejoice: how few of these there are, and how many of the other kind. These last must all hope for the Second Birth, brought on slowly if at all by years of the hardest kind of work, much luck, much self-doubt, many false starts, and the difficult and ultimately moral habit of trying each poem, each line, each word, against the shifting but finally constant standards of inner necessity. As the words come to him, the poet must be eternally and ruthlessly vigilant against claiming what is not really his: against fastening on a good Audenesque or Empsonian line, say, and using it because it occurred to him instead of to Auden or Empson. Through enough such renunciations, he may, if he is fortunate and has the will and the time, come to define and thence to explore his own uniquely human segment of the common consciousness, and if in so doing he develops a characteristic style suited to express his discoveries, he will have succeeded at least to some degree in the essential task of the poet of the Second Birth; he will have obliterated or reduced to unimportance the standing distinction between the "born" and the "made" poet. The poet of the Second Birth must strive all his life to become, in Pierre-Jean Jouve's luminous phrase, " master of a superior secret." The secret does not, of course, reside in a complete originality, which does not and could not exist. It dwells, rather, in the development of personality, with its unique weight of experience and memory, as a writing instrument, and in the ability to give literary influence a new dimension which has the quality of this personality as informing principle. The Second Birth is largely a matter of self-criticism and endless experiment, presided over by an unwavering effort to ascertain what is most satisfying to the poet's self as it develops, or as it remains more clearly what it has always been. That the Second Birth can be attained in our time as in any other, we have as examples W. S. Graham, who rose from perfectly terrible imitations of Thomas to a strong, confident style utilizing elements of Scottish balladry, but based, largely, also, on snatches of conversation overheard in pubs, on street-corners, and in the shipyards of the River Clyde. There is Theodore Roethke, who began as a poet so traditional that even Yvor Winters approved of him, and then, beginning again, ranged through the strange hot-house world of inspired baby-talk and "pre-poetry" of *The Lost Son* back to a formal verse that really counts. Perhaps the most striking case in point is the marvellous John Berryman, who began quite ordinarily as one of the better disciples of Yeats and Auden, and after twenty years of wrestling with the problems of syntax as it operates within the poetic line, emerged to create, in the birth sequence of *Homage To Mistress Bradstreet,* what is to my mind the most daring and successful rendering of human experience ever to appear in American poetry. If we hold the example of these poets enough in mind, the while honouring them for the difficult and valuable thing they have done: if we realize it is not enough simply to write "the best poems of which we are capable," for these are more than apt to sound like (or even to *be*) the second or third-best poems of Empson or Auden or Thomas or someone else: if we hold out, line by line, as if forever, for the poems that are as near as we can get them to being our own, we shall have some chance of saving our age from the fate of inconsequence, adequateness, and imitation that is threatening to render it impotent. The belief in the value of one's personality has all but disappeared from our verse. Yet the inexhaustible vitality and importance of writing are there, and nowhere else. Berryman and Roethke show us this, and so do Robert Penn Warren, Lawrence Durrell, Edwin Muir, and Richard Eberhart. Let the poets of my generation ask as much of themselves.

THEODORE ROETHKE

Theodore Roethke seems to me the finest poet now writing in English. I reiterate this with a certain fierceness, knowing that I have to put him up against Eliot, Pound, Graves, and a good many others of deservedly high rank. I do it also cheerfully, however, for stating his own idiosyncratic and perhaps indefensible views is part of a reviewer's business. I think Roethke is the finest not so much because of his beautifully personal sense of form but because of the way he sees and feels the aspects of life which are compelling to him. The powerful, almost somnambulistic statements of his observations and accountings come to us as from the bottom of the " deep well of unconscious cerebration " itself, or from a Delphic trance where everything one says is the right, undreamed-of, and known-by-the-gods-all-the-time thing that should be and never is said. The best of Roethke's poems are very nearly as frightening and necessary as " darkness was upon the face of the deep," and as simple and awesome as " let there be light." It is this world of perpetual genesis, his own genesis, recurring, continually available if only the perceiver is up to it in mind and body, that Roethke has somehow got down in words. The few objects that define his personality—stones, flowers, sunlight, wind, woman, darkness, animals, fish, insects, birds—tell his entire story, and the changes and similarities he finds among them are his poems. They are simple, tragic, profound, and unutterably joyful. They are, and will be, permanent parts of our perception of reality, and one feels guilty of an unjust act, of a dislocation of nature, in referring to them as " literature " at all.

Words for the Wind, by Theodore Roethke, Indiana University Press, 1961, $1.75.

KENNETH PATCHEN

Often at night, when I see that, indeed, the sky is a "deep throw of stars," I think of a poet named Kenneth Patchen, who once told me that it is. Because of this and a few other passages I remember years after first reading them, I have tried to keep track of Patchen, and have gone through most of his books (all, in fact, except *Sleepers Awake*, which I abandoned in despair). I have heard recently that he has joined the "San Francisco School," but in reality he was its only permanent member twenty years before the group was ever conceived in the impatient mind of Kenneth Rexroth, and is still, despite having produced a genuinely impassable mountain of tiresome, obvious, self-important, sprawling, sentimental, witless, preachy, tasteless, useless poems and books, the best poet that American literary expressionism can show. Occasionally, in fragments and odds and ends nobody wants to seek out any more, he is a writer of superb daring and invention, the author of a few passages which are, so far as I can tell, comparable to the most intuitively beautiful writing ever done. He is a poet not so much in form as in essence, a condition of which we should all be envious, and with which we should never be satisfied. To evoke the usual standards of formal art in Patchen's case is worse than meaningless. He cannot give anything through the traditional forms (those who suggest that he ought at least to try should take a look at some of the rhymed poems in *Before the Brave*). I do not like to read most of Patchen's work, for it seems to me a cruel waste, but he somehow manages to make continuing claims on my attention that other more consistent poets do not. If there is such a thing as pure or crude imagination, Patchen has it, or has had it. With it he has made twenty-five years of Notes, in the form of scrappy, unsatisfactory, fragmentarily brilliant poems, for a single, unwritten cosmic Work, which bears, at least in some of its parts, analogies to the prophetic books of Blake. Yet the words, the phrases, and the lines that are supposed to make up the individual pieces almost never coalesce, themselves, into wholes, because Patchen looks upon language as patently unworthy of the Vision, and treats it with corresponding indifference and contempt. This is the reason he is not a good writer, or a good prophet, either: this, and the fact that his alternately raging and super-sentimental view of things is too violent, centerless, convulsive, and one-dimensional to be entirely convincing. But he has made and peopled a place that would never have had existence without him: the realm of the "Dark Kingdom," where "all who have opposed in secret, are . . . provided with green crowns," and where the vague, powerful figures of fantasmagoric limbo, the dream people, and, above all, the mythic animals that only he sees, are sometimes as inconsolably troubling as the hallucinations of the madman or the alcoholic, and are occasionally, as if by accident, rendered in language that accords them the only kind of value possible to this kind of writing: makes them obsessive, unpardonable, and magnificent. It is wrong of us to wish that Patchen would "pull himself together." He has never been together. He cannot write poems, as the present book heartlessly demonstrates. But his authentic and terrible hallucinations infrequently come to great good among the words which they must use. We should leave it at that, and take what we can from him.

When We Were Here Together, by Kenneth Patchen, New Directions, 1957, $3.50.

HOWARD NEMEROV

I—*The Salt Garden*

Howard Nemerov is a fine poet in the process, here, of becoming a finer one. His is a tough-minded, learned, subtle, and ironic lyricism, determined at all times not to let the world bring in anything poetic form can't handle. There is not a really bad poem in his book. What you do miss, though, is a sense of the poems speaking themselves out, or ever thinking that they ought to speak themselves out, beyond the poet's assured and confident and somewhat predictable idiom into their own uniqueness and necessity. In these tight, nervously off-hand stanzas, the means are too obviously well-satisfied at being " adequate "; there is not enough evidence of the exploratory, the big-thing-just-missed, or got-hold-of-in-part, that we feel we can legitimately expect of a talent as promising as his.

You are inclined to think of Nemerov as a " resourceful " poet, and he is, very. The resources are those you might imagine: Auden, Eliot, and, more pronouncedly, Yeats, but more especially yet, those of a kind of climate of " modern poetry " that these earlier figures have distilled. This weather of custom makes it possible for one to pick his structures and even his attitudes from the air, and it is doubly nice, considering the ease with which this may be done, to be told that one is " in the tradition ": that one is " consolidating " (or even " improving ") what one's predecessors have but indicated. But the " tradition," considered in this sense, makes a very real danger of " adequacy," or idiomatic acceptability: makes it, in fact, a species of shallow and expectant death-bed of originality, of the personal and individuating reaction to things which in large part determines the value of the poet's work. I don't mean to offer Nemerov as a sacrifice to this (perhaps dubious) conjectural machinery, for he is too gifted a poet to be a perfect or even a particularly good example of the tendency I describe. Nevertheless, it seems to me that he would do well to watch himself closely, or abandon himself less shrewdly, perhaps, for the next few years, when he writes.

Nemerov is a very easy poet to read; you like him immediately. He always gives you "something to think about," even in the lighter poems, the *New Yorker*ish ones, and you are inclined to waive the feeling that you have thought about it before, with more vital connections between you and the world, in the work of Yeats and Auden. Despite the uneasy suspicion that many of the poems are better exercises than poems, you do feel, when you have finished the book, that Nemerov is beginning to limit and perfect his own thing, or two things, rather: the satiric song with learned overtones, the resigned, knowing, intellectual lyric, and, on the other hand, the casual-serious meditation from nature, in which the schooled modern intelligence looks through or past its burden of knowledge into the brute Fact of an aspect of the surrounding world.

> . . . these trees were here, are here,
> Before King Hannibal had elephants
> Or Frederick grew his red beard through the table
> Or Mordecai hung Haman at the gate.
> The other Ahasuerus has not spat
> Nor walked nor cobbled any shoe, nor Joseph
> So much as dreamed that he will found the Corn
> Exchange Bank in the baked country of Egypt.
> Not even those burnt beauties are hawked out,
> By the angry Beginner, on Chaos floor

Where they built Pandemonium the Palace
Back in the high old times. Most probably
Nothing will happen. Even the Fall of Man
Is waiting, here, for someone to grow apples;
And the snake, speckled as sunlight on the rock
In the deep woods, still sleeps with a whole head
And has not begun to grow a manly smile.

The poetry of the present age in America, the forties and fifties, has its exemplar in Nemerov, I think. He is in my opinion the best poet under forty-five that we have, with the possible exception of Richard Wilbur. I should like to see him break out a little, though, write a few bad poems, even, and then come at the thing another way, through more " Deep Woods " and " Sanctuaries," keeping one hand on what he has won in the " Dialectical Songs." It may be that the long sequence " The Scales of the Eyes " is the poem I am wishing for him. Certainly it contains many impressive things. It is concerned with spiritual definition: with the Why of belonging " here," at this place and time rather than another. Nemerov's " here " is between the city and the sea, between process and permanence, between the fact and the symbol. The interplay of figures, the star and the pool, the vine, the bloodvessel, the snowfall, the waiting animal, the spider's web, the bird, seems at first a little discursive, but each of these entities comes to hold, through quiet, skillful shading, a powerful and unique particularity.

The low sky was mute and white
And the sun a white hole in the sky
That morning when it came on to snow;
The hushed flakes fell all day.

The hills were hidden in a white air
And every bearing went away,
Landmarks being but white and white
For anyone going anywhere.

All lines were lost, a noon bell
I heard sunk in a sullen pool
Miles off. And yet this patient snow,
When later I walked out in it,

Had lodged itself in tips of grass
And made its mantle bridging so
It lay upon the air and not the earth
So light it hardly bent a blade.

Yet, despite its impressiveness, the poem misses a total, felt unity (though I should not be prepared to argue this with Mr. Kenneth Burke, whose reading of the poem draws on sources of interpretation to which I can pretend no knowledge at all). The individual poems seem to me to achieve more by themselves than the sequence does; the poem is somehow split and portioned out among its symbols and approaches instead of being concentrated, drawn in upon them.

I hope I am not ungrateful to Nemerov in this summary. He is a poet who rouses your fears that he will spend a great deal of time sewing himself a uniform which fits part of him perfectly, provided he exorcises the Fire-Bringer, who is harder to measure. I should like to see Nemerov a Power Among Us, not written off as a " careful minor artisan." The good poems here, " The Sanctuary," most of " The Scales of the Eyes," " Deep Woods," " The Priest's Curse on Dancing," (though when will someone point out that in the much-praised " I Only Am Escaped Alone to Tell Thee," the plaintive " But all that whalebone came from whales " is not really adequate, structurally, to bind the two parts of the central metaphor?) make this by far the poet's best book. It is better, I assume, to say a few hard things of it, hoping they will help the poet even if he sends them off to Hell, than cheerful half-truths, " the nice things one could say " if one looked the book over with an eye toward determining what they might be.

The Salt Garden, by Howard Nemerov, Atlantic-Little, Brown, 1955, $3.00.

II—*Selected Poems*

I am of Howard Nemerov's generation, in age about midway between him and W. S. Merwin. I have never had great hopes for the poets of my time, since it has seemed for years that the writers who came to maturity just before, during, and immediately after the second war were to survive only as human beings, settling into the genteel, face-saving poverty and sterility of academic life and having their poems published simply because they were the only poets there were, and that they (or we) were never to count as poets at all, except as a kind of Georgian era that would be annihilated by some new revolution of the word, much as Pound and Eliot blew the literary world apart around 1912. After reading Mr. Nemerov's *New and Selected Poems,* however, and after noting that James Wright, Jon Silkin, Geoffrey Hill and W. S. Graham are of the same generation: after noting, too, that those poets whose early work I most deplored for its neatness, correctness, and deadness—poets like Merwin and James Merrill—have not died as artists but developed toward other and better modes of expression: after reading the work of the "Beat" poets of the ilk of Ginsberg, Corso, and Ferlinghetti (surely the most ludicrously bad of them all) and the defenses of same by the older Beats like Rexroth, none of whom is fit to appear on the same page (or platform) with Nemerov, Silkin, or any of the others I have mentioned: after all these things I begin to see my generation somewhat differently than before, and am a great deal more encouraged over its possibilities than I have ever been. That a new poetry of some kind is coming I have no doubt. But it will not be the anarchic collectivism of the Beats, nor will it be based on the sentimental eroticism of Rexroth or the bookish pastiche of Olson. It will not be the airless aestheticism of the forties, either. I cannot of course make any sure prediction as to what its outlines might be like, but if it is to prove of any value at all it will have to find a way to use the intelligence at full stretch, and to turn it into an instrument of liberation rather than constriction: a means by which the intellect can function without inhibiting whatever personal vision and imagination the writer may possess. The operation of such an essentially poetic intelligence can be seen in the newest work of Howard Nemerov, and in great and heartening abundance. Nemerov is one of the few poets I have ever encountered who can turn the sometimes rather grim business of reading through the poems of a book into a profoundly enjoyable experience without sacrificing a jot of intensity. He is one of the wittiest and funniest poets we have, and there are whole sections of his book which might easily be passed over as clever light verse by clever, light readers. And it is true, too, that in his most serious poems there is an element of mocking, or self-mocking. But the enveloping emotion that arises from his writing is helplessness: the helplessness we all feel in the face of the events of our time, and of life itself: the helplessness one feels as one's legitimate but chronically unfair portion in all the things that can't be assuaged or explained. And beneath even this feeling is a sort of hopelessly involved acceptance and resignation which has in it far more of the truly tragic than most poetry which deliberately sets out in quest of tragedy. I won't go on and on, and I won't name what I think are Mr. Nemerov's best poems, for I want each reader to find them for himself, and for all opinions to differ and for each beholder to defend his own view, if necessary, with his life. But I do wish to end by saying that Nemerov has earned the best that his poetic intelligence, his imaginative censor, can do for him, and that this censor, far from limiting him by putting up barbed wire at his boundaries, is busy showing him every day just how those boundaries may be pushed back, little by little, so that what stands inside them is earned ground, and will remain his. For what we all want, in the end, is just such a censor: a poetry-knowledgeable and poetry-divining being who could only be ours, and who is a good deal more alive and kicking than we are, is more vitally conscious and certainly more poetically responsible than we, more able to tell the good from the bad, the essential from the inessential, the borrowed from the new. He is, really, all we have: the best of ourselves as writers. The value of the censor, the notion of the censor, lies not with Mr. Auden, who defined him and cleverly gave him a name which I have been using uncleverly: the value is not in the name but in the thing, the demonstration of its timeless importance and purpose: the poems of good poets.

Selected Poems, by Howard Nemerov, University of Chicago Press, 1960, $3.50.

HAYDEN CARRUTH

I—*The Crow and The Heart*

Hayden Carruth has been around a long time, as "younger poets" go. Up to now, I have never been favorably impressed with anything of his I have seen, and have passed him off as one among many of the same. But that is not the way to begin a review of his first book, for as it turns out I *am* very much impressed. As I think of *The Crow and the Heart*, I find myself believing not in its sustained power or concentration of language, but in a carefulness which bursts, once or twice or three times, into a kind of frenzied eloquence, a near-hysteria, and in these frightening places sloughing off a set of mannerisms which in the rest of the book seems determined to reduce Carruth to the level of a thousand other poets who can do, just as easily as he, most of the things he does in about three-fourths of these poems. Often, Carruth appears not to have learned the Gresham's Law of poetry, which states that the more sounds and images you crowd into a line, the less effect they have. He seldom lets you forget that you are reading something which has been written, and written again, and then written some more. These poems strike me as being completely mechanical and lifeless, with more than a hint of academic dilettantism about them. They are Suspect, and I for one, cannot take them seriously. The subjects of the poems are completely obscured in a blur of likely-sounding words.

> This is the white king's palace: snowflakes flounce
> On every draught, dally in secret aisles,

Bow and depart, an instant clap of fury,
And winds, O sparrow, shake your chandelier

That leaps and branches toward the reeling walls.

This is supposed to be a description of a snowfall, but it is a decorator's description, with a great deal more emphasis on the describing than on the snow, and so we get a little shimmer of words and no sense of winter at all. And the same thing happens over and over again.

What kind of thing, here where my mother's flowers
Bark colors only, like a tranced bazaar,
Is my late lingering love for you, which flows
Beyond all those events, past the Azores?

I guess (and I am only guessing) that "bark colors" is intended to indicate that the colors are raucous and irritating, and call attention to themselves mindlessly and unnecessarily. Actually, though, this is not what happens in the beholder's mind. He thinks momentarily only of a preposterous image of flowers like dogs, or like side-show barkers, and then dismisses it, his attention having been retained by neither flowers nor dogs. Because the objects which are called to our attention are vertiginously disembodied in language, considerable doubt is cast on the veracity and imagination of the mind that brought them up and presented them in this way. As Auden says, the poet's job is to find out the images "that hurt and connect," and a great many of Carruth's don't, at least not for me. They are like musical exercises that one wants to hear dissolve into the real playing.

The point where this happens is page 19, for those who wish to consult the text. "On a Certain Engagement South of Seoul" is as fine a poem as an American has ever written about the ex-soldier's feelings, and that takes in a lot of territory. It is only after the Inevitable has clamped us by the back of the neck that we go back and look carefully at the poem, and see that it is written in terza rima. And so, hushed and awed, we learn something about the power of poetic form, and the way in which it can both concentrate and release meaning, when meaning is present. This poem suggests, too, that Carruth is one of the poets (perhaps all poets are some of these poets) who write their best, pushing past limit after limit, only in the grip of recalling some overpowering experience. When he does not have such a subject at hand, Carruth amuses himself by being playfully skillful with internal rhyme, inventing bizarre Sitwellian images, being witty and professionally sharp. And there is much of this. But through Carruth's verses-by-anybody we are led slowly and a little restively, like the true mad, into "The Asylum," surely one of the most remarkable sequences of recent years. It is a low-keyed, extremely intelligent, tremblingly helpless poem about insanity and its terrible cure. It draws conclusions that no one but Carruth could have drawn, and which, by the miraculous process that takes place in poetry as good as this, manages also to speak for the rest of us, too, and for our society. I hope I am not making Carruth's powerful writing appear ordinary by talking about it as I do, but you must let him, and not me, convince you that it is neither. I should like very much to quote long stretches of "The Asylum," but I restrain myself in order to give the poem the chance it deserves of building up in the reader's mind as it was meant to. I suggest, then, that you buy Carruth's book and read "On a Certain Engagement," "The Fat Lady," and "The Asylum." They have done us proud.

The Crow and the Heart, by Hayden Carruth, Macmillan, 1960, $1.50.

II—*Journey To A Known Place*

Carruth's *Journey to a Known Place* is worth waiting for: a real event. I can only give an inadequate, betraying sketch of this beautifully conceived and imagined poem, into which Carruth blends his tremendous and sensitive vocabulary (surely the largest and most precise since Hart Crane's) with a mixture of cold, steady fury and nightmarish passion in the presence of which I can do little more than record my amazement and gratitude. Mr. Carruth's Known Place is the world itself, seen and experienced in and through its classic elements, earth, water, air, and fire. Each of its four sections begins with the protagonist's apprehension of one of the elements and follows him as he goes into it, comes to know it, lives it through a process of primal metamorphosis and then emerges in preparation for his entry into the next element, until all is resolved in fire. Since part of the immense force of the poem depends upon its closely-packed, slow-rolling diction over long stretches, quotation in brief can hardly do more than suggest its quality. But when Mr. Carruth's man-fish goes

> Down, down to the stiller mid-regions
> Where giant sea-snails hung torpid in copulation,
> Half out of their shells, white flesh rolling, exposed
> Obscenely in the slow coiling and cramping of a cruel
> And monstrously deliberate ecstasy

we have had a vision of the blind and necessary horror of nature which is, for my money, very nearly absolute.

Like his man-bird, Mr. Carruth is " skilled now in the/ profound and lovely/necessities," and his wonderful new poem, which begins with a huddle of refugees and ends in the City of the Sun, is bound to be discussed and reread for many years. *Journey to a Known Place* is a painful and magnificent poem; it really hurts and it really sings, and I can only urge readers to buy it and live with it, even though New Directions has put it on the market at $12.50, a price that will unfortunately keep many readers away from what would certainly be a profound and moving experience.

Journey to a Known Place, by Hayden Carruth, New Directions, 1961, $12.50.

RANDALL JARRELL

A. Why are we Two?

B. I find that my opinions of Randall Jarrell's poetry are so violent that I have summoned you, or created you, out of niggling and Opposing Winds, to furnish me with arguments against which my own will stand forth even stronger, which I should like them to do.

A. I am glad you have created me. I think it good for writers to have the most violent possible arguments brought into play against them. Even unfair arguments. If the work is strong enough, all these will be overcome. Now, I was moved by Jarrell's poems even when I was Wind. Now that I am a Voice therefrom, I find I am moved even more, for I am nearer the human things he writes about.

B. I take it, then, that I have brought forth a satisfactory Opposing Self, for you seem to like Jarrell's poems.

A. I do. I think his book is, or should certainly be, the occasion of a Triumph. He has been writing for twenty years now, and this book contains a fair portion of all he will do as a writer: that is, the book is a monument, if not to Jarrell *in toto*, then at least to his "early phase," no matter what he may do later.

B. And why is the book a Triumph, may I ask?

A. Because it is the work of an honest, witty, intelligent, and deeply gifted man, a man who knows more about poetry, and knows it in better, more human ways, than any other of our time. If you add to these other things that he has a rare poetic intelligence which works, not for itself, but totally in the service of human beings, in compassion and love, then you will have an idea of the kind of Triumph I'm talking about. All you can do about a book like this, as Herbert Read said of Dylan Thomas's *Deaths And Entrances,* is to praise it.

B. I must tell you, then, that to me the book is dull beyond all dullness of stupefaction or petrifaction; that when I read it from end to end I know more of boredom than the dead do. " In plain American that dogs and cats can read " the poems are the most untalentedly sentimental, self-indulgent, and insensitive writings that I can remember; when I read them I cry and laugh helplessly all night, over the reputation that has come out of such stuff.

A. I would say, in answer, that you have missed the entire point of Jarrell's contribution, which is that of writing about real things, rather than playing games with words. He is set like a kind of laughing death against the technique-on-principle people that fill the quarterlies. His world is the World, and People, and not the cultivated island of books, theories, and schools. Can't you see that?

B. Would you give me an example of this attitude at work in one of Jarrell's poems?

A. I'll just pick up a random sample. This is from " The Night Before the Night Before Christmas." He speaks of " the big old houses, the small new houses." Don't you see . . .

B. That's real enough, all right, if that's what you mean by real. That is, there *are* big old houses and small new houses, and perhaps this observation tells us something about the economic and social changes that have taken place in the time between the building of the two types of houses. But isn't the statement pretty much of a commonplace? After all, we don't need a poet to point this out to us. Am I to believe that you and Jarrell think that comment of this rather tame and obvious kind constitutes Triumphal Poetry? I should be sorry to think so.

A. You certainly *are* to believe it. It is, for instance, far more important than surrealist poems, or those of Garcia Lorca's "Poet in New York," or any other poetry that uses objects as counters to whirl into and out of bizarre images, simply for the sake of the images, and the bizarreness. Jarrell's poems are far too respectful of experience, of life as it is lived by people, for that to happen. Their world is our world.

B. Now this word " real " : Hadn't we better examine it a little more closely? Is it actually as important as you say to Jarrell's writing?

A. It *is* his writing. He writes about the things we know; that is, he writes about cats, common soldiers, about the dilemmas of children, and . . . and the small man, the man " things are done to," usually by the State, to the man's almost willing detriment and slow consternation.

B. " Reality," though, is what, exactly? The philosophers have gone into cold graves, for ages, still arguing about the nature of Reality, and probably will do so forever. Do you mean to tell me that if I read Jarrell's poems " in the right spirit " I will have the answer to all these vexing questions the Ages have turned back from with only provisional, unsatisfactory solutions?

A. Yes; in a sense, you will. Like any poet's, Jarrell's is an experiential reality. I believe that, without becoming entangled in metaphysics, we can assume that his reality is " the common ground of experience " of twentieth century man, especially the American, but not confined to him. Through poems about what has happened to this man (or to his child) in this time, we get, in an extremely detailed, moving, and " true " way the experience of our time defined. And that is Reality enough.

B. " Reality," then, is what everybody knows and feels it is, since we all have roughly the same experiences as human beings living under (approximately) the same conditions. When there is a war, for instance, we all react to it.

A. That's right.

B. And you think that it's important that Jarrell appeals to others' participation in this common ground of experience: that his poems draw their strength at least in part from this appeal?

A. I do. Can you deny that you have undergone many of the things he writes about?

B. No. I have undergone them. But so have newspapers, mediocre movies, soap operas, and bad poems. So has my old Aunt Virgie, on television. It is not enough that the poet's world be that of "all of us." Of course he must begin there, but that fact doesn't make him a poet, or his writings valuable.

A. Nobody is asserting anything of that kind. You oversimplify much too drastically.

B. Jarrell himself seems to assume something of this nature, though. In his criticism he speaks frequently, even obsessively, of a poet's evoking not "a" but "the" real world; he says of Whitman's world that it "so plainly *is* the world" (italics Jarrell's), and so on.

A. You are still missing the point. The poet must evoke a world that is realler than real: his work must result in an intensification of qualities, you might say, that we have all observed and lived, but the poet has observed and lived most deeply of all. This world is so real that the experienced world is transfigured and intensified, through the poem, into itself, a deeper itself, a more characteristic itself. If a man can make words do this, he is a poet. Only men who can do this are poets.

B. Isn't it, though, what all poets are trying to do? Or at least half of them, anyway. There are some poets who are on the side of the World against Art, like Jarrell, and there are others, like the surrealists, Mallarmé, and

Valéry, who are for Art against the World. Nietzsche said that no true artist would tolerate for an instant the world as it is. Some artists want to characterize the world, and some to change it and make use of it in their own ways. Assuming for the moment that I, like you and Jarrell, think that the world ought to be characterized, let me ask you an important question: does Jarrell's work in fact do this intensifying and typifying you claim for it?

A. You bet it does. His realm is one of pity and terror, of a kind of non-understanding understanding (which I'll explain later), and above all of helplessness. All his people, the wounded soldiers, the children, the cancer patients, all these are people in predicaments that happen all the time. They are the things that our situation as human beings can't help bringing to bear on us. It is through the kind of compulsion that these things force up in us that Jarrell writes his poems. He is saying, in almost every poem, "There is no explanation for what is happening to you. I don't understand why it is; I can tell you nothing. But I know how it must be for you." The poems are moving in the way life is, when these things happen in it. And there is the compassion of a man in them, a man who knows that his helpless pity won't do any good, won't change anything, but who keeps pouring it out anyway because he can't help it. There is your real helplessness, and there is your poet Jarrell. And if you read him in a little less cynical manner than you have done, you would know this; you would become fully Human.

B. But these are *poems* he is trying to write. If you ignore that, you substitute sentimentality and special pleading (admirable though it be) for the poet's true work, which is to put down words in a certain order. You get, in fact, *my* Jarrell. Tell me, my Compassionate friend, with all these fine things that happen to you when you read a Jarrell poem, can you honestly tell me that you think Jarrell has a good ear, or is very perceptive or even accurate in his use of language?

A. Yes, I think he has, and is, in an unexceptional, unobtrusive way.

B. (reads)

> The yaks groaning with tea, the burlaps
> Lapping and lapping each stunned universe . . .

Now, how about those " burlaps/Lapping and lapping "? What put that one past him if not laxity and not-hearing? Come, now; has he really the poet's deep, instinctive feel of language, the sense of language as a *mode* of experience?

A. He has, but he has a more important commitment, which is to humanity. And that is better.

B. Not in poetry, it isn't. Language and experience have got to be interactive at a deeper (or higher) level to make poetry happen. Deeper or higher than Jarrell commands, I mean. I maintain that Jarrell doesn't have in more than the slightest and rather synthetic and predictable degree this kind of grasp on language. He has a good sense of the poetically profitable situation, which by itself is by no means enough. It won't do, when you write a bad poem, a poem that doesn't " raise to consciousness " (to paraphrase Collingwood) a given segment of experience, to say, " Well, the World told me to say it that way. I looked at the Thing, the War, the Child, the Wounded Man, and it looked back, and the World told me, ' Son, what you see, *is*.' And so I put it down without Artifice, or with only a little, and I felt Compassion for the subject, and I had a poem. And that's what poetry is, by gum." No; that won't wash. Let Jarrell write a single phrase that has the harnessed verbal energy of Valéry's " La mer, la mer, toujours recommencée " and I'll begin to see him as a poet. And let me add that that line, as far as I'm concerned, has more of "the World" in it than all of Jarrell's; it has because the poet has put it there.

In Jarrell's poems, the "Real World" is far too often merely called on, and not created at all, by descriptions that would not be remarkable in an ordinary naturalistic short-story or novel. This is in part the case, I suppose, because Jarrell evidently considers it a particular virtue, in his espousal of the "real," to cling like death to the commonplace, as though the Real were only the Ordinary, after all, and the solution that artists have sought for centuries were resolved in that recognition. But when Garcia Lorca says, "Your belly is a battle of roots," is that Ordinary?

A. Jarrell might not admit it as poetry.

B. I can't judge as to that. But *I* admit it. Furthermore, it seems to me to be almost fearfully "real," Jarrell be damned. It comes down to this: I don't think you can impose your own notion of "reality" as everyone's, no matter how much you assume and take for granted that everyone is like you, or should be like you. You can't legitimately offer your personal interpretation of "reality" as though it were universally acceptable, and write criticism and poetry out of an agreement with yourself that this is the case.

A. I suppose I am at liberty to believe in Jarrell's as a real world, as a world that is probably as near as a poet can bring me to the World, whatever that is (but I *feel* it!).

B. You are. Realler, though, than Dylan Thomas's?

A. Well, yes. Not so good, though, as poetry. But Jarrell's world is nearer what I know.

B. How about what Thomas knows? You appear to be willing to accept this business of Ordinariness as Reality. Tell me, then, why you believe Thomas's to be the better poetry?

A. He does something, well, something *else* to the world. Changes it, maybe.

B. Yes; birds fly through water, stars burst out of bearing mothers' ears (this from the prose), hunchbacks turn into tall young women, and so on. He plays pretty fast and loose with your Ordinary Reality, doesn't he?

A. Yes, I guess so. But what you're saying is that anyone who plays fast and loose with things is thereby a poet, which is just as untrue as any of the assumptions you say Jarrell makes.

B. I don't intend that inference at all. Would you admit that Thomas's successes depend at least in part on these qualities of changing and shaping?

A. Yes, and so would Jarrell, probably. He says of Whitman that he is "the rashest, the most inexplicable and unlikely—the most impossible, one wants to say—of poets." Doesn't that knock out almost everything you've said?

B. Not at all. Consider the kinds of individualities he thinks relevant to poetry. All, or almost all the poets he likes, Frost, Williams, Elizabeth Bishop, Robert Lowell, Corbière, even poets mentioned, as it were, in passing, like Adam Drinan and Niccolo degli Albizzi, have what qualities in common?

A. I should say (except possibly of Lowell) that they use simple diction, different kinds of unpoetical offhandness, and are preoccupied largely with . . .

B. Everyday objects, scenes, and so on: brooms, cats, garbage cans, broccoli patches, chickens, squirrels, rabbit-hutches, socks, boxes. If someone has a simile comparing defeated soldiers to ". . . barrels rolling, jolting," Jarrell will be more likely to approve it than if the soldiers were likened to dispossessed kings, unless the kings were homey ones. But mightn't kings be more effective, in some conceivable instances?

A. Aren't you just assuming all this?

B. I don't think I am, entirely. Most of the metaphors Jarrell cites as good are of this type. Almost all of his own are. "His raft's hot-water-bottle weight," for instance. There are hundreds. If you make a metaphor, Jarrell seems to be telling you, the second term of it, the thing the first term is being compared to, must be something homey, something ordinary, or else you are not dealing with "reality" and therefore not writing poetry.

A. Are you asserting that poetry shouldn't or can't be made with these things?

B. Of course not. Only that it can be made with other things as well.

A. Tell me, do you think these objections hold true of the war poems?

B. Yes, more even than of the others, if that is possible. They have all the attitudes that most people think ought to be shown by poets during wars. Can you imagine a poet loving war, or not pitying the individual soldiers?

A. Does that prevent Jarrell from really pitying them?

B. No, and he does pity them. I am disturbed, though, that despite all the pity he shows, none of it is actually brought to bear on any*one*. Did Jarrell never love any *person* in the service with him? Did he just pity himself and all the Others, in a kind of monstrous, abstract, complacent, and inhuman Compassion? I don't think there are really any *people* in the war poems. There are only The Ball Turret Gunner, A Pilot from the Carrier, The Wingman, and assorted faceless types in uniform. They are just collective Objects, or Attitudes, or Killable Puppets. You care very little what happens to them, and that is terrible.

A. It seems to me that Jarrell is writing mostly *about* the impersonal side of war: about the fact that wars are fought, now, almost entirely by machines, and that men suffer more or less as an irrelevant afterthought of the machines.

B. Yes, but men, not Man, suffer. You do get, however, in Jarrell's war poems, some sense of this vast and impersonal aspect of modern warfare, but little of it is realized dramatically. Most of the stuff about aircraft carriers, for instance, is like watching a good film on the subject, like "The Fighting Lady." If I had to choose between the film and the poems, I would choose the film. I can think of no film I would prefer to Thomas's "Ceremony After a Fire Raid." Jarrell's second-hand Reality simply does not do enough. His work is just sophisticated journalism; it is craft, in Collingwood's definition: working up a predictable emotion, and damned poor metrically, too. In these later poems, do you suppose Jarrell cares, any more, that poetry is supposed to display at least some degree of rhythmic concentration?

A. He is *beyond* those considerations. He is not Yvor Winters, you know. He is not your mechanical stress-monger. He is a Man, as he says in the last line of the book. He has broken away from all that petty finger-and-toe-counting, those neat, rectangular stanzas. He is past being concerned with those mechanics. He has attained a realm "where only necessary things are done,/With that supreme and grave dexterity that ignores technique" (though I may be misquoting from Kirkup here, in a word or two).

B. You say he's "broken through" these things, that he knows enough, now, not to have to worry about technical matters. Yet it seems to me that he hasn't really reached them at all, in any significant way, or has fallen progressively away from the very slight acquaintance with them evidenced in his first book. The unstated and insistent principle underlying the later poems is "The situation is enough." But, as I keep saying, he has not the power, or the genius, or the talent, or the inclination, or whatever, to make experience rise to its own most intense, concentrated, and meaningful level, a level impossible without *that* poet's having caught it in *those* words. And there the matter rests, as far as I'm concerned.

A. I can see that there's no arguing with you. But I believe that Randall Jarrell will have something to say to people for a very long time to come, especially as the world tries increasingly to survive by inhumanity (assuming you agree with me on this). The poems give you the feel of a time, our time, as no other poetry of our century does, or could, even. They put on your face, nearer than any of your own looks, more irrevocably than your skin, the uncomprehending stare of the individual caught in the State's machinery: in an impersonal, invisible, man-made, and uncontrollable Force. They show in front of you a child's slow, horrified, magnificently un-understanding and growing loss of innocence in which we all share and can't help: which we can neither understand nor help in ourselves in the hands of the State any more than can the children in our hands. The poems are one long look, through this expression, into a child's face, as the Things of modern life happen around it, happen to it, so that you see the expressions change, and even feel the breath change over you, and you come to be aware that you are staring back in perfect and centered blindness, in which everything to pity is clear as death, and none of the reasons for any of it. Now *that* is our time. It is humanity in the twentieth century. Or whatever is good, worth saving, there. And that is your poet Randall Jarrell, to stand against any objections, even legitimate ones. He gives you, as all great or good writers do, a foothold in a realm where literature itself is inessential, where your own world is more yours than you could ever have thought, or even felt, but is one you have always known.

Selected Poems, by Randall Jarrell, Knopf, 1955, $4.00.

E. E. CUMMINGS

When you judge one of E. E. Cummings' books, you have to judge them all; you have to judge Cummings. Perhaps this is true to some degree of reviewing all poets, but it is entirely true in Cummings' case. His books are all exactly alike, and one is faced with evaluating Cummings as a poet, using the current text simply as a hitherto unavailable source of quotations. Let me make my own position clear right away. I think that Cummings is a daringly original poet, with more virility and more sheer, uncompromising talent than any other living American writer. I cannot and would not want to deny, either, that he dilutes even the finest of his work with writing that is hardly more than the defiant playing of a child, though the fact that he does this with the superb arrogance of genius has always seemed to me among the most attractive of his qualities. I love Cummings' verse, even a great deal of it that is not lovable or even respectable, but it is also true that I am frequently and thoroughly bored by its continuous attitudinizing and its dogmatic preaching. I have often felt that there must be something hiddenly wrong with his cult of spontaneity and individuality, that these attributes have to be insisted upon to the extent to which Cummings insists on them. I feel, also, that "love" and the other well-known emotions that Cummings tirelessly espouses are being imposed on me categorically, and that I stand in some danger of being shot if I do not, just at that moment, wish to love someone or pick a rose or lean against a tree watching the snow-flakes come down. The famous mannerisms, too: aren't they, by now, beginning to pall pretty heavily? Were some of them, even when they were new, worth very much? I can, for example, think of no two literary devices which interest me less than the countless " un "-words Cummings is fond of using, and his wearisome, cute, and mechanical substitution of other parts of speech for nouns (" a which of slim of blue/of here will who/straight up into the where . . ."). Yet when you come on a passage like this, what can you feel but silence, gratitude, and rejoicing?

> now air is air and thing is thing: no bliss
> of heavenly earth beguiles our spirits, whose
> miraculously disenchanted eyes
> live the magnificent honesty of space.

Here is something entirely beautiful, with the odd, arresting, directness-from-another-angle that characterizes the best poetry, and can change your life. One thinks of Blake's observation about the crooked roads without improvement, and is glad of the quotation, and even more glad that Cummings has lived along those roads with vitality and constancy, and has defended them against the cheapjacks of life and of the word with the belligerency and the withering scorn he has. A few years ago, reviewing Cummings' *Poems 1923-1954* in *The New York Times Book Review,* Randall Jarrell deplored Cummings' insistence on his difference from other men. Whether or not Cummings does this to the extent Mr. Jarrell suggests, and I think he does, I am more delighted than dismayed by it. Just this jealous treasuring of his individuality, his uniqueness, has enabled Cummings' personality to flower in a number of perfectly inimitable poems, and in countless passages in other poems beside which the efforts of all but a few other contemporary poets pale into competent indifference. It has encouraged also, I suppose, the various devices and mannerisms for which Cummings is celebrated. The important thing, however, is that Cummings has felt the need, and followed it, of developing absolutely in his own way, of keeping himself and his writing whole, preferring to harbor his most grievous and obvious faults quite as if they were part and parcel of his most original and valuable impulses, which perhaps they are. The poems in *95 Poems* are no better and no worse than Cummings' best and worst poems in his other books, though the percentage of good poems over bad is considerably higher here than is customary. As always, Cummings is his own most distinguished and devastating parodist, able with penetrating wit to hold his own work up to the ridicule some of it deserves, and then, in the next poem, or even in the next line, to restore it to an eminence which seals the critic's mouth and changes him into a more perceptive being than he has been since his fifth year. But how is this done? I attempted to answer this question by doing my best to determine which of the two or three writers present in Cummings I admire most. It is certainly not the one who depends on a number of elementary and quite predictable tricks of typography to make points which could be made more easily, and probably more effectively, by other means. In Cummings' experiments in breaking up words and using syllables in various permutations and combinations on the page, I have only the faintest interest.

l (a
le
af
fa
ll
s)
one
l
iness

There is not much doubt as to what the vertical arrangement of the letters, here, is meant to do. Within the enveloping context of "loneliness," the motion of the leaf, set parenthetically, the initially unexplained "l" which completes the key word when one goes back to it, all show pretty well how this device in Cummings' poems usually operates. Although this treatment (one can hardly call it a technique) has, in addition to a simple kind of puzzle-interest, the slight advantage of approximating kinaesthetically the falling of the leaf, and of literally surrounding it with the human emotion which it connotes or causes, I cannot for the life of me think of this piece as particularly good poetry, or particularly good anything; certainly I do not think of it in the same way I do of some of Cummings' poems. No; I am most drawn to the Cummings whose quirky, indignant sharpness of observation produced the unforgettable pages dealing with Jean le Nègre in *The Enormous Room*, over which no type-setter asked for a raise or cut his throat: to the writer whose fantastic and uncompromising devotion to a spontaneous, outward-going (and typically American, if we would just *be* Americans) view of the world permeates his prose and most of his poems with gorgeous, unpremeditated energy: to the Cummings whose entirely personal daring with diction and image brings us into a Chaplinesque, half-comic, half-holy reconciliation with the events through which we live. His excesses are, most certainly, enormous, as one feels they should be in a genuine poet. Cummings is without question one of the most insistent and occasionally one of the most successful users of pathetic fallacy in the history of the written word. He is one of the most blatant sentimentalists, one of the most absurdly and grandly over-emotional of poets, one of the flimsiest thinkers, and one of the truly irreplaceable sensibilities that we have known, with the blind, irresistible devotion to his exact perceptions, to his way of knowing and doing, and to his personal and incorruptible relation to the English language that an authentic poet must have.

Immediacy and intensity are Cummings' twin gods, and he has served them with a zeal and single-mindedness which we should learn to appreciate even more fully as these traits tend to disappear from our verse, giving way, as they seem to be doing, to a more withdrawn, philosophical, "considered," and altogether safer point of view. I can think of no other qualities so much needed in contemporary poetry as those which Cummings has spent his life discovering ways to make viable. Whether or not successful in every instance, all of Cummings' skill, so special to himself that we cannot imagine anyone else making use of it, has gone to establish and consecrate the moment: the event which is taking place *now*: the thing which will never be repeated in quite this same way, and which, quite likely, would ordinarily not even be noticed as it happens. Cummings' several devices are always means by which to get at this, and to show "what happens" in its pure, inexplicable, purposeless instancy and intensity: in its meaning-beyond-meaning. He has never felt the need to broaden his subject-matter, or to systematize its implications, or even to notice anything beyond the experiences and scenes which attain the highest degree of intuitive meaning for *him*: love, love with sex, sex without love, spring, flowers, snow, death, sunlight, moonlight, leaves, birds, his family, hatred of money and money-makers and public figures. No one would insist that Cummings be a more systematic thinker than he is, because of his spectacular success in feeling responsively and deeply and verbally, but I for one often wish, when reading his poems, that they had somewhat more intellectual structure or firmness under them. I had as well withdraw that statement, though, for poems 48 and 49 in this book are wonderful poems, and are so quite without taking any notice whatever of my objections. Aside from his big *Poems 1923-1954*, this is Cummings' best book; there are so many good things in it that to begin to quote whole poems would necessitate my going on for pages. As a reviewer, I note this with relief, for to point out all the brilliant passages would entail having to indicate ludicrous failures also, and with having to reckon again with the fact that Cummings has long since passed (perhaps with his first poem, perhaps when he was born) the point where writing correctly, well or badly according to other lights than his own, made the slightest difference to him. He is so strongly of a piece that the commentator feels ashamed and even a little guilty in picking out flaws, as though he were asked to call attention to the aesthetic defects in a rose. It is better to say what must finally be said about Cummings: that he has helped to give life to the language, for language is renewed by the best perceptions of its most valuably intuitive and devoted users, and by no other means. Cummings belongs in the class of poets who have done this, not by virtue of his tinkering with typography, but because of his superior insight into the fleeting and eternal moments of existence: not because of words broken up into syllables and strewn carefully about the page, but because of right words with other right words, which say what they do whether they are upside down, right-side up, inside out, backward, or any other way.

to stand (alone) in some
autumnal afternoon:
breathing a fatal
stillness . . .

Cummings is an important poet because he has insisted, by virtue of his fine, irascible talent, on the primacy of the perpetually-happening, never-repeated "natural miracle," and on our feeling with what we see, and seeing with what we feel, spontaneously, thoughtlessly, and totally. I do not in the least mean to slight his typographical innovations, which may well be of greater import than I have been willing to concede; I only wish to reiterate that what I consider Cummings' finest moments are dependent not on these innovations, such as they are, but on combinations of words that deliver the necessary insights regardless of what splintering process may or may not take place among them. These poems, such as "Paris: this April sunset completely utters," and " Always before your voice my soul," show that part or perhaps most of the miracle is in our observing and responding: that it is we who must do the seeing and feeling, unashamedly and faithful to nothing but our actual responses. In poems as strongly charged with as unforeseeable and as unique a personality as Cummings', that is a very great deal.

95 Poems, by E. E. Cummings, Harcourt, Brace, 1958, $4.00.

ELDER OLSON

To my untutored mind, which probably shouldn't be allowed an opinion of this sort, Elder Olson has always appeared the most gifted of the influential University of Chicago " neo-Aristotelian " school of literary aesthetics. From time to time he publishes a few poems, too. I have come to watch eagerly for these, and have noted with especial delight their difference from the complicated and rarefied trafficking with universals that he and his colleagues do in the pages of the learned journals. All of Olson's poems that I have seen are in his new book, together with five short plays which are witty, ingenious, and amusing, but which are not up to even the lesser of the poems in originality and lasting effectiveness. The plays are marred by excessive reliance on literary " gimmicks " and surprises, and do not impress me as being anything more than mildly successful, even within their modest intentions. " Faust," for example, is a humanist parable on the old story, but with the twist that Faust, in quest of youth instead of knowledge, is taken at his word in an entirely different sense from that which he intended, becomes the victim of a purely scientific retribution, and is made to suffer " regressive evolution " back to the state of the primates, and beyond. " The Illusionists " makes use of Huxleyan " illusion machines " which the populace of the earth, habituated for years to illusions by other means such as television, the cinema, and advertising, eagerly adopts, because " real individual happiness is incompatible with the good of the State; besides, it isn't possible." Men no longer see any reason to distinguish reality from illusion, and embrace the illusion machines even though they must pay the machine-masters with their flesh. As may be inferred, these five small plays are exclusively dramas of ideas, with the characters simply serving as a number of stand-ins for various points of view. Once the surprise-packages of their denouements have been opened, they come to seem contrived and a little thin.

The poems are in another class altogether. Obvious influences there are, to be sure, and not all of them good; to note one, the well-known "Ballad of the Scarecrow Christ" is disastrously in the shadow of Dylan Thomas's "Ballad of the Long-legged Bait":

> Look, look! Amid what pomp of water
> He lordly rides like the light of day;
> All the sea-robed waves throng round,
> Sea-foam garlands all his way . . .

This is not Olson's best manner. But "Crucifix," "The Jack-in-the-box," and, above all, "A Nocturnal For His Children" are models of difficult thinking made profoundly clear, and of a power of organization which brings the Great Questions into perfectly convincing rapport with the actual circumstances of everyday life. I am delighted and even awestruck by Olson's capacity to assemble the materials of his poems around the ideas they dramatize, and by the ease with which he wields his verse-forms upon basic and eternal considerations, steadily and evenly.

> Not in God's image was man
> First created, but in
> Likeness of a beast;
> Until that beast became man,
> All travailled in death and pain
> And shall travail still
> Till man be the image of God
> And nothing shall transform
> Man to that image but love;
> And this I believe is God's will.

And all shall work that Will:
Planet and planet shall spin,
Atom and atom, until
The scriptures of heaven and earth
Mountain and ocean, spell
The one unnameable Name
Of One we know nothing of,
Save what we learn from love . . .

Reading this, and many other poems and parts of poems in Olson's book, I keep asking myself why his work is not better known. I can think of no adequate answer, and must leave Olson's relative neglect a mystery, trusting I have done what I could to rectify what seems to me a really unfortunate situation, and hoping to enlist the aid of Time.

Plays and Poems, 1948-58, by Elder Olson, University of Chicago Press, 1958, $4.00.

RICHARD EBERHART

Richard Eberhart has long been an enigma for critics, and doubtless will be so forever. To make things even harder for us, he has all but perfected a number of devices that he employs, cleverly and with increasing skill, to hide the fact that he is one of the most authentically gifted and instinctively poetic minds of our time. If we must choose, and in this case it begins to look as if we must, between the merely formal and uninspired and the unformed and talented—if we cannot have executive form *and* inspiration—we will choose the latter: we will choose Eberhart over Robert Bridges or Howard Baker. That much is or should be plain. Yet Eberhart is often irritating beyond belief; in this book he has indulged himself increasingly in a mannerism which first began to be obtrusive in *Undercliff*: a gabby, jocularly pedantic dialect, largely of his own invention, packed with awkward and ponderously frivolous word-play like " the election of erection " and " Enrapture my blessing/Immediacy of perception." One might imagine the heights to which an untrammelled and enthusiastic use of this procedure might take American poetry, but one does not have to imagine them; they are all reached in *Great Praises*: surely it is hard to believe any of us will ever see again, at least in the book of a sometime superior poet, anything quite like " Superabundant/Faculty manifests sun-burned rarity/As he eschews aridity and valley." It is an irony with aspects of the fabulous that Eberhart's main pre-occupation as a poet—the achievement of true " immediacy of perception "—is made literally impossible by the heap of ill-digested bookish language he uses to try to persuade you that he is, too, writing from the center of the place " where everything is seen in its purity." Without this manner, on the other hand, Eberhart speaks with utter conviction and directness.

> I wanted to give him some gift,
> Small child dying slowly,
> With brave blue intelligent eyes,
> His form withered piteously.
>
> Only in the intelligence of those eyes
> Where life had retreated for a piercing look
> Was the enormous mystery justified,
> As he inhaled the betraying oxygen.

I don't know whether or not this kind of clairvoyant simplicity would be available to Eberhart if it were not for the unnatural and frequently ludicrous excesses of the other poems. I am willing to suppose that it would not, though surely his seems a strange route to take toward the first and only poetic Innocence. Yet there are wonderfully exciting times in which Eberhart does appear to be able to make of himself " flesh without a mind," and to speak with penetrating and involving spontaneity, and we must therefore grant him whatever means he adjudges favorable to such states, for at these times we recognize him for what he assuredly is: one of the writers who are opening up the world to our life, from the inside.

Great Praises, by Richard Eberhart, Oxford, 1957, $4.00.

BROTHER ANTONINUS

Reviewing religious poets, determinedly religious ones, always makes me a little nervous. I feel somewhat as if I were reviewing God, and am intimidated at flying in the face of all that good will with the mere instruments of my own taste and judgment. This is especially true when I came to Brother Antoninus. I remember him from several years back as William Everson, who wrote some of the first poetry I ever truthfully liked. Along with his new book, I went back and read his old one, *The Residual Years*, and found it full of the hatred and necessity of sex, and of a very convincing and powerful, from-inside-the-thing feeling about California farmers and farming.

> Deep sun, deep sky;
> No wind now for the dance of the leaves;
> But the light clean on the shape of the neck;
> And the deep sound of the heart.

Everson is (or was) best in simple, tactile description. His poems in *The Residual Years* are unforced and open, and I renewed my acquaintance with many of them gladly, noting their imperfections and setting them aside in favor of the living quality that these pieces give off. And yet I was also struck, as I had been before, by the author's humorless, even owlish striving after self-knowledge and certainty, his intense and bitter inadequacy and frustration. I suppose I should have known, when I first read him fourteen years ago, that these problems would be resolved in religious orthodoxy, though I could not have guessed that Everson himself would become Brother Antoninus in the Catholic Church. In *The Crooked Lines of God* I encountered a good deal less of what I am pleased to call poetry than in *The Residual Years*, though if there were any justice there would be more. The verse here is of the kind I had hoped not to find: page after page of not-very-good, learned, dry sermonizing which in several places leans toward an attitude which I cannot help believing is somewhat self-righteous and even self-congratulatory. Before the poems proper ever begin, it is disconcerting to hear a writer say that what follows is "tortured between grace and the depraved human heart," as though he were presenting his poems, not as the tentative, hopeful ventures that all poems must be, but as a confident excourse from the mere estate of being human to the extreme Beatification. He talks of "my new poetic vision" as though it were an irrefutable fact. But alas, it is not so. What Brother Antoninus offers, instead of the "vision" he speaks of, is a sober, unimaginative forthrightness and a nagging insistence that he is right and you are, no matter what *else* you may believe, wrong. What I find peculiarly disagreeable in Brother Antoninus' work is his basic dislike of people and of sex, and this seems to me to be based at least as much on secular reasons as on religious, especially considering the fact that he shows the same distastes in *The Residual Years*, though there they are offered simply as personal feelings instead of Enlightenment. It may be that I am being unfair to Brother Antoninus, and if so I hope he will forgive me. Nevertheless, I still must say that the material offered here is much nearer to being apologetics than poetry. Worse; the author's determination to make his subjects as important and impressive as he believes they should be only succeeds in puffing them up into unbelievability.

Good Peter, upside down,
Straddles the Roman sun,

His legs like aqueducts
Bloody the down-hung head.
Already here the packed arena fills;
Its martyrs mount their yardarms.
The starveling lion
Snuffs the blood-stung air,
And the maiden's coif
Mats the tiger's jaw.
All, all are here. Their pain
Reaches already to this swollen Heart
That lugs and labors like a giant sea
Clasping its wounded islands,
Toning its solemn note upon that shore,
To weep out its geologic woe alone.

Unfortunately, as I have said before, the means, risks, and results of poetry are the same for religious verse as they are for any other kind. Hopkins knew this, and he labored mightily to see what the world had to show him. If inspiration is religious, and is also inspiration, the result will be good religious poetry, provided the words are adequate to express it. If the writing is religious in theme, but without the spark that only imagination can supply, the result will be much like the verse of Brother Antoninus and Thomas Merton, all argument, good intentions, and no light. It is too bad that, in verse coming to us from intensely devout, serious, and dedicated men, we get enough solemn, dead metaphors to fill the stuffed owl's mouth for generations to come, enough laborious theology to make us wish Thomas Merton were still an undergraduate Bohemian, and Brother Antoninus still a farmer in the San Joaquin Valley, ploughing God's land with his horses.

The Crooked Lines of God, by Brother Antoninus, University of Detroit Press, 1960, $4.00.

TOWARD A SOLITARY JOY

GARY SNYDER

Somehow it isn't enough, anymore, that there are plenty of good poems around, as there are. What we feel we need now is a poetry good in a way we could not have foreseen: a kind of perceiving and writing which will transcend and destroy our present criteria, open new areas of experience, and release us to our own waiting, hidden potentialities. Not that there haven't been several tries. The "Movement" in England was one, but it has come to surprisingly little. The carefully off-hand, self-effacing, intelligently embarrassed tone so fashionable among young British poets a few years ago now appears to have been only a cultivated way of admitting imaginative bankruptcy. In this country, the "Beats" are, of course, the nearest thing we have to a poetry movement. Though, despite my best efforts, I can't take most Beat poetry seriously, its very existence shows that the well-bred verse of the Schoolmen which dominated the forties and early fifties is exhausted. As a consequence of these developments, every book we read nowadays can be placed in one of three categories, and by means of such placement we can make a fairly accurate guess as to what the writer believes our poetry should be. There are those who assume that academic poetry is as good now as it was in the forties and fifties, when almost nothing else was printed, those who are convinced that academic poetry is dead, and are trying energetically to bury it (the Beats), and those who find themselves in a curious halfway house between academic poetry and Somewhere Else: Beatnikism, or their own hesitantly emerging and personal vision of the New. This last place is where Galway Kinnell, for example, is starting life.

The best of them, Gary Snyder, is not. I don't know

precisely what his relation to the Beats may be, but he is usually published with them, and has certainly taken up a good many of their preoccupations, such as Zen and the rest of the mail-order orientalism of the West Coast crowd. But he is also by far the most interesting of these poets that I have read. What you see about him immediately is his debt to the Pound of the *Cantos:* Pound's fragmented, juxtaposing method, his quotations (with and without quotation marks), and even his irritating use of the ampersand. But what you also see is that this is unmistakably the right technique for Mr. Snyder to use. The Pound style, at the same time so style-conscious and so styleless, can be very bad: disorganized, flat, pretentious, obscure, inconsequential, bookish, and dull. But in Mr. Snyder's work it is none of these. It is, instead, close to what Pound probably thinks it should be: sharp-edged, vivid, detached, concentrated both on the thing shown (the image) and on bringing it into a field of interpretation not explicitly given but formulated by the various quotations woven into the writing. The musing, drifting series of terse, observant statements does fix Snyder's experiences and beliefs in such a manner that they become available for us to live among and learn from. And that is the kind of living and learning—within another's life—that we are always hoping poetry will make possible.

Myths and Texts, by Gary Snyder, Totem Press (New York), 1960, $1.25.

GALWAY KINNELL

I like Galway Kinnell's poems mainly for their wholehearted commitment to themselves, and for what I can only call their innocence. Mr. Kinnell cares quite openly and honestly about almost everything he has ever seen, heard of, or read about, and finds it rather easy to say so. There is nothing very tragic or tearing about him, or nothing very intense, either. He seems to me a natural poet: humanly likeable, gentle, ruminative. But he is dishearteningly prolix. Prolixity is, of course, the foremost and perhaps only natural enemy of the natural poet, and Mr. Kinnell is going to have to do battle with it if he is to realize himself. Some of these pieces are almost too trivial to be believed, and even the best of them keep blurring into each other, since there is no real division, nothing to individualize them, make them separately experienceable. They are just part of the amiable weather of the book. Poetry can do better than this, and so can Kinnell. The last long poem, "The Avenue Bearing the Initial of Christ into the New World," has some beautiful lines about such unbeautiful objects as carp in grocers' tanks and vegetable pushcarts. Here, you feel quite strongly a genuine presence, an integrated personal reality more powerful and more projected than anything else in recent books except Gary Snyder's poems about logging and fire-watching. Kinnell realizes the difference between knowing something because you have been told it is so and knowing it because you have lived it. And this latter kind of knowing is what good poetry can give, and what Kinnell in some of his work gives, too. His first book is not as deep and abiding as we might like; I find myself remembering his themes and a few scattered details, but not the *way* in which they are told, or, as happens with the very best poems, the *words* in which they are told. But Mr. Kinnell has made an authentic beginning, and many poets die without getting even this far. Perhaps to a degree more than is true of other poets, Kinnell's development will depend on the actual events of his life. And it is a life that I think we should watch. It is warm, generous, reflective, and friendly. And as poetry it holds out some promise, largely because of this necessary involvement with the author's life, of being in the end magnificent. It is not entirely impossible that the Wave of the Future may turn out to have begun at Avenue C, or some place within walking distance of it.

What A Kingdom It Was, by Galway Kinnell, Houghton Mifflin, 1960, $3.00.

JOHN LOGAN

In the only lines of his I have ever found memorable, Kenneth Rexroth says that the poet is " one who creates /Sacramental relationships/That last always." I have often been struck by the profundity and necessity of this statement, and I have also wondered why it is that the creation of sacramental relationships takes place so rarely in the work of most of our religious-oriented poets, men of good intent and life-long devotion to God and to writing, like Thomas Merton, Daniel Berrigan and Brother Antoninus. A sense of the sacred, which these men labor to make available, is probably the most important quality that poetry can possess, and it is not, I think, excessive to say that all poets, regardless of their orthodoxies, beliefs or unbeliefs, are trying to embody and project such a sense according to their various lights and abilities.

John Logan's approach to the problem of sacramentalism in poetry is an interesting one. To begin with, he is on the surface a very literary poet, drawing constantly on quotations from church fathers, ecclesiastical writers and also others, like Lorca and Rimbaud (you would think, from the number of poets who attach Rimbaud's words to their poems as though they were *mana*, that he made his living writing epigraphs), and in his present book not only precedes his poems with multiple quotations but also furnishes them with explanatory afterthoughts (" After Antonia Valentin and after a memorial to Heine in Kilmer Park") a practise that I simply loathe, and which I fervently wish that Logan would forget about. From a description of the subject matter of most of Logan's poems—a description citing their preoccupation with saints, with the sacred writings, with holy days, and with ecclesiastical rituals—one would be tempted to think that his approach to the creation of sacramental relationships is based exclusively upon an eminently orthodox symbology, and that it would thus run some chance of failing to convey this sense to those not of like faith and persuasion. One might conclude, also, that an habitual use of such time-worn symbols and images from an age of greater and more universally acknowledged faith would result, even at best, in a kind of museum or textbook poetry based upon matter which no amount of sincerity or ingenuity could ever restore to its former urgency. Though it is true (at least in my opinion) that his poems about saints and martyrs are not his best, the surprising thing about this part of Logan's work is that the churchly bookishness is not dry and dead; it is oddly alive and felt, for in addition to being a Catholic, Logan is a man for whom intellectual excitement exists. Even so, to a religious outsider like myself, his formidable and detailed knowledge of church history and ritual is rather forbidding, and there are a good many times when I get lost in it. If one is patient, however, one comes to see that Mr. Logan's sense of what is sacred in his own experience is by no means limited to what is officially supposed to be sacred; it does not in the least depend on his having read Saint Augustine or on any of the rest of his orthodox or unorthodox learning. His poems at their best—and Mr. Logan's work is remarkably " level," with few peaks and declines—convey to a remarkable degree that degreeless and immeasurable and unanalysable quality which Albert Schweitzer has called, in our century's greatest phrase, " reverence for life." In the face of this feeling, which is constant throughout Mr. Logan's writing, one does not really care much about talking of his literary means. His technical abilities are relatively slight, and really begin and end with an uncommon capacity for coming up with a strangely necessary and urgent observation and setting it among others by means of ordinary, unemphatic but rather breathless language which makes his lines read something like a nervous, onrushing prose. The heavy machinery of his religious symbology looks at times a little incongruous in this setting, but Logan himself never does. The day will come, I am sure, when he will lay less stress upon the symbols provided by his church, and rely more upon what he has so abundantly and joyously: the spirit of love without which all the dogma of Christianity would be valueless. I know of no other writer of my generation who so consistently is able to project this quality, and Logan does so entirely without recourse to that awful and professionally useful kind of " love " that is no more than a word on a page, and is often mistaken for the spirit that infrequently underlies it. Logan mentions love very few times in his two books, but it informs, illuminates and transfigures everything he writes about. One closes Logan's books—particularly the present one, markedly superior to the first—thinking, "Yes, this is what poetry can sometimes do; this is what it can sometimes be." One understands what the religious faculty in man really is, and the human miracles it can perform even in its impure modern environment.

Mr. Logan's poems have not, perhaps fortunately, been widely or well reviewed; perhaps they could not have been. His strange kind of innocence, walking in and out of his ecclesiastical and literary knowledgeableness, is not an easy thing to talk about, though anyone who reads Mr. Logan cannot fail to be excited and uplifted by it. He is very much out of place, too, in the pathetic and vicious jostling and literary back-scratching for prizes and favorable notices that shows his generation of American poets at its ineffectual worst. He is far beyond the Idols of the Marketplace, and works where the work itself is done out of regard for the world he lives in and the people he lives among because he is helplessly and joyously what he is. As (and if), in Logan's work, the letter of religion fades away in favor of its spirit, he stands, in my opinion, an exciting chance of being one of the finest poets we have ever had in this country. (It might help, also, if he could find a less prosaic way of writing, and if he would explore a little among the dynamics of language, always retreating when they became too interesting for their own sake). It might be given to Logan to show in exultant urgency and truth what so many have labored and failed to show, but only said: that the spirit that makes Christianity Western Man's greatest triumph and hope is always and perpetually available in everything the human creature is privileged to do, from bringing children to birth to caressing the head of a dog.

Ghosts of the Heart, by John Logan, University of Chicago Press, 1960, $2.75.

W. S. MERWIN

W. S. Merwin is probably the most widely published poet of his generation. That he is a fine writer I have no doubt at all, and that in his new book he displays signs of a power I had not hitherto noticed is equally true. Even at his most ornamental he has never been near the obvious and busy emptiness of so many other American poets his age, though one has certainly remarked the low-keyed monotony of some of his descriptive poems and the endless fascination that the mechanical problems of writing verse have always had for him. What he has lacked up to now, and still lacks, is intensity, some vital ingress into the *event* of the poem which would cause him to lose his way among the intricacies of what is so easy for him to say concerning almost anything on earth and suffer a little at the hands of his subjects: in a word, *earn* them emotionally. Control of one's material is one thing, and dictatorship over it is another. It is this, I suppose, that led " Crunk," the critic of the *The Sixties,* to speak of Merwin as being " like a great general born into the world again as a member of the animal kingdom." It seems to me, also, that Merwin has never given enough of himself to his subjects: of the self that somehow lies beyond the writing self. He has always seemed so sure, so utterly sure of the things he knew and what he could tell about them that the strokes out of Heaven, or out of the subjects themselves, have never quite managed to hit him between the eyes. One of the difficulties about Mr. Merwin's writing generation has always been just this, as I have noted before: the dominations and powers of poetry itself—of the surface effects and the learnable manipulations as opposed to the profound marriages of technique and personality that make up the poems we remember—are constantly in danger of becoming a kind of mask which takes, automatically, a more or less pleasing, predictable shape, but which also with tremendous effectiveness obscures and kills what the poet should want to get at: those areas which only he is capable of discovering. In a land where all poems are masks, good ones or bad ones, it behooves the poet to construct the best faces for himself that he can. And yet when the right kind of simplicity reveals itself, how artificial all such construction and its products come to seem!

I think that his own kind of simplicity is now becoming available to Merwin, and the fact that it is slowly emerging from the techniques of one of the master prosodists of our time makes its advent doubly worth watching. There is still far too much gilded stuffing rounding out the contours of Mr. Merwin's poems, and I can't yet see his features clearly through his various masks, but I hope that one day in the not-too-distant future I shall be able to do so. After a prodigal beginning Merwin may now seem to be stalled. But it is my impression that he is gathering force. The title poem here and " One-Eye " avail themselves of an odd kind of roughed-up, clunking diction and meter that I found quite attractive, and which involved me in their poems more than in any of Mr. Merwin's others that I have read. With tools like these and with the discoveries about himself that this book shows him intent on making, Merwin should soar like a phoenix out of the neat ashes of his early work.

The Drunk In The Furnace, by W. S. Merwin, Macmillan, 1960, $1.25.

WILLIAM STAFFORD

There are poets who pour out rivers of ink, all on good poems. William Stafford is one of these. He has been called America's most prolific poet, and I have no doubt that he is. He turns out so much verse not because he is glib and empty, but because he is a real poet, a born poet, and communicating in lines and images is not only the best way for him to get things said; it is the easiest. His natural mode of speech is a gentle, mystical, half-mocking and highly personal daydreaming about the landscape of the western United States. Everything in this world is available to Mr. Stafford's way of writing, and I for one am very glad it is. The things he chooses to write about —I almost said " talk "—seem in the beginning more or less arbitrary, but in the end never so. They are caught up so genuinely and intimately in his characteristic way of looking, feeling, and expressing that they emerge as fresh, glowing creations; they *all* do, and that is the surprising and lovely fact about them:

The well rising without sound,
The spring on a hillside,
The ploughshare brimming through deep ground
Everywhere in the field—

The sharp swallows in their swerve
Flaring and hesitating
Hunting for the final curve
Coming closer and closer—

The swallow heart from wing beat to wing beat
Counselling decision, decision:
Thunderous examples. I place my feet
With care in such a world.

Let Mr. Stafford keep pouring it out. It is all good, all to his purpose.

A characteristic Stafford poem makes itself felt with soft, delicate insistence; one somehow becomes stiller on reading it, convinced from the first few words that one must miss nothing of what is being so quietly and confidently said:

> On the third finger of my left hand
> under the bank of the Ninnescah
> a muskrat whirled and bit to the bone.
> The mangled hand made the water red.
>
> That was something the ocean would remember:
> I saw me in the current flowing through the land,
> rolling, touching roots, the world incarnadined,
> and the river richer by a kind of marriage.
>
> While in the woods an owl started quavering
> with drops like tears I raised my arm.
> Under the bank a muskrat was trembling
> with meaning my hand would wear forever.
>
> In that river my blood flowed on.

West of Your City, by William Stafford, The Talisman Press, 1960, $5.00 (cloth), $2.50 (paper).

DAVID IGNATOW

I—*The Gentle Weightlifter*

David Ignatow writes a flat near-prose which sometimes helps his poems toward the kind of innocence and legendary strangeness they try for. The ultimate effect of its use, however, is numbing. Through repetition, understatement loses the sense of the deliberately left-out or held-down that should enhance the suggestiveness of the individual poem, and the poems tend to blur and run together.

The best pieces in *The Gentle Weightlifter* might be called " Secret Histories." Oedipus, Aeneas, Achilles, King David are seen moving confidently and unsuspectingly through their familiar roles, to become resigned and incredulous at the end-results. The reader, too, thinks, " Why, anyone could have made that mistake, and now look what's come of it." The perfectly human actions of these people have somehow been chosen to become fabulized and " illustrative," but Ignatow's interest and sympathy lie with the human beings who must, unknowingly, act out the myths, and suffer as men their final point. His is a kind of parable-poetry, emphasizing the individual act and its effect on the participant rather than the generalizing or transcendent power of the episode.

> At Colonnus Oedipus complained;
> Antigone attended him. He thought
> The sun too hot, she shielded him;
> His enemies too strong, she fought
> For him; his life bitter, she soothed him;
> And hope gone, like all things.
> His blinded eyes pained him, she bathed them;
> And when he left, by decree forced to,

She went with him, her arm supporting him;
And where he lay at the end of his strength,
Stretched out upon the forest floor,
His head pillowed in her lap,
His arms at his sides trembling,
She thought surely some cover
Could be found for him.

Aside from the flatness, which is only in a very rudimentary sense a technique, Ignatow does almost completely without the traditional skills of English versification. He makes no effort to assure his lines rhetorical effectiveness; the import of each poem is thus far too dependent upon *what* is said, given in a low, gentle, spell-breaking murmur. At his best, however, Ignatow often seems a real primitive, with the small, serene vision of the Douanier Rousseau or of Bombois. His narrative gift appears to me to be worthy of encouragement, and I look forward, queerly, since concision and concentration are integral to Mr. Ignatow's successes here, to longer work.

The Gentle Weightlifter, by David Ignatow, The Morris Gallery, 1955, $3.00.

II—*Say Pardon*

David Ignatow is in a strange and necessary category; his own. I have liked his work for a very long time, ever since his *Gentle Weightlifter,* and have watched the poems in the present book come out in various places with the growing conviction that they would make a superb showing when they were collected. They do. This is one of the three or four best books—with James Wright's *Saint Judas,* Robert Francis' *The Orb Weaver* and Louis Simpson's *A Dream of Governors*—that Wesleyan has brought out, and these four titles alone give that house the most exciting poetry list in current American publishing. Ignatow's poems are in no sense inferior to the best of Wright's or Francis's, which is to say that they rank with the most authentic now being written. What gives them their unique power is a kind of strange, myth-dreaming vision of modern city life, and the ability to infuse the decor of the contemporary city with the ageless Old-Testament fatality of death and judgment: to make the traditional moral issues of the race count in an environment where seemingly they have ceased to, and to give them a fitting dramaturgy of symbol and image which not only brings the reader into the situations Ignatow writes about, but makes him subject to the same unchangeable laws: judges him, doesn't let him get away untouched. There is no obvious brilliance of language such as the academic poet is straining to achieve; in Mr. Ignatow's use, words are merely a vehicle for recounting what happened: what happens. The dramatic impact of each poem hits you foursquare, always convincingly, and the whole thing, the incident, the judgment, is what you remember. Mr. Ignatow's is a " total poetry " in a different sense from that in which the term is ordinarily used; not like that, say, of Hopkins or Dylan Thomas or Mallarmé. Rather than being word-oriented, it is an inspired and brilliantly successful metaphysical reportage, with an " I-was-the-man " authority that shakes the involved beholder to his bones.

> Someone approaches to say his life is ruined
> And to fall down at your feet
> And pound his head upon the sidewalk.
> Blood spreads in a puddle.
> And you, in a weak voice, plead
> With those nearby for help;

Your life takes on his desperation.
He keeps pounding his head.
It is you who are fated;
And you fall down beside him.
It is then you are awakened,
The body gone, the blood washed from the ground,
The stores lit up with their goods.

Say Pardon, by David Ignatow, Wesleyan University Press, 1960, $1.25.

TOWARD A SOLITARY JOY

The battles of art are silent, bloodless, and usually result in defeats more total than any others. This is especially true of poetry, where the writer has virtually no audience at all, and puts in his hours, almost always after work, in dogged misery, determined to realize himself and to communicate even if there is no one to communicate with. It is heartbreaking, truly. And yet, like everything else, it has its good side. Nothing else on earth can equal the profound and upsurging sense of personal justification that a good line or a good poem gives one, and, in the dead quiet after midnight or the groggy dawn when the poet seizes whatever time he can to get that new, promising poem together, he can be assured that this feeling will come again, maybe tomorrow, maybe next month, maybe next year, if he sticks at it. The carping of critics matters very little beside this, though critics are doubtless bothersome enough, for the poet's "place in the literature of his time," his place in the anthologies and textbooks that are his only Valhalla, are largely determined by what people, professionally knowledgeable people, think and say about him in public. Yet literary vanity disappears in the light of the truly creative moment; the hardscrabble labour of writing poems is quite literally its own reward. The major good of writing a poem is done to the poet, and if a faint radiation of this central good gets as far away as somebody else, that is extra. But nobody can really count on it. Therefore, without being asked, I encourage all bad poets as well as good ones to write, and for the rest of their lives, for whatever is in it for them. My comments, such as they are, can't touch *them,* really, and I only offer what seems to be reasonable advice to help some of them toward that lonely, unfathomable rising of joy between teaching Chaucer and freshman composition, or at night after grading papers, or on the commuter train to Scarsdale.

Why, indeed, do people write poetry? Especially, why do increasing numbers of them write it now, in an age wherein poetry is supposed to be kicking weakly in its final throes? For every poem in these books there must be thousands and thousands in manuscript, written by housewives, teachers, school-children, porters, clerks, secretaries, advertising executives (even), lawyers, salesmen. Why? All of these poems, one imagines, come out of the unconscious conviction that significant emotions must, somehow, not be lost, and that they surely will be, if action of a kind is not taken. Almost everyone believes that at least a few moments of his life belong uniquely to *him;* that these, in fact, *explain* his life, and must be protected from or made to stand against the monstrous manipulation of human interests for gain; the treatment of humanity as " the consumer," and the terrible attendant rationalizations by the Powers that have it so (" But we're helping them get what they want!") The least of these poets, the most unschooled and desperate, have nothing to do but moan or howl. A few cuts above these are the writers who have dimly sensed that Form has something to do with the quality and the communicability of what they wish to say. These are beginning the essential journey, though as poets they die by thousands along the way, many of them after taking no more than a step or two. A third group—the artisans—are consciously seeking all their lives to forge the great key of a style, and, if successful, to employ it as extensively and wisely as possible. Though a few of the poets here discussed have entered the City of Artisans, none has stood in the " artifice of eternity " with Yeats, or made or become the golden singing bird. Lacking greatness, however, there is much variety here: strong dedication, devotion to a medium and, one must conclude, love. To read even a dreadful poet like Tennessee Williams after watching an evening of give-away programs and " true-life dramas " on television, or looking with half-persuaded and fascinated disgust at the rest of the comfortable and deadening "Consumer's Paradise" around us, where every means is used to persuade us that life, American life, consists, doesn't it, of the radiant happiness of the clean, pretty, harmless, and helpful things we buy, and of the nice, fun-loving people that we ourselves should (no; *must*) want to be: to read even Williams, or Allen Ginsberg, is to have one's eyes fill with tears. At times the hardest of the reviewer's tasks is to keep himself from saying to his little stable of poets, regardless of his likes and dislikes: " Yes! Yes! Go on and do what you're doing: write. You're all wonderful ! You've declared in favor of humanity, and that fact itself must endear even your faults to anyone who sees what you are trying to preserve. I take your hands! I bless you all!" It is with the cold knowledge that he would, by such an attitude, be depriving the writers of whatever small help (perhaps none) he could be to them, in their effort to belong to " the opening world," to move among the vital potentialities of life and proclaim them, that the critic sinks back with a sigh on his own opinions, and takes up again the hard and frequently bitter business of discrimination, which is not the wildness but the practicality of hope. The sworn enemy of such hope is the Suspect, who, like the Devil, is always with us. And, like the Devil, he (or it) is infinitely various, and can take every form but God's. For every reader there are poems to which he responds with no prompting from criticism or from his tutored, knowledgeable self. Let us cleave hard to those, and, because they betray nothing, neither us nor the world nor their poets, let us be doubly ruthless to the Suspect, and deny him whenever he may arise, offering us a synthetic apple.